Oracle SQL:
101 Frequently Asked Questions

Gary M. Lewis and Alex Sirota

Komenda Publishing Co.
Boulder, CO

Published by
Komenda Publishing Company
PO Box 21583
Boulder, CO 80308-4583
Telephone: (303)543-8540
Facsimile: (303)543-8546
Email: glewis@komenda.com

Considerable care was taken in the preparation of this book. Nevertheless, Komenda Publishing Company assumes no responsibility for any errors, omissions, or inaccuracies that remain in the book. Neither the publisher nor the authors assume any responsibility for damages resulting from the use of information obtained in the book.

The following are trademarks or registered trademarks:
LaserJet — Hewlett-Packard Company
SAS — SAS Institute Inc.
SQL*PLUS, PL/SQL, SQL*FORMS, SQL*LOADER, ORACLE — Oracle Corporation
SQR — Management Information Technology, Inc.
VAX and VMS — Digital Equipment Corporation
Windows 95, MS-DOS, Notepad, Word, and Excel — Microsoft Corporation
PumpItUp Lite — Client Server Factory
All other products and brand names are trademarks of their respective holders.

First printing March 1997
10 9 8 7 6 5 4 3 2 1
Printed in the United States of America

Library of Congress Catalog Card Number 96-94143
ISBN 0-9644912-7-3

Publisher's Cataloging in Publication Data
Lewis, Gary M.
    Oracle SQL: 101 frequently asked questions / Gary M. Lewis and Alex Sirota.
    p. cm.
    Includes bibliographical references and index.
    ISBN 0-9644912-7-3
    1. Oracle (Computer file) 2. SQL (Computer program language) 3. Relational databases. 4. Data base management -- Computer programs. I. Title. II. Sirota, Alex.
    QA76.73.S67 L492 1997   96-94143

With great respect and love,
to my daughter Heather Lewis
Gary Lewis

To my loving and patient wife Lara,
my incredible parents David and Mila,
and my awesome brother Eric
Alex Sirota

Contents Summary

Contents

Preface

Someday people will query Oracle databases considerably differently than they do now. When that day arrives, expect to see vice-presidents, clerks, department managers, secretaries, and board members asking questions of organizational databases, receiving answers, and asking additional questions until they get their arms around whatever problem they currently confront. The central feature is that people without any database experience will directly and routinely use databases to address job-related questions. They will do so without any programming and without any intermediary to translate the ad hoc query into language understandable by the database. The process of asking ad hoc queries will approach the ease and convenience of speaking with another person. It's just that in this case the conversation will occur with a database containing information that can help solve day-to-day operational or longer-range policy and strategic issues.

It's helpful to have a vision of future ad hoc queries. But getting from the reality of today to the promise of that vision entails considerable work and great uncertainty as to how, exactly, we can move forward. Today, ad hoc queries are primitive by comparison with the scenario sketched above. Questions, of course, arise naturally in the course of a job. But most are triaged before they're even uttered aloud, simply because the person asking the question does not personally have the capability to query the database and because the process of actually getting an answer to the query involves so much effort. Normally, a query must be asked through proper channels, defended as to priority and importance, and queued with other queries to be programmed by information systems staff. Most questions simply wither rather than face this process; organizations suffer a hidden cost from questions unasked.

The present tools for ad hoc querying are also primitive compared with those which surely must evolve. Present query tools generally fall along a continuum. Programming tools exist at one end of the spectrum. These include SQL, SQL*PLUS, procedural extensions like PL/SQL, and procedural languages like SQR that provide embedded SQL. End-user tools dominate the other end of the continuum. Typically these tools are characterized by point-and-click, graphical interfaces that shield users from database complexity.

Both extremes exact penalties. SQL and procedural languages permit direct access to transactional databases, yet only programmers and analysts can invest the time required to use these tools proficiently. Organizations using these tools typically funnel ad hoc queries through intermediaries, who then write the query and return an answer. Much of the success in this approach depends on the skill of the intermediary — how well she knows the business rules and can interpret the original query correctly, how well she understands the database tables and their idiosyncrasies, how good a programmer she is, how persuasively she can present the findings, and how fast she can process the scores of questions queued for her.

The intermediary model is far from ideal. Not even the best of intermediaries can provide the real-time response needed for query, response, requery, response and so on. Intermediaries also can endanger an organization by creating points of brittleness. If nearly all queries of a particular type pass through one person, the organization becomes heavily dependent on that person. All it takes is a better job elsewhere and the conduit into the database suddenly disappears.

Graphical end-user tools solve some of these problems but create their own costs. These tools were developed with ease of use in mind. While many of the early efforts merely slapped a graphical interface over a programming language, several end-user query tools do now make data more accessible to nonprogrammers. The downside is that these tools cannot handle the complexity of fully normalized relational databases.

Perhaps an example is in order. One of us works for a college that uses an administrative database implemented with Oracle7 products. To comply with federal regulations, the college must distinguish new students from continuing students and, among new students, must distinguish freshmen from transfers. You might think these distinctions would be easy, but the federal definitions of transfer students actually make it difficult to identify these students until well into their first term of enrollment. The query that makes this distinction uses simple but convoluted logic that need not be detailed here. Suffice it to say that the query requires about 50 lines of SQL, two correlated subqueries, one UNION, and a complex DECODE across correlating criteria. The question is simple, the SQL is not; but even this SQL is relatively modest compared with other queries.

End-user query tools are not equipped to handle complex queries or even simple queries against complex relational databases The solution generally has been to change the database — to create special data warehouses and extracted data tables intended only for querying. Data get copied, cleaned, reexpressed, combined, organized, filtered, moved, and inserted into the query-only data tables, which are then suitable for use with the end-user tools. For large warehouses, the expense can be enormous.

Clearly, something better must evolve, something that retains and improves on the ease-of-use of the end-user tools yet includes the power and flexibility of programming languages. This will require movement from both extremes — the end-user tools must incorporate more power, while the programming tools must incorporate greater ease-of-use. Perhaps eventually a product will emerge that allows people to converse conversationally with databases while performing their work.

This book addresses the gap that presently exists in ad hoc query tools by improving the ease-of-use of programming languages used for queries. For several years now, we've collected the questions and answers posted to online Oracle support groups about ad hoc queries. Principally, this involved monitoring the oracle-l listserv and, to a lesser extent, the Usenet group comp.databases.oracle. We also benefited from postings to the Oracle forum on CompuServe and to other online lists designed for specific products that use Oracle databases.

When printed and stacked, the assembled postings cast a formidable shadow. But even a cursory review of the postings showed that some questions get asked repeatedly or with slight variation. These frequently asked questions (or FAQs as they're called in the online lexicon) form the basis for this book.

We hope by having available to them a single resource that discusses the most frequently encountered ad hoc query problems, query writers will find it easier to access and use Oracle databases. There are, however, several important implications of our decision to focus on frequently asked questions.

- First, this book is not meant to be an exhaustive handbook of query techniques. The questions that get asked during online sessions clump around certain topics and leave other topics untouched. These gaps are reflected in the book. The categories of questions do prove interesting, however. For example, who could have predicted that among SELECT clauses the ORDER BY clause would generate the most problems?

- Second, the questions are somewhat time dependent, often relating to product cycles and enhancement schedules. For example, when Oracle version 7 first shipped, a flurry of questions appeared about the differences between CHAR and VARCHAR2. More recently, this question has disappeared as general familiarity with version 7 has improved. In this book we have restricted the questions to Oracle version 7. Specifically, the release versions we used were SQL*PLUS Release 3.2.2.0.1, PL/SQL Release 2.2.2.3.1, and Personal Oracle7 Release 7.2.2.3.1. The operating system was Windows 95.

- Third, many ad hoc query problems relate to a specific operating system and to specific hardware platforms. We have ignored all such questions and concentrated instead on questions concerning SQL, SQL*PLUS, and PL/SQL.

- Fourth, people who frequent online listservers have widely varying experience with Oracle products. Consequently, some questions reflect the efforts of people just learning ad hoc query techniques. Other questions pose problems stumbled on by people pushing a query product to its limitations. Most posted questions, however, fall somewhere between these two extremes. This book mirrors this distribution, with most questions falling somewhere in the middle of the degree of difficulty scale.

- Fifth, any book requires that organization be imposed on the topic. This organization, however, can have a profound effect on how easily a book serves as a query writing reference. We first organized the online postings in lumpy categories that evolved into chapters and then into subgroups that became section headings. However, this is only one organization among many possible ones, and it may not conform well with the way a particular query writer experiences a query problem. Consequently, we tried several techniques to make the material accessible. Each individual query problem concludes with a section entitled "See Also" that points to other sections in the book dealing with related material. We also paid special attention to the index and included extensive cross-classifications and multiple headings for the same topic in an effort to make the index a really useful search tool.

We expect that shortly after print publication Komenda Publishing will provide a Web site devoted to the book. You will be able to browse the FAQs, search on keywords, download programs, email the authors, and review new material added after the book's publication.

Finally, a word about the conventions you'll find when reading this book. In the text we identify SQL, SQL*PLUS, and PL/SQL reserved words in SMALL CAPITALS. Whenever new concepts are first introduced, the defined words appear in *italics*. Many figures show the results of queries — which frequently occur in practice as computer printouts. To distinguish computer printouts, we've used the `OCRB monospaced font that looks like this`. All table names are shown in uppercase, bold, italic like ***ADDRESS***. All examples utilize simulated data, as opposed to any actual data that may have been posted to a listserv when a question was originally asked. Finally, one note of a grammatical nature. To avoid the awkward difficulty of maintaining gender neutrality (e.g., using "he or she"), we have simply alternated the use of masculine and feminine pronouns.

We've already been asked if there are really 101 questions in this book. The answer is no; there are actually 121 questions. We use "101" to mean a large number, but not yet large enough to qualify as 1001. Perhaps some day, as we add FAQs to the Web site, we may need to revise the book's subtitle.

This book is a modest effort, but we hope that query writers will find it a useful step toward the future of ad hoc queries that lies ahead.

Gary M. Lewis
Boulder, CO

Alex Sirota
Mississauga, Ontario

Acknowledgments

This book owes a great debt of gratitude to the many people who frequent Oracle-related electronic forums and lists. Here, questions get asked and suggestions, opinions, and knowledge get freely provided in a extraordinary exchange of group problem-solving. Some of these problems concern ad hoc queries. The people who asked questions about ad hoc queries or who offered responses to these questions provided the intellectual grist for this book. Exposure to these people truly deepened our own understanding of, and appreciation for, the art in crafting ad hoc queries. To remove the specific context within which query problems first appeared online, we have generalized both the questions and discussions that appear in this book.

We specifically wish to thank Dave Aman, Bambi Bellows, J.R. Benson, Peter Brenner, Lito Dizon, Charles Dye, Greg Grimes, Altan Khendup, Suresh Manyam, John Peterson, Paul Picciotta, Phil Pitha, Tom Robbins, and Jared Still, who volunteered their time and knowledge to review and comment on portions of the book. They provided many useful suggestions that made the book stronger. At Oracle Corporation, Peter Vasterd coordinated the review of technical portions of the book. We thank him, Thomas Kurian, and Linda Willis for their cooperation and helpful comments.

We tried mightily to remove any errors or inaccuracies that filtered into the book, but undoubtedly a few will remain to be uncovered as the book gets used. None of the people acknowledged above bears responsibility for these errors.

Chapter 1
Preliminaries

Before you can actually write ad hoc queries, there are some preliminaries that must receive attention. This chapter discusses the most frequently asked questions about issues that occur prior to actual query writing.

Query writers experienced with a specific database bring a wealth of information to bear on an ad hoc query. This information accrues over time in the form of database documentation, assembly of procedural manuals and institutional data standards, discussions with data entry staff and business policy makers, and much play and experimentation with the data. For the most part, a query writer does this on his own.

However, a formal part of the information gathering includes assembly of a set of tools that every query writer should own. This chapter begins by discussing the tools that will help you explore a database — simple queries that produce reports on table owners, table descriptions, data column dictionaries, index inventories, and constraint conditions. You'll refer to these reports frequently as you write queries.

Probably the most obvious indicator of a novice query writer is the absence of standards applied to the queries. The queries are unstructured and difficult to read; they're not modularized for ease of understanding and reuse; they don't utilize powerful techniques for simplifying the code; and they're not well documented. No generally recognized ad hoc query standards exist, but this chapter discusses several good programming practices that each query should employ.

To accommodate individual idiosyncrasies in preferred working style and to produce consistent environments for printed or screen reports, you'll want to customize the SQL*PLUS environment. This chapter discusses the options available and then concludes with an interesting problem that can arise when you're actually trying to run a query.

Exploring the Database

Whether you're new to a database, to a functional area within the database, to a data table, or even to a data column, you need to explore, play with, and learn about the unknown.

This section provides several tools that make the exploration easier. It includes reports on owners, tables, data dictionaries, indexes, and constraints — all items essential for writing ad hoc queries.

How do I get an overview of the database?

How can I get a broad overview of a new database I'm working with — just something to help orient me?

Approach

Understanding a database is a bit like peeling an onion. Aside from the tears that well up in your eyes occasionally, each time you peel back a database layer there's another layer underneath.

Data in Oracle databases is stored in tables, and tables have owners. Lists of owners and tables serve as helpful guides to the database landscape — a way of peeling back that first layer.

Owners

Run the program owners.sql listed in Appendix A (page 319). This produces a frequency distribution that counts the number of tables by owner and sketches the database at a high level of aggregation (see Figure 1-1). In database systems comprised of modules such as a finance module or a human resource module, table owners often distinguish the modular areas. The number of tables provides a rough indication of complexity.

```
Summary of table owners

owner                count
----------------     ------
GLEWIS                   1
KOMENDA                 21
OR2                      3
SYS                     79  ◀
SYSTEM                   2
                     ------
sum                    106
```

Figure 1-1: Sample report of table owners produced by owners.sql.

Comments

▶ SYS and SYSTEM owners appear in all Oracle databases, providing considerable information about the database itself. SYS, for example, owns the views used to produce both the owner and table reports that appear in this section.

Tables

Run the program tables.sql listed in Appendix A (page 320). The report lists all tables and views for a specified owner and includes a description of the table or view if it's available. Figure 1-2 shows an example of this type of report.

```
Summary of OR2 tables

name        type    owner  comments
----------  ------  -----  ------------------------------
ADDRESS     TABLE   OR2    Table of Addresses
CADDRESS    TABLE   OR2    Code Table of Address Types  ◀
NAME        TABLE   OR2    Table of Names
```

Figure 1-2: Sample table report produced by tables.sql.

Comments

▶ Table descriptions, unfortunately, are not required items during database design. So you may run the tables SQL script and find blank table descriptions. If this happens, talk to your database administrator about adding comments that describe the tables.

See Also

1. Chapter 6 on page 174 discusses frequency distribution reports in more detail.

2. Several SYS views appear in this book, including ALL_TAB_COMMENTS used to produce the report in Figure 1-2. Check the index under SYS *views* for a listing.

How do I get a dictionary for a table?

When I DESCRIBE a table, the result doesn't actually describe the contents of each data column. How can I get a data dictionary for a table that would provide more information?

Approach

Lists of owners and tables won't take you very far when you write ad hoc queries. You'll quickly need to identify what data columns exist in the tables you intend to use and determine what data are stored in these columns. A data dictionary gives you a place to begin this exploration. It defines the data columns in a table and provides a brief description of the data each column contains.

You're likely to find, however, that a complete understanding of a data column requires that you also consult office procedural manuals, written or de facto input and maintenance standards, users familiar with the data entry, or programmers who actually use the data column.

Dictionary

Run the program tabldict.sql listed in Appendix A (page 322). The SQL prompts you for a table name and a table owner and produces the type of report shown in Figure 1-3.

```
                              ▼
08-MAY-1996  08:08                 TABLE: ADDRESS                    Page:     1
Report: address.dic                 Owner: OR2              SQL: tabldict.sql
                                 Table of Addresses

Column Name            Type      Width  Scale Nulls      Column comments
===============================================================================
ADDRESS_ID             VARCHAR2     5         NOT NULL   ID of person
ADDRESS_TYPE           VARCHAR2     2         NOT NULL   Code for address type
ADDRESS_STREET         VARCHAR2    25         NULL       Street address
ADDRESS_CITY           VARCHAR2    20         NULL       City of address
ADDRESS_LOC            VARCHAR2     5         NULL       State/province/etc of address
ADDRESS_PCODE          VARCHAR2    10         NULL       Postal code of address
ADDRESS_COUNTRY        VARCHAR2     3         NULL       Country code of address
ADDRESS_SERIESNO       NUMBER       2       0 NOT NULL   Sequential number for
                                        ▲                addresses of a specified
                                        2                address_type
```

Figure 1-3: Sample data dictionary produced by tabldict.sql.

If you run the report and find that the comments are blank, this means that the database designer or table owner did not document the columns properly. In such cases, we can only give you the standard response — talk to your database administrator.

Comments

▶ The data dictionary is date and time stamped and includes page numbers, the type of object (a table or view), its name and owner, and a description of the table or view. Documentation in the header also includes the name of the SQL program that produced the report (tabldict.sql) and the name of the report output file (here it's address.dic).

▶ Most of the columns appearing in the data dictionary are self-explanatory. The only one that needs additional detail is the report column labeled "Scale". The NUMBER datatype is used to store numeric data. NUMBER includes two parameters, one defining the *precision* of the data and the second defining its *scale*. Precision is the total number of *significant* digits a numeric value may contain; scale is the number of digits to the right of the decimal point. Significant digits exclude any leading zeroes and any trailing decimal zeroes. For example, a data column with the datatype NUMBER(5,2) can contain up to five significant digits, with two of the digits being to the right of the decimal point. The numbers 123.45 and 12345.00 both qualify.

In the *ADDRESS* data dictionary, the datatype for address_seriesno is NUMBER(2,0). A scale of zero means the number is an integer. Negative scales are also possible. For example, a datatype of NUMBER(5,−2) means that data values get rounded to the nearest hundred.

In data dictionaries produced by tabldict.sql, the report column labeled "Width" indicates the precision of NUMBER datatypes and the maximum possible characters that can be stored in CHAR or VARCHAR2 columns.

See Also

1. Report titles for the data dictionary in Figure 1-3 were created with the TTITLE command. See the index under TTITLE *command* for other examples of its use.

2. Data column comments for dictionaries appear in the SYS view called ALL_COL_COMMENTS. See the index under SYS *views*.

How do I identify the indexes for a table?

One of my queries takes a long time to run, and I'd like to ensure I'm using indexes effectively. How can I identify what indexes exist for a table?

Approach

Indexes serve an obvious purpose when tuning a query to improve its performance. But indexes also serve a second important function. For queries in which you expect one row returned for each population item, examining the unique indexes in joined tables can provide clues about the best way to structure the query so that row singularity is maintained.

Appendix A (page 324) lists a program called indexes.sql that produces a formatted report for all indexes on tables with a specified owner. The program produces a report like the one shown in Figure 1-4.

```
Indexes on tables owned by: OR2
Date: 10-MAY-1996       Time: 10:53                                           Page:     1
Report name: OR2.idx                                          SQL name: indexes.sql

 table             index                      uniqueness column                     pos
 ---------------   ------------------------   ---------- -------------------------   ----
 ADDRESS           PK_ADDRESS                 UNIQUE     ADDRESS_ID                    1
                                                         ADDRESS_TYPE                  2
                                       ◀①                ADDRESS_SERIESNO              3

                   UK_ID_ZIP                  UNIQUE     ADDRESS_ID                    1
                                                         ADDRESS_PCODE                 2
                                                                                             ◀②
 CADDRESS          PK_CADDRESS                UNIQUE     CADDRESS_CODE                 1

 NAME              NAMES                      NONUNIQUE  NAME_LAST                     1
                                    ①                    NAME_FIRST                    2

                   PK_NAME                    UNIQUE     NAME_ID                       1
                                                         NAME_SERIESNO                 2
```

Figure 1-4: Sample index report produced by indexes.sql.

Comments

▶① Oracle7 creates an index on any data column or combination of data columns identified as *unique keys* or *primary keys*. The difference between the two types of keys is subtle but important. A table can have only one primary key, while many unique keys are possible. In either type of key, no two rows in a table may contain the same values for the data columns comprising the key. However, data columns appearing in a unique key may contain NULL values; this is not true for data columns in primary keys. In fact, if a row contains NULL values in all the data columns in a unique key, it automatically meets the uniqueness criteria — implying that two or more rows may contain NULL values in the key columns and the uniqueness constraint will not be violated.

The distinctions between primary and unique keys mean one thing — queries involving table joins through unique keys require that you pay attention to NULL values.

In the *ADDRESS* example shown above, an index called pk_address was created on the primary key composed of address_id, address_type, and address_seriesno. An index called uk_id_zip was created on the unique key composed of address_id and address_pcode (i.e., in this example no two rows in the *ADDRESS* table may have the same combination of address_id and zip code). Note, too, that the *NAME* table includes a non-unique index based on the data columns name_last and name_first. Obviously, two people can have the same names.

Constraint reports (see Figure 1-5 on page 8) allow you to distinguish primary keys from unique keys.

➤ When tuning a query, you'll frequently need to consider the *leading edge* of an index. The index report shown in Figure 1-4 includes a position indicator for data columns that appear in an index. For example, the pk_address index includes address_id in position 1, address_type in position 2, and address_seriesno in position 3. The full index includes data columns in positions 1, 2, and 3. The leading edge of the index, however, only includes data columns in position 1 or in positions 1 and 2.

If you construct a query without referring to the columns in the leading edge of an index, the query cannot use the index. Improving performance often requires that you rewrite the query to take advantage of the leading edge of an index.

See Also

1. A discussion of the special problems presented to query writers by NULL values begins in Chapter 5 on page 144.

2. Data columns included in an index appear in the SYS view ALL_IND_COLUMNS. The indexes themselves appear in ALL_INDEXES.

3. For other examples of primary keys, see Chapter 9 on page 254.

How do I find the constraints for a table?

I'm having trouble joining some of the tables needed for a query. How do I find out what primary and foreign keys exist for a table?

Approach

Run the constrnt.sql program listed in Appendix A (page 326). This produces a report identifying all the *integrity constraints* placed on a table. An integrity constraint is a rule that limits the values that may appear in one or more data columns in a table. Primary and foreign keys are only two types of integrity constraints that exist. Others identify unique keys and describe the check conditions enforced on individual data columns.

Figure 1-5 shows an example of the report produced by constrnt.sql.

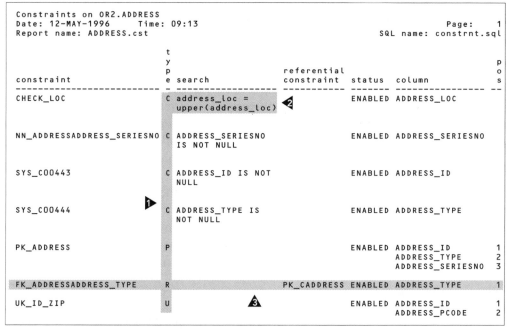

```
Constraints on OR2.ADDRESS
Date: 12-MAY-1996      Time: 09:13                                               Page:    1
Report name: ADDRESS.cst                                        SQL name: constrnt.sql


                           t
                           y
                           p                            referential                           p
constraint                 e  search                    constraint   status  column          o
                                                                                              s
------------------------   -  ------------------------  -----------  -------  --------------- --
CHECK_LOC                  C  address_loc =                         ENABLED  ADDRESS_LOC
                              upper(address_loc)

NN_ADDRESSADDRESS_SERIESNO C  ADDRESS_SERIESNO                      ENABLED  ADDRESS_SERIESNO
                              IS NOT NULL

SYS_C00443                 C  ADDRESS_ID IS NOT                     ENABLED  ADDRESS_ID
                              NULL

SYS_C00444                 C  ADDRESS_TYPE IS                       ENABLED  ADDRESS_TYPE
                              NOT NULL

PK_ADDRESS                 P                                        ENABLED  ADDRESS_ID       1
                                                                             ADDRESS_TYPE     2
                                                                             ADDRESS_SERIESNO 3

FK_ADDRESSADDRESS_TYPE     R                            PK_CADDRESS ENABLED  ADDRESS_TYPE     1
UK_ID_ZIP                  U                                        ENABLED  ADDRESS_ID       1
                                                                             ADDRESS_PCODE    2
```

Figure 1-5: Sample constraint report produced by constrnt.sql.

Comments

▶ Different types of integrity constraints exist. Those coded C in the report identify *check constraints*, those coded P or U identify primary or unique keys, respectively, and those coded R identify *foreign keys* (i.e., *referential constraints*).

▶ *Check constraints* place conditions on data columns. For example, each data column where NULL values are not permitted will have a constraint that prohibits NULL values. Check constraints can conveniently enforce many business rules. In Figure 1-5, the state address (address_loc) has a check condition that ensures that all state abbreviations appear in uppercase characters.

▶ A *referential constraint* identifies a *foreign key*, which is composed of one or more data columns that appear as a primary or unique key elsewhere in the database. Usually the primary or unique keys appear in other tables, but this need not be the case. To satisfy a referential constraint, one of two conditions must be met: (1) the values that appear in the foreign key must exist in the referenced primary or unique key, or (2) one or more of the data columns in the foreign key must be NULL.

In Figure 1-5, the *ADDRESS* table contains one foreign key (fk_addressaddress_type). This ensures that a value in the address_type data column must exist as a primary key (pk_caddress) in the table that maintains address codes (i.e., *CADDRESS*).

See Also

1. Integrity constraints placed on a table appear in the SYS view ALL_CONSTRAINTS. See the index under SYS *views* for examples using this view.

Query Standards

It's real easy to make a mess of your ad hoc queries. Yet, if you apply a few simple standards, you'll find queries much easier to construct, test, debug, and maintain.

This section discusses how to format a query to improve legibility and understanding, how to simplify a query so that its meaning is not lost in a maze of SQL, and how to document a query so that you or others have some hope for maintaining the SQL at a later time.

How do I format a query?

Sometimes when I need to revise an SQL query written weeks previously, I have trouble deciphering what the program does. Is there any way to structure a query so that it's easier to understand and maintain?

Approach

The Oracle engine can be very forgiving about some SQL syntax, making it possible to write valid queries that are equivalent to run-on sentences. Consider two versions of the same SQL program shown in Figure 1-6 and Figure 1-7. One uses a freeform unstructured approach; the other incorporates a few simple standards to structure the query.

```
column name format a30
select n1.name_id,n1.name_last||', '||n1.name_first
"name",address_city,address_loc
from address,name n1
where n1.name_seriesno = (select max(n2.name_seriesno) from
name n2 where n2.name_id = n1.name_id) and
address_id = n1.name_id and address_type = 'PR' order by 2;
```

Figure 1-6: Example of unstructured SQL.

The SQL programs themselves are identical, and either version produces the same report. But the unstructured version invites confusion, whereas the structured version makes the intent of the query much clearer. Revising an unstructured query of several hundred lines can be a daunting task if you return to the query weeks after it was first written.

No standards exist for structuring SQL queries. It would be convenient, in fact, if a utility existed that would parse a query and format it. Such a tool could produce a physically structured program. It also might convert all SQL and SQL*PLUS reserved keywords to uppercase characters.

```
COLUMN name FORMAT a30
SELECT  ◀1
    n1.name_id,
    n1.name_last||', '||n1.name_first "name",
    address_city,  ◀2
    address_loc
FROM
    address,
    name n1
WHERE
    n1.name_seriesno =
        (SELECT MAX(n2.name_seriesno)
        FROM name n2                          ◀3
        WHERE n2.name_id = n1.name_id)
    AND address_id = n1.name_id   ◀4
        AND address_type = 'PR'  ◀
ORDER BY 2;  ◀5
```

Figure 1-7: Example of a structured query.

Comments

▶ Highlight each of the six possible clauses (i.e., SELECT, FROM, WHERE, GROUP BY, HAVING, and ORDER BY) by placing each on a separate line at the left margin. Indent everything else.

▶ Place each data column and expression that appears in the SELECT and GROUP BY clauses on a separate line. Place each table in the FROM clause on a separate line.

▶ Structure all subqueries using the same standards that apply to the main query, or, as shown above, compress the subqueries slightly to conserve space but retain the meaning.

▶ Indent the WHERE clause to highlight every table join. Keep together all join criteria related to a single table, with one condition per line.

▶ Whenever possible, use numbers in the ORDER BY clause. These numbers refer to the positions of the data columns or expressions in the SELECT clause. Of course, if you sort by a data column or expression that does not appear in the SELECT clause, then you'll need to use the column name or the expression.

See Also

1. Chapter 4 (beginning on page 107) discusses the principal clauses of the SELECT command.

How do I make queries easier to construct?

My queries are often a jumble of SQL and SQL*PLUS commands. How can I simplify the programs so that they're easier to write and understand?

Approach

Using good programming practices can improve your ability to write and maintain programs. Two concepts are key — modularize and reuse. That is, write smaller program components that can be employed in a variety of situations.

There are no standards that can be cited, but here are some practices that we've found helpful.

Shell and retrieval programs

Rather than writing queries as one long program, break them up into at least two programs — one that formats the report and a second that actually retrieves the data. We call the first type of program the *shell* (or *main*) program because it calls the second data retrieval program.

Figure 1-1 on page 2 showed one way to explore a database through a frequency distribution of table owners. The shell program that generated the report is shown in Figure 1-8.

```
SET TERMOUT OFF
START &&object.\clears
START &&object.\printer
START &&object.\date        ◀1
START &&object.\time
START &&object.\owncol

TTITLE 'Database tables and views by owner' skip 1 -
    LEFT 'Date: ' xDate '        Time: ' xTime -
    RIGHT 'Page: ' FORMAT 999 SQL.PNO SKIP 1 -
    LEFT 'Report name: owners.lis' -
    RIGHT 'SQL name: owners.sql' SKIP 2;

SPOOL &&query.\owners.lis
    START &&tool.\xowners    ◀2
SPOOL OFF

START &&object.\clears       ◀3
START &&object.\screen
```

Figure 1-8: Example of a shell program.

Note the considerable use of other smaller SQL and SQL*PLUS programs, acting much like procedures in procedural programming languages. Modularizing the shell makes it much easier to see what's actually happening in the program. Appendix A describes in detail what function each of these modular programs performs.

Comments

▶ Each START command executes a separate SQL or SQL*PLUS program. These programs are all stored in a directory whose name is stored in the SQL*PLUS variable &&object defined at the time of login. The programs clean up any existing mess made by previous queries, specify printer characteristics, and retrieve the date and time so that they can be used in the report title.

▶ The data retrieval program gets executed in this statement.

▶ Prior to exiting from the shell, the cleanup program is rerun, and settings appropriate for work at the screen get activated.

PL/SQL functions

By building reusable PL/SQL functions, you also can modularize and simplify ad hoc queries. Figure 1-7 on page 11 showed a query for a simple name and address report. The query included a correlated subquery that retrieved the most recent name for any individuals with name changes.

This correlated subquery surely will recur in other programs. You could reenter the subquery each time it's needed, but you also could write a PL/SQL function that has the same effect (see Figure 1-9).

```
CREATE OR REPLACE FUNCTION name_now
     (id VARCHAR2)
RETURN NUMBER
AS
name_now  NUMBER(2);

CURSOR main_cursor (p_id VARCHAR2) is
    SELECT MAX(name_seriesno)
    FROM name
    WHERE name_id = p_id;

BEGIN
    OPEN main_cursor(id);
    FETCH main_cursor INTO name_now;

    IF main_cursor%NOTFOUND THEN
          name_now := NULL;
    END IF;

    CLOSE main_cursor;
    RETURN name_now;
END;
/
```

Figure 1-9: Function that identifies most recent name data.

With the name_now function, you can revise the SQL query in Figure 1-7. This substantially reduces the WHERE clause criteria, making the program simpler and easier to understand (see Figure 1-10).

```
COLUMN name FORMAT A30
SELECT
    name_id,
    name_last||', '||name_first "name",
    address_city,
    address_loc
FROM
    address,
    name
WHERE
    name_seriesno = name_now(name_id)    ◀
    AND address_id = name_id
        AND address_type = 'PR'
ORDER BY 2;
```

Figure 1-10: Revised SQL from Figure 1-7 using name_now function.

Comments

▶ The PL/SQL function name_now replaces a correlated sub-query to retrieve the most recent name information; one line of code replaces several lines. Conceptually, the query suddenly becomes less complex. Choosing a meaningful function name also makes it easier for people to understand its purpose.

Views

Carefully constructed views also can improve your ability to write queries easily. The danger with views is that they tend to grow uncontrollably. Information systems (IS) staff create a view, it gets used for a time, but then users begin requesting revisions. The request generally starts this way: "View xyz has most data columns I need, but it's missing one thing." So IS staff add another table join into the view. Over time this incremental growth deteriorates query performance because, even if a specific query does not require all tables in the view, all table joins still occur.

It's far better to construct specialized views that perform very narrow functions and then employ these views in data queries. Here's an example. The query in Figure 1-10 will return multiple addresses with address_type of PR (permanent residence). Suppose you only wished to see the most recent permanent address as identified by the last row added or updated. This requires a correlated subquery that makes the query messy. However, if you create a view of the most recent addresses, the correlated subquery gets included in the view and need not appear in the query. Figure 1-11 shows an example of such a view called *RECENTAD-DRESS*. Now you need only join to the view and specify an address_type.

```
CREATE VIEW RecentAddress
     (RA_id,
      RA_type,
      RA_street,
      RA_city,
      RA_loc,
      RA_pcode,
      RA_country,
      RA_seriesno,
      RA_datestamp)
AS
SELECT * FROM address a1
WHERE                                        ▼
      a1.address_datestamp =
      (SELECT MAX(a2.address_datestamp)
      FROM address a2
      WHERE a2.address_id = a1.address_id
           AND a2.address_type = a1.address_type);
```

Figure 1-11: View that returns most recent addresses.

Comments

▶ The correlated subquery returning data on most recent addresses appears in the *RECENTADDRESS* view. Using this view means that the subquery need not appear in the query itself, making the query simpler and easier to understand.

One very nice feature of Oracle7 Release 7.2 and later releases is that subqueries can appear in the FROM clause of queries. In effect, this allows the query writer to construct data views "on the fly" instead of relying on IS to develop and maintain views. Later chapters provide several examples where such implicit views are used.

SQL segments

Sometimes you'll find yourself writing a query that uses nearly the same code that you wrote for a previous program. If you save and generalize these code fragments, then they're available for use in later queries. In a previous book by one of us, these code segments were called SQL *objects* and played a central role in simplifying ad hoc queries. To better distinguish SQL objects from other Oracle objects (especially when Oracle8 arrives), we now call these code segments SQL *segments*. The American Heritage Dictionary defines a segment as "any of the parts into which something can be divided." There is also a nice analogy to biology where segments mean differentiated subdivisions of an organism. Any sql query has these subdivisions, defined most obviously by the major clauses but then further defined as clause fragments.

Query writers can use SQL segments in many creative ways. A segment might define an adjective commonly used in the business (e.g., an "international" student at a college). SQL segments also can provide standard table joins based on a desired effect. For example, each of the following situations requires a different join to an address table: (1) return all addresses of a specified type if they exist, (2) return only the most recent address of a specified type if it exists, and (3) return the most recent address of a specified type if it exists or return NULL values if no such address exists. The join criteria used with the address table cannot be predetermined; you need to understand the intent of the query. By building an SQL segment for each situation, you can retrieve the appropriate one when constructing a new query.

SQL segments also find considerable use in defining business populations. Figure 1-12 shows an SQL query that counts the number of applicants who were accepted for college admissions.

```
SELECT COUNT(*)
FROM
      applicant
WHERE
      applicant_term = '199709'
              AND applicant_level = 'UG'        ◀1
              AND applicant_college = 'AS'
 ▶2 AND EXISTS
      (SELECT 'x'
      FROM
              cdecision,
              decision
      WHERE
              decision_id = applicant_id
                      AND decision_applicant_term = applicant_term
                      AND decision_applicant_seriesno =
                              applicant_seriesno
              AND cdecision_code = decision_code
                      AND cdecision_accept_ind = 'Y');
```

Figure 1-12: Applicants accepted for admission.

Comments

▶ The query includes codes for the term (e.g., Fall 1997), level (e.g., Undergraduate), and college (e.g., Arts & Sciences).

▶ A messy correlated subquery captures the business rules that identify an applicant accepted for admission. If the criteria EXISTS, then the applicant qualifies as accepted for admission.

By creating a simple PL/SQL function and generalizing the hardcoded values, you can create an SQL segment that defines accepted applicants. This segment can be reused in subsequent queries. Figure 1-13 shows one possible version of the segment.

```
applicant_term = '&&term'            ❼
        AND applicant_level = '&&level'
        AND applicant_college = '&&college'
AND accepted(applicant_id, applicant_term,
    ❷ applicant_seriesno) = 'Y'
```

Figure 1-13: SQL segment that defines an accepted applicant.

Comments

▶ The SQL segment replaces each of the hardcoded values that appeared in Figure 1-12 with a substitution variable. At runtime, the query prompts for these variables. This segment can now be used in queries that specify different terms, levels, and colleges.

▶ The PL/SQL accepted function (not shown) requires three arguments — an applicant's ID number, the term, and a sequence number if more than one application was submitted for a given term. The correlated subquery in Figure 1-12 makes clear why these three values must be specified.

The SQL segment shown in Figure 1-13 is more versatile, more compact, and more easily understood than the query in Figure 1-12.

See Also

1. Appendix A (beginning on page 313) includes several examples of shell programs. Also see Chapter 6 (Figure 6-27 on page 207).

2. See the discussion later in this chapter on page 24 showing the use of a login.sql file to define path names at time of login.

3. See the index under PL/SQL *functions* for examples of other PL/SQL functions used in this book.

4. Chapter 10 (Figure 10-15 on page 305) shows another example of view creation.

5. Report templates make wonderful SQL segments. Save the templates and reuse them whenever you need a similar report. Chapter 6 (beginning on page 173) discusses many such templates.

How do I place comments in a query?

My queries would be easier to understand if I could put comments in them to document the intent of a particular section. Is this possible?

Approach

Including documentation is another good programming practice that you should incorporate into your queries. Programs with ample comments are much easier to maintain than programs without comments.

Figure 1-2 on page 3 listed the tables for a specified owner. The shell program that produced this report appears in Figure 1-14.

```
SET TERMOUT OFF
/*
    sql:        tables.sql
    date:       22-mar-1994
    author:     glewis                                          ◀①
    use:        list of tables for a specified owner
*/
START &&object.\clears      -- clear break, compute, column
START &&object.\printer     -- report in landscape 8pt
START &&object.\date        -- retrieve date                    ▲②
START &&object.\time        -- retrieve time

START &&object.\getowner    -- prompt for table owner
START &&tool.\deftabl       -- define xReport (report name)

TTITLE 'Tables for owner: ' xOwner SKIP 1 -
    LEFT 'Date: ' xDate '        Time: ' xTime -
    RIGHT 'Page: ' FORMAT 999 SQL.PNO SKIP 1 -
    LEFT 'Report name: ' xReport -
    RIGHT 'SQL name: tables.sql' SKIP 2;

SPOOL &&query.\&&xReport
    START &&tool.\xtables   -- data retrieval program
SPOOL OFF

START &&object.\clears      -- cleans up after program run
START &&object.\screen      -- sets vars for work at monitor
```

Figure 1-14: Shell program for table report.

Comments

▶① sql comment delimiters /* and */ are useful when you want to provide multiple lines of documentation. This type of comment may appear separately (as here), on an sql*plus command line, or embedded within an sql command.

▶② ANSI/ISO comments begin with a double hyphen (--). They may not span multiple lines but can appear on separate lines by themselves or embedded within SQL commands. They may not, however, be used on the same line as an SQL*PLUS command.

Data for the table report get retrieved by the program xtables.sql. Figure 1-15 lists this program and illustrates several types of comments.

```
REM sql:        xtables.sql
REM author:     glewis
REM date:       15-may-1996
REM use:        retrieve data for tables report    ◀1
REM
        -- wrap comments at end of words
COLUMN comments FORMAT a40 WORD_WRAP
        -- skip line between table types    ◀2
BREAK ON type SKIP 1
SELECT
     t.table_name "name",
     t.table_type "type",
     c.comments "comments"
FROM
                    /* retrieves only those tables    ◀3
                    available to the user */
     ALL_TAB_COMMENTS c,
     ALL_CATALOG t
WHERE
     t.owner = '&&xOwner'    -- xOwner defined in shell
     AND c.owner = t.owner
          AND c.table_name = t.table_name
          AND c.table_type = t.table_type
ORDER BY 2, 1
;
```

Figure 1-15: Program that retrieves data for table report.

Comments

▶1 The SQL*PLUS REMARK command also can be used for comments. Each must appear on a separate line and cannot be embedded within an SQL command.

▶2 An ANSI/ISO comment cannot appear on the same line as an SQL*PLUS command.

▶3 SQL comments can span multiple lines even within a query.

Comments cannot appear on the same line as the SQL terminator, which is usually the semicolon unless it's been reset to another character.

See Also

1. The SQL*PLUS SET command controls many system variables, including the SQL terminator. See the discussion on page 22 that describes how the SET command affects the SQL*PLUS environment.

How do I create default column headings for reports?

I find it time consuming to create column headings and formats each time I write a query. It's also confusing because I'll give a column one heading in a report and a second heading in another report. Users sometimes ask how the two columns differ. Can I create default column headings and formats that would be in effect automatically for my reports?

Approach

It makes sense to eliminate the repetitious creation of column formats and to standardize headings so that they're consistent from report to report. Fortunately, this is easy to do.

Typically, query writers concentrate in one section of a large database, perhaps in one functional area like human resources or even in a subset of tables within a functional area. The same data columns appear frequently in reports. For those data columns which you use most often, create a COLUMN command that defines a heading and specifies a format. Then place the COLUMN commands in an SQL*PLUS file that you can start from the shell of each query. This effectively creates default column information for each query. It relieves you from creating the headings and formats repeatedly and also standardizes the appearance of your reports.

Whenever you write a query that uses new data columns or expressions, add the COLUMN commands to your SQL*PLUS command file. Over time, you'll build an impressive collection of default headings and formats. Figure 1-16 illustrates how default column settings can be created.

```
/* name */
COLUMN name_id HEADING 'id'
COLUMN name_last HEADING 'last|name'
COLUMN name_first HEADING 'first|name'
COLUMN name_middle HEADING 'middle|name' FORMAT a6
COLUMN name_seriesno HEADING 'name|seqnum' FORMAT 999999

/* address */
COLUMN address_id HEADING 'id'
COLUMN address_type HEADING 'address|type' FORMAT a7
COLUMN address_street HEADING 'street|address'
```

Figure 1-16: Command file that creates default column headings and formats.

See Also

1. See Appendix A on page 315 for another discussion of how to create default column headings.

How do I run multiple reports without format changes interfering?

Sometimes when I run several queries in one SQL*PLUS session, my reports contain weird formatting problems. This is particularly true when I intermingle reports that display at the screen with reports intended for the printer. How can I prevent this from happening?

Approach

Typically, reports display in one of two places — at the screen or at the printer (or a file that will be printed). The SQL*PLUS environments suitable for these two report types differ considerably. Thus, as you run several queries, any changes you make to system variable settings, column headings and formats, BREAK actions, and COMPUTE actions all compound. With interactions possible, you can get some bizarre results.

Unfortunately, there is no single SQL*PLUS command or system setting that reestablishes the defaults in operation when you first login to the SQL*PLUS environment. You could always exit and login between each query, but this quickly becomes tiresome. Therefore, you're left with the task of ensuring that you clean up after every query.

The shell program in Figure 1-8 on page 12 coordinates several programs to accomplish the cleanup function. The clears.sql program gets started before and after the main query. This clears all BREAK, COMPUTE, and COLUMN commands. The owncol.sql program reestablishes default column headings and formats. The printer.sql program runs prior to the main query, disables system settings appropriate for screen displays (e.g., where PAUSE is ON), and enables settings appropriate for print displays. Then, after the query completes, screen.sql disables the settings appropriate for print displays and reenables settings for the screen.

These programs will help avoid strange formatting effects in reports, but they won't prevent them from occurring. You'll still need to be aware whenever you manually override a system variable or define a user variable to create a special effect in a report. When exiting the query, you'll want to undo the special actions, for example, by resetting the altered system variable to its default or by undefining a user variable.

See Also

1. Beginning on page 313, Appendix A shows the program listings for the utility programs clears.sql, date.sql, time.sql, owncol.sql, printer.sql, and screen.sql.

SQL*PLUS **Environment**

When you write queries, your home base is normally a monitor and the SQL*PLUS environment. To reflect your preferred way of working, you can customize this environment. Some of the changes may be cosmetic, but others serve functional roles.

This section describes how to change the SQL prompt to provide more information than the default (SQL>). It also illustrates ways that the SQL*PLUS environment can be customized automatically at login.

How do I change the SQL *prompt?*

I work with several different Oracle databases. Is there some way I can modify the SQL prompt to identify which Oracle instance I'm working with?

Approach

By default, the SQL prompt is set as SQL>, but you can define it many other ways using the SQL*PLUS command SET SQLPROMPT 'text'. You also can add the current time to the SQL prompt merely with SET TIME ON.

The program in Figure 1-17 shows one way to retrieve the current Oracle instance, store it in a user-defined variable, and then use that variable to set the SQL prompt. If, for example, the instance is a production database called PROD, then instead of SQL> the prompt becomes PROD>.

```
COLUMN instance NEW_VALUE xInstance NOPRINT   ◀1
SELECT
     SUBSTR(GLOBAL_NAME,1,INSTR(GLOBAL_NAME,'.')-1) "instance"
FROM GLOBAL_NAME;
SET SQLPROMPT &&xInstance.>   ◀3                      2
```

Figure 1-17: Program that redefines SQL prompt as the current Oracle instance.

Comments

▶1 The program defines a user variable called xInstance that contains the name of the current Oracle instance. If you know the value for a user variable, the DEFINE command is the most direct method of defining a variable. However, when the value of a user variable must be retrieved from the database, other methods are required. The procedure shown here is one such method. It uses a simple SELECT query to return the instance name. The NEW_VALUE option in the COLUMN command creates an implicit DEFINE of the user variable xInstance.

▶ The name of the Oracle instance is extracted from GLOBAL_NAME, but it is also available in other views like V$DATABASE if you have the appropriate access rights. You could save and then run the program in Figure 1-17 whenever you wished to change the SQL prompt, or you could add the program to your login.sql file so that it got executed automatically whenever you logged into the SQL*PLUS environment. The next section discusses the login.sql file.

▶ The SET command changes the SQL prompt to the value contained in xInstance followed by the greater than (>) sign. The double ampersands (&&) identify the beginning of the substitution variable xInstance. The period (.) identifies the end of the substitution variable.

See Also

1. You'll find considerable use for implicitly defined user variables when writing ad hoc queries. It's the technique used, for example, to capture the date and time that datestamp a report. See the index under *user variables* for several examples.

2. GLOBAL_NAME is another SYS view. See the index under SYS *views* for examples of its use.

3. Beginning on page 36, Chapter 2 describes substitution variables and discusses several problems that arise with their use.

4. Another SET command (SET CONCAT) controls the character used to end a substitution variable. See the index under SET *commands*.

How do I ensure a consistent look to the SQL*PLUS environment?

Each time I login to the SQL*PLUS environment I need to reset some of the default system variables so that they work the way I prefer. For example, I always SET PAUSE ON so that output displayed on the monitor appears one screen at a time. Is there a way to automatically configure the SQL*PLUS environment to my liking?

Approach

SQL*PLUS supports something called a *site profile*, which is an SQL*PLUS command file generally named glogin.sql that allows the database administrator to create a default SQL environment for all users. The default name and location are system dependent.

SQL*PLUS also supports a *user profile*, which is a command file named login.sql that's run after glogin.sql. Each time you enter the SQL*PLUS environment, login.sql gets executed from your current directory if it exists or from a system-dependent path if it's not in your current directory. The login.sql program may contain SQL, SQL*PLUS, or PL/SQL commands that allow you to customize the SQL*PLUS environment to your choosing.

Figure 1-18 shows a simple login.sql file. Note that it uses the SQL*PLUS START command to execute other programs. By modularizing login.sql in this manner, it is easier to understand and easier to revise.

```
SET TERMOUT OFF
DEFINE object = d:\orawin95\komenda\objects     ◀1
DEFINE tool = d:\orawin95\komenda\tools
DEFINE query = d:\orawin95\komenda\query

START &&object.\getuser
START &&object.\getinstc
SET SQLPROMPT &&xUser.@&&xInstance.>     ◀2

DEFINE _editor = c:\windows\notepad.exe     ◀3

START &&object.\screen
```

Figure 1-18: Example of a login.sql automatically run at login.

Comments

▶ The login program first defines several system-dependent local path names. This has two advantages: (1) by making a single change in the path definition in login.sql, you can change the location of commonly used utility programs without making changes to each individual SQL query, and (2) if the defined names are short, they're much more convenient to use at the SQL prompt than longer path names.

▷ The SQL prompt gets changed from SQL> to a string formed by concatenating the user name, the @ character, and the Oracle instance. If, for example, the user is glewis and the instance is PROD, then the SQL prompt becomes glewis@prod>. Note in the SET SQLPROMPT command that the two periods each identify the end of a user-defined variable (xUser and xInstance).

▷ The login program defines a default editor that will be used whenever you use the EDIT command at the SQL prompt. This allows you to use an editor of your own choosing. In Figure 1-18 the default editor is defined as the Windows Notepad editor. The user variable must be named _editor (or _EDITOR) in the DEFINE command.

getuser.sql

This program determines the user name for the person making the SQL*PLUS login. The value for the user name then gets used to change the SQL prompt (see Figure 1-19).

```
COLUMN user NEW_VALUE xUser NOPRINT
SELECT LOWER(user) "user" FROM DUAL;
```

Figure 1-19: Program getuser.sql that retrieves current user name.

Comments

▷ The NEW_VALUE option in the COLUMN command coordinates with the SELECT query to implicitly define a variable called xUser that contains the current user name. This procedure is exactly analogous to the implicit DEFINE of the Oracle instance in Figure 1-17 on page 22. It's a somewhat convoluted way to define a user variable, but if the value must be retrieved from the database, this procedure conveniently captures the value.

getinstc.sql

This program retrieves the current Oracle instance, using the same technique shown in Figure 1-17 on page 22. The instance name then gets used along with the user name to set the SQL prompt (see Figure 1-20).

```
COLUMN  instance  NEW_VALUE  xInstance  NOPRINT
SELECT
    LOWER(SUBSTR(GLOBAL_NAME,1,INSTR(GLOBAL_NAME,'.')-1))
            "instance"
FROM  GLOBAL_NAME;
```

Figure 1-20: Program getinstc.sql that retrieves current Oracle instance.

screen.sql

In the last step, login.sql runs a program called screen.sql that sets several system variables so that the SQL*PLUS environment is suitable for working from the monitor. Many of these settings reflect personal preference, so you may wish to change them to match your own preferences (see Figure 1-21).

```
SET  PAUSE  "ENTER  to  continue  ..."    ◀1
SET  PAUSE  ON
SET  LINESIZE  80    ◀2
SET  PAGESIZE  24
TTITLE  OFF
SET  ESCAPE  OFF    ◀3
SET  ECHO  ON
SET  TERMOUT  ON
```

Figure 1-21: Program screen.sql that sets system variables for monitor work.

Comments

▶ When working from the monitor, you generally want reports to pause at the end of the screen as opposed to scrolling from begin to end. The screen.sql program sets the PAUSE on and provides a prompt to the user that the next page of the report may be seen by pressing the enter (or return) key.

▶ Page and line sizes depend on the monitor being used. The setting of 80 characters by 24 lines is common for monitors. But if you're using a monitor with other capabilities, then revise these settings.

▶ SQL*PLUS uses the backslash (\) as an escape character that says essentially "the next character in the string is valid, so ignore any special uses it may have." With ESCAPE set on, a command of DEFINE x = 'AT\&T' will define x as 'AT&T'. But with ESCAPE set off, SQL*PLUS will assume that the ampersand identifies the beginning of a substitution variable. If you work on operating systems that use the backslash as a valid character in path names, then it's important to redefine the escape character or to set it off. The default setting is off, but including a SET ESCAPE OFF in screen.sql ensures this to be the case in SQL*PLUS sessions where you've previously activated the escape character.

The counterpart to screen.sql that controls the SQL*PLUS environment when you want to print reports is illustrated in the shell program in Figure 1-8 on page 12. A listing of the printer.sql program appears in Appendix A (page 315). It turns off pausing so that the report spools continuously from begin to end; sets the PAGESIZE and LINESIZE characteristics to suit the printer, font, and orientation you've chosen; activates title lines; and deactivates the echoing of the SQL and any summary timing statistics that are more appropriate when working at the monitor.

See Also

1. The SET command controls many features of the SQL*PLUS environment. See the index under SET *commands* for other illustrations of its use.

Executing Queries

It can be frustrating when you've tested, debugged, and tuned a query only to experience problems when attempting to generalize the query for wider use. This section discusses problems that commonly occur when passing values to a query through command line arguments.

How do I pass values to a query?

Sometimes when I run a query by using arguments in the @ or START command, I get an error message. Obviously, the values specified in the arguments are not being passed correctly. How can I avoid this problem?

Approach

The START and @ commands allow optional arguments that get passed to parameters in a query. Elements in the argument list are separated by blank spaces. For example, "START test.sql 15 A" passes the values 15 and A to parameters &1 and &2, respectively, in a query called test.sql.

Argument errors depend on several factors: (1) how the arguments are specified, (2) how the query is written, and (3) whether you're running the query from the SQL*PLUS environment or from the operating system.

Specifying arguments

Blank spaces commonly produce errors when used in argument lists for any reason other than as a delimiter. The confusion probably occurs because blanks can be included when a user is prompted for data values at runtime. Figure 1-22 illustrates this interaction in a simple query prompting for ID numbers.

```
SQL> START test5
SQL> SELECT * FROM name WHERE name_id IN &&1;

Enter value for 1: ('a330', 'a505')  ◀
old   1: SELECT * FROM name WHERE name_id IN &&1
new   1: SELECT * FROM name WHERE name_id IN ('a330', 'a505')


      last            first       middle     name
id    name            name        name       seqnum
----- --------------- ----------- ------     -------
a505  Carrington      Thomas      J          1
a330  Vincent         Caroline               1
a330  Healey          Caroline    V          2
```

Figure 1-22: Query where user is prompted for data values.

Comments

▶ When prompted for a data value, you can use embedded blanks, and they produce valid SQL.

However, note what happens in Figure 1-23 when you enter the ID numbers as arguments from the SQL command line.

```
SQL> START test5 ('a330', 'a505')  ◀
SQL> SELECT * FROM name WHERE name_id IN &&1;

old   1: SELECT * FROM name WHERE name_id IN &&1
new   1: SELECT * FROM name WHERE name_id IN ('a330',
SELECT * FROM name WHERE name_id IN ('a330',
                                           *
ERROR at line 1:
ORA-00936: missing expression
```

Figure 1-23: Query where argument improperly includes an embedded blank.

Comments

▶ When used in arguments from the SQL command line, embedded blanks delimit argument values. The error occurs because the blank space in the argument makes SQL*PLUS believe that you've passed two data values — and the value it believes is &&1 produces invalid SQL. You'll need to enclose any arguments containing blanks within double quotes to avoid errors.

Type of query

How you write a query influences how the argument must be specified. Some queries require arguments that are more easily specified than others. Consider a simple query in which the user must specify an address type. Figure 1-24 shows one method of specifying the substitution variable. Note that the substitution variable is embedded in single quotes.

```
SQL> START test9 BU
SQL> SELECT * FROM address WHERE address_type = '&&1';  ◀

old   1: SELECT * FROM address WHERE address_type = '&&1'
new   1: SELECT * FROM address WHERE address_type = 'BU'

        address  street                            city               state/  postal
id      type     address                           address            prov    code
-----   -------- ------------------------------    -----------------  ------  ----------
aB&N    BU       3501 Western Ave                  Cambridge          MA      02140
a330    BU       McArthur and Phillips             Westchester        CO      80312
```

Figure 1-24: Query where character arguments are easily specified.

Comments

▶ When passing character data values to queries, structure the query so that the argument does not need a single quote in position 1. In this example the substitution variable is embedded in single quotes and the argument that gets passed is simple (i.e., BU).

Figure 1-25 shows exactly the same query with a slightly different way of handling the substitution variable. Instead of being embedded in single quotes, the substitution variable stands by itself. This method requires the user to pass the single quotes to avoid an error. Note that the argument that produces a valid SQL query is more complicated than the one in Figure 1-24. With the additional complication, it is harder to remember the correct syntax to use when passing arguments and therefore easier to generate errors. Choose the simpler method in Figure 1-24; it will make generalizing queries more enjoyable.

```
SQL> START test10 'BU' ◀①
SQL> SELECT * FROM address WHERE address_type = &&1;

old   1: SELECT * FROM address WHERE address_type = &&1
new   1: SELECT * FROM address WHERE address_type = BU
SELECT * FROM address WHERE address_type = BU
                                           *
ERROR at line 1:
ORA-00904: invalid column name


SQL> START test10 "'BU'" ◀②
SQL> SELECT * FROM address WHERE address_type = &&1;

old   1: SELECT * FROM address WHERE address_type = &&1
new   1: SELECT * FROM address WHERE address_type = 'BU'


      address street                        city            state/ postal
id    type    address                       address         prov   code
----- ------- ----------------------------- --------------- ------ ----------
@B&N  BU      3501 Western Ave              Cambridge       MA     02140
@330  BU      McArthur and Phillips         Westchester     CO     80312
```

Figure 1-25: Query where character arguments are difficult to specify.

Comments

▶ Revising the query so that the substitution variable is not embedded in single quotes complicates the argument. Note that when 'BU' is used as the argument, an error occurs because the single quotes get stripped from the argument before insertion into the program. This produces invalid SQL and generates error ORA-00904 (invalid column name) because the parsing process believes that BU is a data column and cannot locate it in the tables that appear in the FROM clause.

▶ To enter a valid argument, you'll need to use "'BU'". The double quotes get stripped before insertion in the query, and this produces valid SQL. It's easier just to write the query as shown in Figure 1-24 on page 29 and then use BU as the argument.

Command level

You can start SQL queries from either the SQL*PLUS environment or from the operating system command line. The syntax differs slightly when you use the operating system form. In general, the syntax is sqlplus uid/pwd @qname [arg . . .], where uid is the username, pwd is the password, and qname is the query command file started with the @ command. Note, that in some systems the executable may not be named sqlplus (e.g., it may be plus32 or some other variation).

Errors generated from improperly specified arguments can be minimized if you again pay attention to how you write the SQL query. Try to avoid writing parameters so that the first character in the data value that you want to pass to the query is a single quote. Figure 1-26 shows one way to pass an argument from an operating system command line that only invites trouble.

```
D:plus32 uid/pw @test6 "'a330','a505'"                  ◀ 1
SQL> SELECT * FROM name WHERE name_id IN (&&1);

old   1: SELECT * FROM name WHERE name_id IN (&&1)
new   1: SELECT * FROM name WHERE name_id IN (a330)

SELECT * FROM name WHERE name_id IN (a330)
                                        *
ERROR at line 1:
ORA-00936: missing expression


D:plus32 uid/pw @test6 \"'a330','a505'\"                ◀ 2
SQL> SELECT * FROM name WHERE name_id IN (&&1);

old   1: SELECT * FROM name WHERE name_id IN (&&1)
new   1: SELECT * FROM name WHERE name_id IN ('a330','a505')


      last            first        middle      name
id    name            name         name        seqnum
----- --------------- ------------ ------      -------
a505  Carrington      Thomas       J                1
a330  Vincent         Caroline                      1
a330  Healey          Caroline     V                2
```

Figure 1-26: Query requiring complex argument from operating system.

Comments

▶ Passing character arguments from the operating system command line can be quite complicated unless you write the query properly. In this example, note that the user specified an argument that would have produced valid SQL if run from within SQL*PLUS. However, from the operating system command line (Windows 95 here) it produces an error. The problem occurs because the query, while valid, made it difficult to specify arguments. Avoid errors by rewriting the query so that the arguments are easier to construct.

▶ Correctly specifying the argument for the query requires that you use backslashes in nonintuitive ways when executing the query from a Windows 95 system prompt. The format for the argument is system-dependent. Unless you like a challenge, revise the query to accept a simpler argument.

Revising the SQL query so that the argument need not start with a single quote, as shown in Figure 1-27, makes passing the argument much easier and less likely to produce errors.

```
D:plus32 uid/pw @test5 ('@303','@505')
SQL> SELECT * FROM name WHERE name_id IN &&1;   ◀

old   1: SELECT * FROM name WHERE name_id IN &&1
new   1: SELECT * FROM name WHERE name_id IN ('@330','@505')


      last             first        middle     name
id    name             name         name       seqnum
----- ---------------- ------------ ------     -------
@505  Carrington       Thomas       J               1
@330  Vincent          Caroline                     1
@330  Healey           Caroline     V               2
```

Figure 1-27: Query requiring simple argument from operating system.

Comments

▶ This query simplifies the argument. Note that no double quotes or backslashes are required.

See Also

1. All the examples in this section used the default system setting which lists the text of a SQL statement containing a substitution variable. Since the default lists the SQL statement both before and after making the substitution, you get the statement listed twice. You can

avoid these listings with SET VERIFY OFF. For an example, see Chapter 2 (Figure 2-9 on page 50).

2. Properly using single quotes in queries can be tricky. For another example, see Chapter 2 (Figure 2-3 on page 42) to see the machinations needed during a query to concatenate a single quote to a string.

Chapter 2
Building Blocks

The ability to use SQL as a reporting tool owes considerable credit to SQL*PLUS commands. It is these commands that allow you to interact with users at runtime, configure the reporting environment for display at the screen or at the printer, document reports with top and bottom titles, provide special column formatting instructions, compute summary statistics, structure the report output to produce different types of reports like frequency distributions, and create a variety of other effects.

Many frequently asked questions about ad hoc queries deal in some way with SQL*PLUS. Sometimes the solution is straightforward and involves only a single command; other times the solution is more complex and involves the coordination and interaction of several SQL*PLUS commands. This chapter deals with both types of questions.

Based only on the questions, there's little to distinguish the simple SQL*PLUS problems from the more complex ones. Producing one report from two queries turns out to be a simple problem, while sequencing page numbers across multiple reports that each begin on a new page turns out to be more complicated. Often, however, you can solve a complex problem once, save the result as an SQL*PLUS command file, give the file some meaningful name, and then reuse it whenever you want to achieve a certain effect.

It's this collection of single or multiple SQL*PLUS commands that provides query writers with building blocks useful for constructing queries. Do you need to configure an HP LaserJet printer, eliminate unwanted blank lines in a report, capture users' runtime responses for documentation, align pages for preprinted forms, or create a format for producing an ASCII output file? SQL*PLUS commands can handle all these problems and others.

Single Commands

Often a single SQL*PLUS command solves a query problem. One command in particular, the SET command, contains literally dozens of options that allow you to customize reports to achieve certain effects. Use SET to change page dimensions, determine the amount of space between report columns, force formfeeds in printed reports, eliminate trailing blanks from flat file output, pause between pages displayed at the screen, and solve other reporting problems. This section illustrates some of the many uses of the SET command.

The section also includes examples of the BREAK and COLUMN commands used in simple ways to double-space a report, reduce the display of redundant information, and hide columns from appearing in a report.

How do I concatenate a suffix to a substitution variable?

I've written a query that prompts the user for a data column value (e.g., 'F97'). I'd like to concatenate the string 'term.lis' to the user's response so that I can name the output file in a SPOOL command. I've tried '&&1'term.lis, but the single quotes get interpreted literally. How can I add a suffix to a substitution variable?

Approach

One of the SQL*PLUS system variables is CONCAT. This determines the character that ends a substitution variable when it's used in a longer string. By default, CONCAT is set to the period (.). To add a prefix or suffix to a substitution variable, use the CONCAT character as in the following command:

```
SPOOL &&yr.term.lis
```

The first period in the SPOOL command tells SQL*PLUS that the name of the substitution variable is 'yr' rather than 'yrterm.lis'.

See Also

1. Each of the shell programs in this book uses the CONCAT character to distinguish subdirectory path names. See, for example, Chapter 1 (Figure 1-8 on page 12).

How do I use a valid ampersand in a query?

I've written a query that includes an ampersand in one of the WHERE conditions. The ampersand is a legitimate part of the string comparison. Yet, when I run the query, I get prompted for a substitution variable. How can I designate the ampersand as valid?

Approach

Ampersands identify the start of an SQL*PLUS substitution variable. To use data column values like 'AT&T' or 'R&D' in the query, you'll need to alter the scanning for substitution variables. Several methods exist:

- Use the command SET DEFINE OFF to disable scanning for substitution variables. The older command SET SCAN OFF accomplishes the same thing.

- Change the character that identifies a substitution variable from an ampersand to something else. For example, 'SET DEFINE ~' changes the substitution character from an ampersand to a tilde.

- Precede the ampersand in your query with the system escape character. In effect, this tells SQL*PLUS that the next character is valid. By default, the system ESCAPE feature is off. When ESCAPE is set on, the default character is the backslash (\). With SET ESCAPE ON, the following query would produce valid SQL matching name_id with 'B&N':

```
SELECT * FROM name WHERE name_id = 'B\&N';
```

See Also

1. The backslash ESCAPE character can also present problems. For example, HP printers use both ampersands and backslashes as part of the escape sequences that control print characteristics. In this case, you must tell SQL*PLUS that both the ampersand and the backslash are valid. See the discussion later in this chapter on page 66.

How do I reset substitution variables?

I've written a query that uses a substitution variable. The first time a user runs the program, she gets prompted for a value and the query completes correctly. But if she wishes to run the query again with another value for the substitution variable, the first query just reruns. What's going on here?

Approach

Substitution variables come in two flavors depending on how many ampersands precede them. An undefined substitution variable with one ampersand (e.g., &var1) generates a prompt each time it's encountered in the program. An undefined substitution variable with two ampersands (e.g., &&var2) only generates a prompt the first time it's encountered. This latter feature is convenient in queries that use the same substitution variable more than once.

Since you're always prompted for a value of an undefined single-ampersand substitution variable, it would not produce the problem described in the question above. However, double-ampersand substitution variables generate an implicit DEFINE that is in effect until you redefine or UNDEFINE the variable. This would create the query behavior described in the question.

Your query could PROMPT and then ACCEPT a value into a substitution variable; this redefines the variable. Or you could simply issue an UNDEFINE command (e.g., UNDEFINE var2) at the start or conclusion of the query. Either method allows you to run the query multiple times with new values each time.

See Also

1. Figure 2-9 on page 50 for an example of the use of PROMPT and ACCEPT commands.

How do I double-space a report?

Users sometimes complain that single-spaced reports are difficult to read if they're used for extended periods of time. They'd prefer double-spaced or even triple-spaced reports. How can I do this?

Approach

Use the BREAK command to skip lines. The following command breaks after each report row and skips one line before the next row displays, producing a double-spaced report:

> BREAK ON ROW SKIP 1

A triple-spaced report would require SKIP 2.

See Also

1. You can skip to a new page using the BREAK command with the SKIP PAGE option. See Chapter 6 (Figure 6-12 on page 190) for an illustration of this technique.

How do I sort on a data column but not print it in the report?

A user requested a report that contains a data column with sensitive information. He doesn't need to see the actual values in this column, but the report does need to be sorted by the column so that he can identify who is in the top decile. How can I sort on a column but not print it?

Approach

This problem has an easy solution. Simply include the data column in the ORDER BY clause, but do not include it in the SELECT clause.

There may be other times, however, when more elaborate measures must be taken to hide a column that must be included in the SELECT clause for other reasons. In these cases, use the NOPRINT option in the COLUMN command. Figure 2-1 demonstrates how this works.

```
COLUMN salary NOPRINT  ◀
SELECT
      name_id "id",
      name_last||', '||name_first||' '||name_middle "name",
      comp_salary "salary"
FROM
      compensation,
      name
WHERE
      name_seriesno = name_now(name_id)
      and comp_id = name_id
ORDER BY 3 DESC;  ◀

id      name
-----   ------------------------------
@330    Healey, Caroline V
@226    Sacco, Danielle
@505    Carrington, Thomas J
@133    Berger, Vincent
```

Figure 2-1: Hiding a data column by suppressing its printing.

Comments

▶ The query sorts results by salary. However, the NOPRINT option in the COLUMN command suppresses the printing of salaries.

See Also

1. See Chapter 4 (Figure 4-11 on page 123) for another example where NOPRINT is used to suppress the printing of a column.

2. The PL/SQL for the name_now function used in Figure 2-1 appears in Chapter 1 (Figure 1-9 on page 13).

How do I eliminate blank lines from a report?

In reports where wrapping occurs in one of the columns, I get blank lines that I'd like to remove. Is this possible? Figure 2-2 shows the problem.

```
22-MAY-1996  05:28                  TABLE: ADDRESS                          Page:    1
Report: ADDRESS.dic                 Owner: OR2                  SQL: tabldict.sql
                                 Table of Addresses

Column Name            Type      Width  Scale Nulls      Column comments
==================================================================================
ADDRESS_ID             VARCHAR2     5          NOT NULL   ID of person
ADDRESS_TYPE           VARCHAR2     2          NOT NULL   Code for address type
ADDRESS_SERIESNO       NUMBER       2        0 NOT NULL   Sequential number for
                          ▼                              addresses of a specified
                                                          address_type

ADDRESS_STREET         VARCHAR2    25          NULL       Street address
ADDRESS_CITY           VARCHAR2    20          NULL       City of address
ADDRESS_LOC            VARCHAR2     5          NULL       State, province, or other
                                                          location of address

ADDRESS_COUNTRY        VARCHAR2     3          NULL       Country code of address
ADDRESS_DATESTAMP      DATE         7          NULL       Date of entry or last update
```

Figure 2-2: Blank lines occurring after wrapped text.

Comments

▶ The blank lines break the report into sections that detract from its appearance.

Approach

Two SQL*PLUS system variables cause the effect shown in Figure 2-2. Both variables refer to *record separators*, which are single lines that separate rows in a report. The character used to create a record separator is defined by the system variable RECSEPCHAR. By default, this character is a space, meaning that the record separator will appear as a blank line. The second system variable, RECSEP, controls when the record separator actually appears. By default, the setting is WRAPPED, meaning that a record separator only occurs after wrapped lines. Other options for RECSEP are EACH and OFF. EACH creates a record separator after every report row; OFF turns off the record separator feature.

You can eliminate blank lines after wrapped text simply by including in your query the command SET RECSEP OFF.

See Also

1. Figure 2-13 on page 58 shows an example where RECSEP was set off to eliminate blank lines after wrapped lines.

How do I use a valid single quote in a query?

I've written a query that includes a single quote in one of the WHERE conditions. The single quote is a legitimate part of the string comparison. Yet, when I run the query, I get an error message. How can I designate the single quote as a valid part of the string?

Approach

Single quotes in SQL*PLUS can get pretty confusing. The following SQL, for example, generates an error:

```
SELECT * FROM name WHERE name_last = 'O'Leary';
```

Doubling the single quote produces valid SQL:

```
SELECT * FROM name WHERE name_last = 'O''Leary';
```

The need to double-up legitimate single quotes can produce some strange looking queries. Figure 2-3 shows a section of the program that produces data dictionaries (see Appendix A on page 322 for a complete listing). The program retrieves table comments from ALL_TAB_COMMENTS for use in the report title. Note the use of the four successive single quotes used in two places. The net effect is to place one single quote at the start and one at the end of the table comment.

```
/* get several column values from all_tab_comments */

COLUMN tabletype NEW_VALUE xType NOPRINT
COLUMN table_comments NEW_VALUE xTable_desc NOPRINT

SELECT
    table_type "tabletype",
    DECODE(comments, NULL, 'No description available',
        ''''||comments||'''') "table_comments"
    FROM
        ALL_TAB_COMMENTS  ▲
    WHERE
        owner = UPPER('&&xOwner')
        AND table_name = UPPER('&&xTable');
```

Figure 2-3: Concatenating a single quote to a string.

Comments

▶ Concatenating a single quote to a string requires four single quotes in succession. The two inner quotes produce a string containing one single quote. The two outer quotes are then needed to concatenate the quote to another string (e.g., the comments data column in Figure 2-3). To produce the string O'Henry would require `'o'||''''||'Henry'`.

See Also

1. Quotes and blank spaces also figure prominently in problems encountered when passing arguments to SQL programs. For a discussion, see Chapter 1 on page 28.

How do I suppress the printing of redundant information?

Some of my reports contain duplicate information. For example, in a name and address report, if someone has two addresses that appear in the report, then the name also appears twice (see Figure 2-4). Is there some way to eliminate the redundant information and make the report easier to read?

```
                                      address  city                         state/  postal
 id     name                          type     address                      prov    code
 -----  ----------------------------  -------  ---------------------------  ------  --------
 a133   Berger, Kimberley      ▼      PR       Ipswich                      MA      01938
 a505   Carrington, Thomas            PR       Crary Mills                  NY      13310
 a330   Healey, Caroline              BU       Westchester                  CO      80312
 a330   Healey, Caroline              PR       Glen Falls                   NY      12750
 a330   Healey, Caroline              PR       Westchester                  CO      80310
 a226   Sacco, Danielle               BU       Charleston                   IL      60954
```

Figure 2-4: Name and address report with redundant information.

Comments

▶ In this report, Caroline Healey has three addresses — two permanent addresses (i.e., address_type is PR) and one business address. As a result of the multiple addresses, her ID number and name each appear three times. Furthermore, the PR address_type appears twice. Removing these redundancies would improve the legibility of the report and improve its understanding.

Approach

What constitutes redundant information depends on the ORDER BY clause. The report in Figure 2-4 is apparently sorted by name and then by address type. You can remove duplicate information using a BREAK command that essentially mirrors the action of ORDER BY. Figure 2-5 illustrates this function of BREAK.

Comments

▶ Redundant information appears in the name_id, name, and address_type columns. BREAK on each of these columns in the order they appear in the ORDER BY clause.
▶ Coordinating the BREAK and ORDER BY removes the duplicate information and makes the report cleaner.

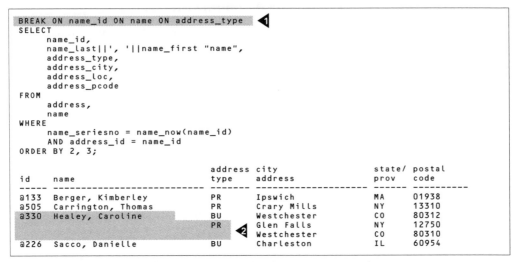

Figure 2-5: Redundant information removed with BREAK command.

See Also

1. Another example where the ORDER BY and BREAK commands co-ordinate to remove redundant information appears in Chapter 6 (Figure 6-14 on page 192).

2. The PL/SQL for the name_now function appears in Chapter 1 (Figure 1-9 on page 13).

How do I run two queries to produce one report?

For some reports I can't include all the summary information I'd like. For example, in Figure 2-6 I'd like to include an overall average sales. I can get this value easily enough in a second query, but the results always print on a new page. Is there some way I can combine the two reports?

```
Average sale by product

product          xavg          count
--------    ----------    ----------
MA1401              40             2
WK3224              10             1
********                  ----------
Tot Num                            3
```

Figure 2-6: Report missing overall average sale.

Approach

Under the default system settings, each report normally begins on a new page. However, you can disable this feature with the following command:

    SET EMBEDDED ON

This allows a report to begin anywhere on a page. Thus you could run one query, then SET EMBEDDED ON, and then run a second query. The second report would begin immediately following the first query.

Figure 2-7 illustrates this technique.

Comments

▶ Use the SET TRANSACTION statement with the READ ONLY option to ensure that no changes committed by other users affect multiple queries. The SET TRANSACTION statement must be the first statement in your transaction. Ensure that this is the case by issuing a COMMIT or ROLLBACK before running the query. The COMMIT at the end of the two queries does not actually commit anything to the database; it merely ends the read-only transaction.

▶ With the EMBEDDED system variable on, two or more reports can be combined into what visually appears as one report. Note that HEADING was set off in the second report to suppress the display of header information, thus making it appear as if the second report is actually part of the first report.

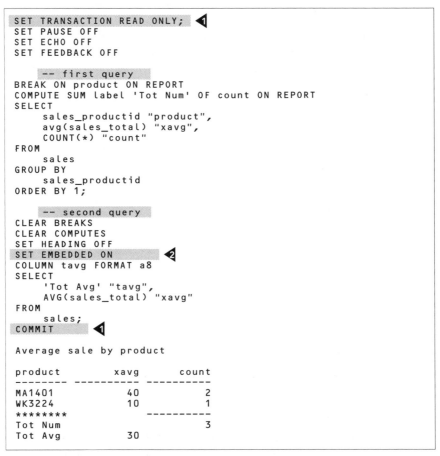

```
SET TRANSACTION READ ONLY;  ◀1
SET PAUSE OFF
SET ECHO OFF
SET FEEDBACK OFF

      -- first query
BREAK ON product ON REPORT
COMPUTE SUM label 'Tot Num' OF count ON REPORT
SELECT
      sales_productid "product",
      avg(sales_total) "xavg",
      COUNT(*) "count"
FROM
      sales
GROUP BY
      sales_productid
ORDER BY 1;

      -- second query
CLEAR BREAKS
CLEAR COMPUTES
SET HEADING OFF
SET EMBEDDED ON          ◀2
COLUMN tavg FORMAT a8
SELECT
      'Tot Avg' "tavg",
      AVG(sales_total) "xavg"
FROM
      sales;
COMMIT  ◀1

Average sale by product

product          xavg          count
--------  ----------    ----------
MA1401             40               2
WK3224             10               1
********              ----------
Tot Num                              3
Tot Avg            30
```

Figure 2-7: Two queries combined into a single report.

See Also

1. The SET TRANSACTION command is useful whenever you have multiple coordinated queries. The COMMIT ends the read-only transaction. Chapter 8 (Figure 8-8 on page 241) shows another example of its use, where a bind variable gets defined in an anonymous PL/SQL block and then used in a SQL query.

2. For another EMBEDDED example, see Figure 2-18 on page 69.

3. Set HEADING off when you need total control over column headings. Block reports require this type of control. See Chapter 6 on page 186 for a discussion and illustration of this.

How do I force a formfeed in a report?

I have a preprinted form that I want to complete with results from a query. Yet, when I print the report on the form, the page doesn't eject correctly so nothing lines up properly. How can I force a formfeed after each row in the query gets printed? Figure 2-8 shows the query I'm using.

```
TTITLE 'Page: ' FORMAT 99 SQL.PNO;
SET HEADING OFF
COLUMN xrow FOLD_AFTER
COLUMN last FOLD_AFTER

SET PAGESIZE 7
BREAK ON ROW SKIP PAGE          ◀

SELECT
     NULL "xrow",
     NULL "xrow",
     LPAD(' ',5),
     name_id,
     NULL "xrow",
     LPAD(' ',8),
     name_last "last",
     LPAD(' ',8),
     name_first||' '||name_middle
FROM
     name
WHERE
     name_seriesno = name_now(name_id)
ORDER BY 2;
```

Figure 2-8: Query without a physical page break.

Comments

▶ Ignore for now the actual SQL query that illustrates techniques for spooling results to a preprinted form. Chapter 6 discusses this in more detail. The misalignment problem occurs because the query relies on the PAGESIZE setting and the SKIP PAGE action in the BREAK command to align each new physical page correctly in the printer.

Approach

You need to distinguish between a page, as defined by SQL*PLUS, and the physical piece of paper in your printer. For SQL*PLUS, a page dimension is PAGESIZE lines high and LINESIZE characters wide. Each line in the top title, the bottom title, and the query results and any blank lines preceding the top title (i.e., NEWPAGE) count as lines in PAGESIZE.

The query in Figure 2-8 relies on the SKIP PAGE action in the BREAK command to print each result row on a new page. When SQL*PLUS skips a page, it does so by skipping PAGESIZE (7) lines, which effectively moves to a new SQL*PLUS page. However, it may not be a new physical page unless PAGESIZE 7 adequately describes the preprinted form being used. Often you'll find yourself fiddling around to find the PAGESIZE setting that's consistent with the physical page.

It's safer to simply force a formfeed between pages. This is easily accomplished with the following command:

> SET NEWPAGE 0

This produces a physical page break by sending a formfeed to the printer between each SQL*PLUS page, thus ensuring consistency between the top of a physical page and the top of an SQL*PLUS page.

See Also

1. If you'd like to know what's going on in the SELECT clause of the query in Figure 2-8, see the discussion on preprinted forms in Chapter 6 on page 190.

2. The PL/SQL for the name_now function appears in Chapter 1 (Figure 1-9 on page 13).

Coordinated Commands

Frequently the effect you wish to create in a report requires the use and coordination of several SQL*PLUS commands. Sometimes this is straight-forward, as when coordinating the PROMPT and ACCEPT commands to provide runtime instructions to users and to capture their responses as user variables. However, at other times the coordination is more subtle, as when implicitly defining variables with the NEW_VALUE option in a COLUMN command.

This section discusses several common query problems, including ways to compress data columns so that they'll fit within the physical dimensions of a report, how to embed escape sequences in reports that will configure an HP LaserJet printer, how to use runtime responses from users to retrieve other database information, and how to creatively display NULL values in reports.

How do I customize runtime prompts for user variables?

Sometimes the default prompt that SQL*PLUS generates when I use substitution variables in queries is not particularly clear. I'd like to provide the user with more information about what kind of response is expected and valid. Is this possible?

Approach

Two SQL*PLUS commands make customizing runtime prompts straight-forward. These commands are PROMPT and ACCEPT.

Appendix A (page 329) includes an SQL utility program that determines the report linesize needed to accommodate requested data columns. The program prompts the user for data column names that must be entered in a specific format or the SQL generated will not produce valid results. Figure 2-9 shows this portion of the program.

```
SET VERIFY OFF   ◀❶
SET TERMOUT ON

PROMPT Enter data columns using format: owner.table_name.column_name
PROMPT Use single quotes around entries and enclose within ().
PROMPT   ◀❷

ACCEPT ColumnName PROMPT 'Enter column names: '   ◀❸
SET TERMOUT OFF
```

Figure 2-9: Example of custom prompts for runtime user variables.

Comments

▶ By default, SQL*PLUS lists the portion of SQL containing substitution variables both before and after the substitution is made. Disable this setting with SET VERIFY OFF.

▶ The default prompt for a substitution variable is "Enter value for varname:". Use the PROMPT command to add detail to the runtime request for user information. The line in Figure 2-9 that includes PROMPT without any text produces a blank line.

▶ When the user responds to the prompt, the value is accepted into a variable (called ColumnName in Figure 2-9). By default, SQL*PLUS makes the datatype of the user variable character, but you also can specify DATE or NUMBER. The maximum length of a character response is 240.

See Also

1. For another example where the PROMPT and ACCEPT commands get used to interact with a user, see Chapter 4 (Figure 4-12 on page 124). This figure illustrates how to sort query results based upon criteria set by the user at runtime.

How can I use runtime user responses to retrieve other information?

I'd like to construct new variables or retrieve additional report documentation based on the responses that users provide to runtime prompts. For example, if the query prompts for a table name and the user responds in lowercase, how can I use an uppercase table name in the report title?

Approach

There are many situations when user variables provide opportunities for further processing that would add value to the report. Examples include

- Cleaning the response for display, as when converting mixed-case responses to uppercase.

- Combining two or more responses into a single variable, as when concatenating an owner and table name into an owner.tablename or converting two numeric responses into a ratio.

- Verifying the accuracy of a response, as when the response should be a valid value in one of the database code tables.

- Retrieving additional information based on the response, as when accessing table comments based on the table name.

Chapter 1 discussed a useful SQL program that produces a data dictionary for a specified table. The listings for this program appear in Appendix A (page 322). The program contains two examples in which user variables are processed to provide additional information for the report.

Figure 2-10 shows one of the two examples from the data dictionary program. The technique implicitly defines a new variable called xReport that contains a report name constructed by concatenating the file extension '.dic' to the user-identified table name.

```
COLUMN reportname NEW_VALUE xReport NOPRINT
SELECT '&&xTable'||'.dic' "reportname" FROM DUAL;
```

Figure 2-10: Implicit define of a new variable.

Comments

▶ To implicitly define a new variable, you'll need to coordinate the COLUMN command and a simple query. The query processes the user variable, in this case concatenating a file extension to the table name, and assigns this expression an alias. The alias is referenced in a COLUMN command containing the NEW_VALUE option to define a new user variable (called xReport).

The query in Figure 2-10 occurred against DUAL. This is convenient for simple processing of a user variable. However, you also may wish to access data in other tables or views. Figure 2-11 shows an example in which user responses are used to access ALL_TAB_COMMENTS.

```
    /* define table type and table comments
    from all_tab_comments */

COLUMN tabletype NEW_VALUE xType NOPRINT
COLUMN table_comments NEW_VALUE xTable_desc NOPRINT

SELECT
    table_type "tabletype",
    DECODE(comments, NULL, 'No description available',
          ''''||comments||'''') "table_comments"
    FROM
        ALL_TAB_COMMENTS
    WHERE
        owner = UPPER('&&xOwner')
        AND table_name = UPPER('&&xTable');
```

Figure 2-11: Implicit define of two user variables from data view.

Comments

▶ A COLUMN command with the NEW_VALUE option coordinates with the query to define two new user variables named xType and xTable_desc.

▶ Aliases used in the COLUMN command are identified in the SELECT query.

▶ The user was prompted for a table owner and a table name. The runtime responses to these prompts provide the information needed to access ALL_TAB_COMMENTS and retrieve the table type and comments that describe the table.

See Also

1. The DUAL table is owned by SYS. It contains only one data column and one row. You can use DUAL in many creative ways; for example, to create header lines in ASCII flat files for exporting to a word processor for mail merges, or to create escape sequences that control HP laser printers. See the index under DUAL *table* for specific examples.

How do I compress columns to fit the report linesize?

Frequently, the amount of information I want to include in a report exceeds the linesize my printer can handle. Are there any tricks to fitting data columns into limited report dimensions?

Approach

A variation of Murphy's law holds true for ad hoc reports — the amount of information requested by the user expands to fill (and just exceed) the amount of space available on the printed page. When this happens, you'll need the query writer's equivalent of the shoe horn to slip that extra column into a report.

First, ask the big questions:

• Did the user request so much information that there's no hope for including it in the standard row-and-column report? If so, then you have basically two choices: (1) create a block report (see Chapter 6) in which data values appear in block format underneath each other instead of across the page in columns (e.g., an address on an envelope is blocked), or (2) use a procedural program to achieve total control over the placement of data values on the printed page.

• Is the report truly bound by the LINESIZE? Can you change printers, for example, to a laser printer with compressed print? Or can you import the report file into a word processor and change the font and type size so that the report linesize is increased?

Let's assume that the linesize is truly limited. You could, for example, be stuck using standard greenbar paper with a maximum of 132 characters. Or, in the case of the reports that appear in this book, the limits of legibility are reached at 85 characters given the physical dimension across the page and the font used for the reports. Let's use an 85 linesize limit and work through an example of compressing reports.

Suppose you've been asked to produce a name and address report with information on ID number; last, first, and middle names; and street, city, state, and zip code address. Also include the type of address and its sequence number if more than one address of a single type exists.

linesize.sql

Appendix A (page 328) includes a utility program called linesize.sql that lets you quickly compute the minimum linesize needed to accommodate all the data columns a user has requested. If the value it returns is less than the available report linesize, then there's no problem. However, if the computed minimum linesize exceeds what you've got available, then it's time to get out that shoe horn.

When you run linesize.sql, you'll be prompted for the data columns to appear in the report. Enter the column names in the format that concatenates owner, table_name, and column_name separated by periods, as in owner.table_name.column_name (e.g., or2.name.name_id). The program assumes that the default value of the COLSEP system variable applies so that one space separates each of the columns in the report. The program then uses the following algorithm to compute the minimum line size needed to include all requested data columns in the report.

1. For data columns with CHAR or VARCHAR2 datatypes, the default display width used by SQL*PLUS is the width of the column in the database. The utility program (linesize.sql) accesses ALL_TAB_COLUMNS and retrieves this information for the column.

2. For data columns with the NUMBER datatype, the default display width used by SQL*PLUS is the greater of the following two values: (a) the width of the column heading, which defaults to the column name, or (b) the value in the NUMWIDTH system variable, which defaults to 10. A column named address_seriesno, for example, with a NUMBER(2) datatype will display at 16 characters because the column heading (address_seriesno by default) contains 16 characters and this is larger than NUMWIDTH. The linesize.sql program assumes that you'll change these defaults to use the minimum column size that's still wide enough to display any valid data. It computes this minimum size as the precision of the data column plus one character for a sign (+ or −) and, if the number is real, one character for a decimal point. Thus a column with datatype number(5,3) would display in 5 + 1 + 1 = 7 columns. Use the COLUMN command to change the format of NUMBER data columns accordingly.

3. For data columns with the LONG datatype, the default display width used by SQL*PLUS is the smaller of the two system variables LONG or LONGCHUNKSIZE. The utility program sets each of these system variables to 80 and uses that value in its computations.

4. For data columns with the DATE datatype, the default display width used by SQL*PLUS depends on the National Language Support (NLS) parameters in effect. The utility program accesses

NLS_SESSION_PARAMETERS and determines the length of NLS_DATE_FORMAT. It then uses this value in its computations. For example, if the format is DD-MON-YY, a display width of 9 is used.

Example

Running linesize.sql shows that we'll need a minimum of 116 characters to include all the data columns in the example discussed on page 54. With the report linesize limited to 85, we're left with the problem of compressing the report by 31 characters.

Several strategies exist for reformatting data columns so that they'll fit within a restricted space. These include

- Reformat all NUMBER data columns to the minimum display size computed with the algorithm in linesize.sql.

- Whenever possible create expressions that would shorten CHAR or VARCHAR2 data columns. For example, concatenate last, first, and middle names into a name expression.

- Use creative headings that do not exceed the default display width for character data columns. For example, suppose a data column person_gender is VARCHAR2(1). If you set the heading as "sex", then you'll need to reset the format as A3 to include the entire heading. Alternatively, you can make use of the HEADSEP system variable to create a heading of "s|e|x", which only requires an A1 format. In this case, each letter of the heading appears on a separate line, one under the other.

- Reformat DATE data columns so that they require less space. For example, if the default format is DD-MON-YYYY, you can conserve display width by changing the format to DD/MM/YY or MM/DD/YY.

- Use the WORD_WRAPPED option for CHAR, VARCHAR2, and LONG data columns and use a format smaller than the default value. For example, you could reformat a varchar2(40) data column as A25 with the WORD_WRAPPED option activated.

- If you object to wrapped report lines, then run a simple query to determine the maximum length of values in the data column for the report population. If address_city is VARCHAR2(30) but nobody in the report population has a city address that exceeds 20 characters, then reset the format as A20. Obviously, this is a one-time solution.

Figure 2-12 shows the final report from the machinations needed to cram 116 characters into 85 spaces.

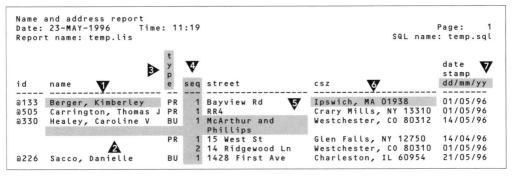

Figure 2-12: Report that illustrates several techniques for conserving display space.

Comments

▶ The report concatenates name data columns into an expression to save space.

▶ Redundant information is suppressed. While this doesn't conserve display width, it does create more white space and make the report easier to read.

▶ Rather than use an A4 format and the heading "type", the report uses the HEADSEP system variable to limit the format to A2.

▶ The datatype for address_seriesno is NUMBER(2). As an integer, the minimum display width is 2 + 1 = 3. The report sets a format and heading consistent with this minimum display width.

▶ Street address is WORD_WRAPPED to conserve display space. RECSEP is set off to eliminate blank lines after wrapped lines.

▶ The report concatenates city, state, and zip code data columns into an expression.

▶ The default date format was DD-MON-YY. The report uses a different format that conserves some space.

The SQL query that produced this report appears in Figure 2-13.

Comments

▶ The BREAK command suppresses the printing of redundant information on name, ID, and address type. Setting RECSEP off prevents blank lines from being inserted after wrapped lines.

```
BREAK ON name_id ON name ON address_type     ◀1
SET RECSEP OFF
COLUMN name_id HEADING 'id'          ▼2
COLUMN name FORMAT a20                        ▼3
COLUMN address_type HEADING 't|y|p|e'
COLUMN address_seriesno HEADING 'seq' FORMAT 99
COLUMN address_street HEADING 'street' FORMAT a18 WORD_WRAPPED
COLUMN csz FORMAT a22
COLUMN xdate HEADING 'date|stamp|dd/mm/yy' FORMAT a8    ▲4
SELECT
    name_id,
    name_last||', '||name_first||' '||name_middle "name",   ◀5
    address_type,
    address_seriesno,
    address_street,
    address_city||', '||address_loc||' '||address_pcode "csz",
    TO_CHAR(address_datestamp, 'dd/mm/yy') "xdate"
FROM
    address,                    ▲6
    name
WHERE
    name_seriesno = name_now(name_id)
    AND address_id = name_id
ORDER BY 2, 3;
```

Figure 2-13: Query that produced the report in Figure 2-12.

▶2 The HEADSEP character helps retain meaningful headers whenever the width of the header would exceed the format used on the data column. Here, a "type" header would require A4 for the data column, but using the HEADSEP character allows you to use the default A2 instead.

▶3 A format of 99 and a heading "seq" displays the integer values for address_seriesno in a column 3 characters wide (1 is for a sign). To control the display width for numeric data, you need to consider both the heading width and the data column format. If you don't specify either a format or heading, address_seriesno displays in 16 characters (the length of the data column name). If you specify only a heading and the length of the heading is less than NUMWIDTH, then address_seriesno displays in 10 characters (the default NUMWIDTH). If you specify only a format, address_seriesno again displays in 16 characters because it defaults to the larger of NUMWIDTH or the length of the data column name. In short, specify both a heading and a format for numeric data columns.

▶4 Wrapping character data at words retains meaning yet allows you to use a smaller format than the default.

▶5 Concatenating character data columns usually reduces the display space needed.

▷ The TO_CHAR function reformats the date column address_datestamp.

Creating formats and headers for data columns can be a real pain, especially when you need to squeeze too much information into too small a physical space. Make sure you save these COLUMN commands in the SQL*PLUS command file you use to create default headers for queries. Having created the column settings once, there's no reason to relive the experience.

See Also

1. Chapter 6 on page 186 discusses block reports.

2. LONG datatypes create special problems when you wish to display them in reports. See Chapter 5 on page 168 for a discussion.

3. The PL/SQL for the name_now function used in Figure 2-13 appears in Chapter 1 (Figure 1-9 on page 13).

4. By creating a command file with column headings you use frequently, you improve consistency between reports. The command file can be started from the shell of your queries. For a discussion, see Chapter 1 on page 20.

How can I display a value instead of a NULL in a report?

One of my users objects to the blank spaces in reports when the query returns NULL values. How can I display an 'unknown' instead?

Approach

Several methods provide control over the display of NULL values. The methods differ on how they affect the display globally. To change the display of NULL values at the most global level, for all data columns, change the default NULL system setting to include the text of your preference:

SET NULL 'unknown'

If you only want to change the display of NULL values in a single data column, specify the text to display by including the NULL option in a COLUMN command (e.g., COLUMN name_middle NULL 'not available').

And if you only want to change the display of NULL values for specific values in a report, use the DECODE or NVL functions to establish the criteria and display text.

The Figure 2-14 illustrates the three methods of controlling the display of NULL values.

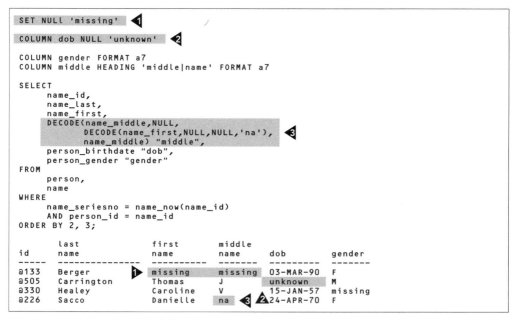

```
SET NULL 'missing'    ◄1

COLUMN dob NULL 'unknown'    ◄2

COLUMN gender FORMAT a7
COLUMN middle HEADING 'middle|name' FORMAT a7

SELECT
        name_id,
        name_last,
        name_first,
        DECODE(name_middle,NULL,
                DECODE(name_first,NULL,NULL,'na'),    ◄3
                name_middle) "middle",
        person_birthdate "dob",
        person_gender "gender"
FROM
        person,
        name
WHERE
        name_seriesno = name_now(name_id)
        AND person_id = name_id
ORDER BY 2, 3;

        last            first       middle
id      name            name        name       dob          gender
-----   -------------   ---------   -------    ---------    -------
a133    Berger     1►   missing     missing    03-MAR-90    F
a505    Carrington      Thomas      J          unknown      M
a330    Healey          Caroline    V          15-JAN-57    missing
a226    Sacco           Danielle    na    ◄3 ▲2 24-APR-70   F
```

Figure 2-14: Three methods for displaying NULL values.

Comments

▶ NULL values appear by default as blank spaces in reports. You can change this default by setting the NULL system variable as some character string of your choice (e.g., 'missing' in this example). This change affects all data columns unless you specifically override the command.

▶ You can override the global treatment of NULL values in the COLUMN command. In Figure 2-14 if the date of birth is NULL, the report overrides the global setting and displays 'unknown'.

▶ You also can override global or column NULL settings by evaluating individual data values with a DECODE function. Based on the DECODE criteria, you can display NULL values in a variety of ways. In Figure 2-14 the DECODE checks the middle name. If middle name is NULL, the DECODE then checks the first name. If a first name exists, then a 'na' displays on the report for the NULL middle name; otherwise, the middle name is left as NULL and the global or column setting takes over.

See Also

1. NULL values frequently create problems for query writers. Beginning on page 144, Chapter 5 discusses several of these problems.

2. The PL/SQL for the name_now function used in Figure 2-14 appears in Chapter 1 (Figure 1-9 on page 13).

How can I easily format query output as an ASCII flat file?

I've written a query that produces a comma-delimited ASCII flat file. To format the query so that there aren't any titles, headers, or other extraneous lines, however, I need to set a bewildering array of system variables. Is there some easy way to do this?

Approach

No single system variable creates an SQL*PLUS environment suitable for producing a flat file that contains only the query results. However, one command does help considerably:

    SET PAGESIZE 0

Setting PAGESIZE at 0 suppresses headers, top and bottom titles, and any blank lines that normally print before the top title. It even disables pausing. However, it does not affect feedback lines, timing statistics, or the echoing of SQL commands. You'll still have to disable each of these.

Figure 2-15 illustrates the use of PAGESIZE 0.

```
SET HEADING ON
SET NEWPAGE 4
SET PAUSE ON                          ◀①
TTITLE 'top title' SKIP 2;
BTITLE 'bottom title' SKIP 2;

SET ECHO OFF
SET FEEDBACK OFF    ◀②
SET TIMING OFF

SET PAGESIZE 0
SET LINESIZE 40     ◀③
SET TRIMSPOOL ON

SELECT
      name_id||','||
      name_last||','||
      name_first||','||
      name_middle||',x'
FROM name
WHERE name_seriesno = name_now(name_id);

a505,Carrington,Thomas,J,x
a133,Berger,Kimberley,,x
a330,Healey,Caroline,V,x
a226,Sacco,Danielle,,x
```

Figure 2-15: System variable setting suitable for producing an ASCII flat file.

Comments

▶ PAGESIZE 0 suppresses each of these system settings and title commands.

▶ You'll still need to disable the echoing of SQL commands, the display of timing statistics, and any feedback information on the number of rows returned by the query.

▶ When producing an ASCII flat file, set the LINESIZE large enough so that it exceeds the maximum characters in a single output row. Setting TRIMSPOOL on trims trailing blanks from each output row.

See Also

1. See Chapter 6 on page 212 for a discussion of how to produce an ASCII flat file suitable for use with mail merges in word processors.

2. The PL/SQL for the name_now function appears in Chapter 1 (Figure 1-9 on page 13).

How do I format a report for output to an HP LaserJet printer?

Many of my reports get printed on a Hewlett-Packard (HP) LaserJet. I almost always print the reports in landscape orientation with compressed pitch and a right margin setting so that I can get at least 160 characters on each line. Is there any way that I can control these characteristics from the output report without having to manually set them on the printer or first import the report into a word processor and format it there? In other words, I'd like to simply print the file and have it properly formatted without requiring any other steps.

Approach

HP LaserJet printers use escape sequences to control many printer functions, including such things as page orientation, typeface families, margins, and font characteristics such as pitch and weight. By embedding the escape sequences in the report itself, you can control the printer without manual intervention.

You'll need two kinds of escape sequences embedded in your report — one to turn on the printer characteristics and a second to turn them off again so that the next person using the printer doesn't get surprised when her report prints all crazy. There are different methods you can use to embed the escape sequences. One convenient method embeds them in titles, using TTITLE to turn on the printer characteristics and BTITLE to turn them off. This toggles the escape sequences on and off for each page of the report.

Figure 2-16 illustrates this method of controlling an HP LaserJet printer.

Comments

▶ The TTITLE and BTITLE each include a user-defined variable; xLandcomp is the escape sequence that places an HP LaserJet IIIp in landscape orientation with compressed pitch (16.67 characters per inch), while xReset reactivates the default settings. These two variables get defined in the program landcomp.sql (see Figure 2-17). The precise escape sequence will depend on which printer you use.

▶ If you examine the report output file, it will contain escape sequences in the top and bottom titles. These sequences configure the printer; they will not appear on the printout. Note that in Figure 2-16 the ■ character denotes the escape character (ASCII

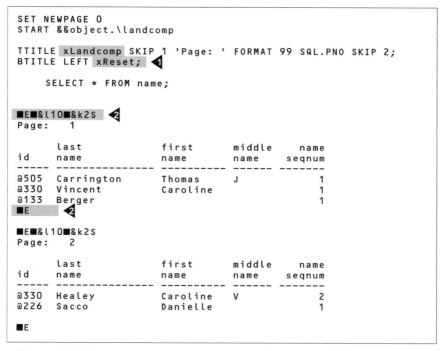

```
SET NEWPAGE 0
START &&object.\landcomp

TTITLE xLandcomp SKIP 1 'Page: ' FORMAT 99 SQL.PNO SKIP 2;
BTITLE LEFT xReset; ◀1

        SELECT * FROM name;


■E■&l10■&k2S ◀2
Page:    1

          last              first       middle      name
id        name              name        name        seqnum
-----     --------------    ----------  ------      -------
a505      Carrington        Thomas      J               1
a330      Vincent           Caroline                    1
a133      Berger                                         1
■E            ◀2

■E■&l10■&k2S
Page:    2

          last              first       middle      name
id        name              name        name        seqnum
-----     --------------    ----------  ------      -------
a330      Healey            Caroline    V               2
a226      Sacco             Danielle                    1

■E
```

Figure 2-16: Using escape sequences to an configure HP LaserJet printer.

character code 027). Other escape sequences determine other print characteristics. For example, the question indicated a preference for printing 160 characters on a line. You can set the right margin in an HP LaserJet printer with an escape sequence so that there are 160 characters per line.

The program landcomp.sql actually defines the escape sequences that appear in top and bottom titles. Figure 2-17 shows how this is done.

Comments

▶ HP LaserJet printer escape sequences sometimes contain ampersands. Yet SQL*PLUS uses ampersands (&) to identify the start of a substitution variable. When you need to use an ampersand as a valid character in a string, you must alert SQL*PLUS to that fact by preceding the ampersand with the system ESCAPE character. Here ESCAPE is set to the # character.

```
SET ESCAPE #    ◄1

COLUMN landcomp NEW_VALUE xLandcomp NOPRINT
SELECT
     CHR(27)||'E'||
     CHR(27)||'#&l1O'||
     CHR(27)||'#&k2S'    "landcomp"    ◄2
FROM DUAL;

COLUMN reset NEW_VALUE xReset NOPRINT
SELECT CHR(27)||'E' "reset" FROM DUAL;

SET ESCAPE OFF
```

Figure 2-17: Defining escape sequences for HP LaserJet printers.

▷ This series of escape characters sets an HP LaserJet IIIp to landscape orientation with compressed pitch. Note that in two of the sequences a # character precedes an ampersand to signify that the ampersand is valid and is not the start of a substitution variable. The defines of xLandcomp and xReset occur implicitly using the same technique shown earlier in Figure 2-10 on page 52, by coordinating the NEW_VALUE option in the COLUMN command with the query aliases.

The procedures shown in Figure 2-16 and Figure 2-17 are useful if you typically print on one HP LaserJet. If you have several different HP LaserJet models, however, and they use different escape sequences for the same function, then you may find it more convenient to create an Oracle table with data columns for the printer name (e.g., LJ3p), escape sequence name (e.g., reset), and escape sequence (e.g., CHR(27)||'E'). Then, instead of landcomp.sql, you would create an exactly analogous query against your Oracle printer table instead of DUAL. The query would contain substitution variables that prompt for printer name and escape sequence name. When it's run, the query defines the appropriate escape sequences needed in the top and bottom titles of your report to configure the printer.

See Also

1. The character used to prefix substitution variables can be changed with the SET DEFINE command. By doing so, you could use valid ampersands without needing to precede them with the system ESCAPE character.

2. You can use the DUAL table in many creative ways. See Chapter 6 (Figure 6-32 on page 213) for an example where DUAL produces a header line in an ASCII flat file. Also see Chapter 8 (Figure 8-4 on page 236) where DUAL gets used in a UNION compound query to force a specific sort order when you cannot use ORDER BY (e.g., in subqueries).

How do I sequence pages numbers across multiple reports?

I have several queries that run nightly in batch from a single command file. Each query includes a page number in the top title. The page number resets to 1 for each new query even though I consider the queries all part of the same report. I'd prefer that the page numbering continue sequentially across queries. Is there some way I can do this?

Approach

When a query produces output, SQL*PLUS tracks the current page number (SQL.PNO) and line number (SQL.LNO). Under default system settings, the start of each new query resets the current page number and line number. Each display line in the report increments the current line number by 1. If more output remains after the current line number reaches the PAGESIZE setting, then the current page number gets incremented by 1, the current line number gets reset, and the process begins again.

Sequencing page numbers across reports requires the coordination of several SQL*PLUS commands. Figure 2-18 illustrates how this works.

Comments

▶ To increment page numbers across reports, SET EMBEDDED ON after the first query. Also ensure that the BTITLE command is active. Note in this example that the PAGESIZE was set at a small value (9) only for demonstration. Setting NEWPAGE 0 forces a formfeed between report pages.

▶ Setting EMBEDDED ON disables the reset of SQL.PNO and SQL.LNO that normally occurs between queries. This creates the incremented page numbers across multiple reports. However, it also means that the second and subsequent reports would start on the line immediately following the ending of the previous report. Sometimes this is desirable, but in this situation it is not. Each query should start on a new page (i.e., SQL.LNO should reset); it's only the page numbers that should continue to increment. Here's where the BTITLE command comes into play. With EMBEDDED ON, the BTITLE forces each new query to begin on a new page. The two commands coordinate to produce the desired effect.

▶ Note that pages are numbered continuously.

▶ With BTITLE on and PAGESIZE set at 9, each page has 9 lines.

▶ In this query, where the bottom title is only one line long, line 9 on each page contains the title.

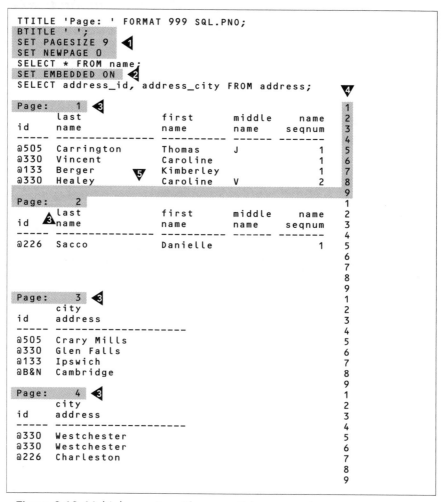

Figure 2-18: Multiple queries with sequential page numbers.

See Also

1. See page 46 in this chapter for another example where EMBEDDED gets used to produce a single report from two queries.

2. See page 48 for discussion on forcing formfeeds with NEWPAGE.

How can I put the value of a bind variable into a report title?

I've written a query that declares and then assigns a value to a bind variable that gets referenced in an anonymous PL/SQL block. I'd like to document my report by including the value of the bind variable in the report title. Is this possible?

Approach

Unlike a substitution variable, you cannot use a bind variable directly in the top and bottom title commands. You'll need to first implicitly define a user variable that contains the value of the bind variable. This can be done using the technique demonstrated earlier in Figure 2-10 on page 52.

The query in Figure 2-19 reports name information for a specified ID number. Two bind variables get declared, one for the value of the ID number to use in the report and a second that references a PL/SQL cursor that actually retrieves data for the report. Note that the ID number appears in the top title of the report, placed there after first defining a user variable called 'xvar' that contains the value of the ID number used in the report.

```
VARIABLE e REFCURSOR
VARIABLE id VARCHAR2(5)       ◀1
EXECUTE :id := 'a330'
DECLARE
     TYPE name_cursor IS REF CURSOR RETURN name%ROWTYPE;
     lc name_cursor;
BEGIN
     lc := :e;
     OPEN lc FOR SELECT * FROM name WHERE name_id = :id;
END;
/


SET TERMOUT OFF
COLUMN var NEW_VALUE xvar NOPRINT       ◀2
SELECT :id "var" FROM DUAL;

SET TERMOUT ON
TTITLE LEFT 'ID is: ' xvar;       ◀3
PRINT e   ◀4

ID is: a330   ◀3
           last              first        middle       name
id         name              name         name         seqnum
-----      ---------------   ----------   ------       --------
a330       Vincent           Caroline                      1
a330       Healey            Caroline     V                2
```

Figure 2-19: Using a bind variable in a report title.

Comments

▶ The SQL*PLUS VARIABLE command declares a bind variable named 'id'. The EXECUTE command assigns a value to the variable.

▶ The bind variable gets used in a query against DUAL. The COLUMN command defines the user variable 'xvar' as the value in the bind variable.

▶ Including 'xvar' in a TTITLE command places the value of the bind variable into the report title.

▶ Note that the SQL*PLUS PRINT command actually displays the report results retrieved by the PL/SQL cursor (named 'e').

See Also

1. Bind variables frequently get used in ad hoc queries that require more than one pass at the data. For example, you can use bind variables effectively when computing a median, percentage distributions, a top *N* report, or when sampling a row from a table. See the index under *bind variables* for examples that demonstrate the variety of their uses.

Chapter 3
Functions

As implemented by Oracle, SQL contains more than 80 functions that each manipulate data values and return results. These functions provide a rich opportunity for creative query writing. This chapter examines some of the ways that you can use functions individually or in combination to achieve special effects with your queries.

Functions come in two varieties based on how many rows they process. As the name implies, single-row functions operate on data one row at a time. An example is the UPPER function that converts character data to uppercase, doing so for a specified data column in each row of the query result set. Conversely, group functions operate on multiple rows grouped according to some criterion. They return a characteristic of the entire group. Examples include functions that compute averages, sums, counts, and variances.

You generally see single-row functions more finely categorized by the datatype accepted in the function argument. Number functions process NUMBER datatypes, date functions process DATE datatypes, and so on. When classified like this, there are five major types of single-row functions: number, character, date, conversion, and miscellaneous. Conversion functions convert data values of one datatype to values of another datatype, often using optional formats. Miscellaneous functions include those functions which cannot be categorized elsewhere.

Query writers most frequently ask questions about two types of SQL functions, with a miscellaneous set of remaining questions. The two principal query concerns are DATE functions and the DECODE function. Both receive considerable attention in this chapter.

Dates

If sheer quantity of questions indicates an area of uncertainty among
query writers, then dates and date arithmetic evidently pose considerable
query problems. Many of the questions that appear in this section arise
repeatedly among query writers.

How do I determine if a date occurred on a Monday?

I'm writing a query to select events that occurred on Mondays. I know
that some of the events did occur on a Monday, yet my query returns no
rows. The WHERE condition in my query uses the TO_CHAR function to
convert the event dates to the day of the week; i.e., TO_CHAR(event_date,
'Day') = 'Monday'. It seems real simple. What's going on here?

Approach

This is one of those "gotcha" problems that torment query writers. Just
when you think you understand query writing, a seemingly illogical element in SQL or SQL*PLUS pops up to humble you. Maybe that's good.

When the TO_CHAR function converts dates using a 'Day' format, it
right-pads the name of the day to a length of 9. Thus the condition in the
question above fails because the TO_CHAR function returns Monday
right-padded with three blank spaces. Any of the following conditions
will work:

```
TO_CHAR(event_date, 'Day') = 'Monday   '

RTRIM(TO_CHAR(event_date, 'Day'),' ') = 'Monday'

TO_CHAR(event_date, 'FMDay') = 'Monday'
```

In the first case, the literal (i.e., Monday) is right-padded with three spaces; in the second case, the RTRIM function trims trailing blank spaces; in
the third case, the FM (Fill Mode) format modifier suppresses blank spaces returned to the TO_CHAR function.

See Also

1. The DAY format model can also be used to achieve other effects.
For example, if you want to recode days into weeks you can use the
DAY format with the TRUNC function. This collapses all days during
a week into the first day of the week. See page 84 in this chapter or
Chapter 10 on page 298 for a discussion of this recoding technique.

How do I create begin-end date ranges from a series of begin dates?

Our training classes run monthly beginning the first day of each month. The table of class information includes a begin date but no end date. I'd like to write a query that displays both a begin and an end date for the training classes. Is there an easy way to do this?

Approach

The ADD_MONTHS function allows you to add or subtract a specified number of months from a date. With just the slightest tweak, you can create monthly date ranges using this function. Figure 3-1 illustrates how this is done.

```
SELECT
    training_code "class",
    training_start_date "begin",
    ADD_MONTHS(training_start_date,1) -1 "end"
FROM
    training
ORDER BY 2;

class begin        end
----- ---------- ----------
A101  01-FEB-96  29-FEB-96
A100  01-JAN-97  31-JAN-97
R950  01-APR-97  30-APR-97
```

Figure 3-1: Creating monthly date ranges with add_months.

Note that adding a month normally yields the same day one month later (e.g., adding one month to 15-APR-97 returns 15-MAY-97). However, if the begin date is near the end of a month and there is no comparable date the next month, the last day of the next month is returned (e.g., adding a month to 30-JAN-97 yields 28-FEB-97 except in a leap year).

Comments

▶ The general form of the ADD_MONTHS function is ADD_MONTHS(date, n), where n is any integer. In Figure 3-1, subtracting 1 in the end date expression produces the correct date as the last day of the month.

See Also

1. The ADD_MONTHS function is one of many date functions. Check the index under *date functions* for examples of other date functions.

How do I calculate age based on SYSDATE and a birth date?

I've written a query that computes a person's age using the MONTHS_BETWEEN function and the following algorithm:

```
FLOOR(MONTHS_BETWEEN(SYSDATE, person_birthdate)/12)
```

Will this formula produce accurate ages in years?

Approach

The algorithm works fine for computing years between two dates. People normally report their age in years by truncating the months and days, so someone is 10 years old until the next birthday that makes him 11. The FLOOR function in the formula corresponds to this common convention. You also could use TRUNC.

The MONTHS_BETWEEN function always returns integers for two dates having the same day of the month (e.g., 11-SEP-97 and 11-AUG-97 are 1 month apart). It also produces integers for two dates that are both the end of the month (e.g., 30-APR-97 and 31-MAR-97). Fractional months are based on a 31-day month. Thus you can get some strange answers when examining results in terms of days. For example, 1996 was a leap year. The MONTHS_BETWEEN 31-MAR-96 and 28-FEB-96 is 1.09677419; that is, there is 1 month between 28-MAR-96 and 28-FEB-96, plus another 0.09677419*31 = 3 days. The days component is wrong, of course, but then this is not the purpose of the function. Used to compute months or larger units like quarters or years, the MONTHS_BETWEEN function will provide accurate results.

See Also

1. FLOOR(arg) is a number function that returns the largest integer equal to or less than arg (e.g., floor(4.2) returns 4). For another example of its use, see Figure 3-4 on page 82.

How do I specify a date value in the year 2000 or later?

I've written several queries that prompt users for dates in a DD-MON-YY date format. Will I have problems with these queries when the next century starts?

Approach

Data values stored with DATE datatypes include the century as well as the year, month, day, hour, minute, and second. Thus the year 2000 won't present any insurmountable problems. However, depending on how your queries are constructed, they may return inaccurate results.

Figure 3-2 includes two training classes that both begin at midnight on 01-APR, but one in the year 1900 and the second in the year 2000. The query prompts the user for a begin date. Suppose you want the row for the training class that begins in the year 2000. The results depend on how the query is constructed.

```
class   begin                   end
-----   --------------------    --------------------
X20a    01-APR-1900    ◀1       01-APR-1900
R111    01-APR-2000             01-APR-2000

SELECT * FROM seminars                                            ▼2
WHERE TO_CHAR(seminar_start_date,'dd-MON-yyyy') = '&date';
Enter value for date: 01-APR-2000
class   begin                   end
-----   --------------------    --------------------
R111    01-APR-2000             01-APR-2000

SELECT * FROM seminars
WHERE seminar_start_date = '&date';   ◀3
Enter value for date: 01-APR-00
class   begin                   end
-----   --------------------    --------------------
X20a    01-APR-1900             01-APR-1900

SELECT * FROM seminars                                            ▼4
WHERE seminar_start_date = to_date('&date', 'dd-MON-rr');
Enter value for date: 01-APR-00
class   begin                   end
-----   --------------------    --------------------
R111    01-APR-2000             01-APR-2000

SELECT * FROM seminars                                            ▼5
WHERE TO_CHAR(seminar_start_date, 'dd-MON-rr') = '&date';
Enter value for date: 01-APR-00
class   begin                   end
-----   --------------------    --------------------
X20a    01-APR-1900             01-APR-1900
R111    01-APR-2000             01-APR-2000
```

Figure 3-2: Specifying dates after the year 2000.

Comments

▶ The data includes two seminars that begin on 01-APR. One begins in the year 1900 and the second in the year 2000.

▶ If you use a TO_CHAR function to format the date column with a four-digit year (i.e., 'YYYY'), then the query will always return accurate results. This means prompting users with the new date format, however.

▶ If the query is constructed in its simplest form with no conversion functions like TO_CHAR or TO_DATE and the user specifies a date with a two-digit year, then the query returns rows for dates in the current century (assuming that NLS_DATE_FORMAT is 'DD-MON-YY' or some variation that uses a two-digit 'YY' year format). In Figure 3-2, the training class in 1900 was returned because the query was run in 1996. This query is obviously wrong if you want the class that begins in 2000. You would experience a similar problem after the year 2000 if the user specified a two-digit year and the training class you want is in the 1900s.

▶ The two-digit 'RR' year format solves several problems associated with dates in different centuries. How it behaves depends on SYSDATE. If the present year ends in 00 to 49 and the user specifies a two-digit year between 00 and 49, the present century is implied. The same holds true if the present year ends in 50 to 99 and the user specifies a two-digit year within this range. Thus, if the year is 1996 and the user specifies a date of 12-DEC-99 with a 'DD-MON-RR' format, it is assumed the user means 1999.

However, if the present year and the two-digit year specified by the user fall within different half-century categories, different centuries are implied. For example, assume that the present year is 1997. Specifying a date as 25-AUG-02 implies the twenty-first century. Similarly, if the present year is 2005, specifying a date of 19-SEP-92 implies the twentieth century.

A query constructed with the TO_DATE function using an 'RR' year format will return the correct results most of the time. It will produce inaccurate results whenever SYSDATE and the date you want are in different centuries and more than 50 years apart. For example, assume that the SYSDATE year is 2005 and the user specifies a date as 10-OCT-23, where she means the year 1923. The query will search for dates in the year 2023 and return the wrong rows.

Note that if your database administrator sets the parameter NLS_DATE_FORMAT as 'DD-MON-RR', you won't need to use the TO_DATE function to get the same results as shown in this query in Figure 3-2.

▶ The two-digit 'RR' year format does not behave differently from the 'YY' format when used in the TO_CHAR function. In either case, the query returns the wrong results.

The long and the short of all this discussion about dates and the year 2000 is that you're better off revising the queries so that they require the user to specify a four-digit year. Then there is no ambiguity. However, if your queries are unlikely to ever confront the date problems possible with the two-digit 'RR' year format, then encourage your database administrator to change the NLS_DATE_FORMAT to use this format.

See Also

1. The NLS in NLS_DATE_FORMAT means National Language Support. Throughout the world, common conventions for the display of dates vary. The parameters that control the default display of dates can be found in the SYS view NLS_SESSION_PARAMETERS.

2. In Chapter 2, the utility program that computes minimum linesize needed for a report used the NLS_DATE_FORMAT to determine the space required for date columns. See Chapter 2 on page 55 for a discussion of this.

3. See the discussion later in this chapter (page 84) on NLS_TERRITORY and the definitions which identify the day a week begins (e.g., in the AMERICA territory a week begins on Sunday).

How do I return all rows where a column equals a specified date?

I'm writing a query to retrieve all training classes that begin on a specific date. The WHERE conditions seem simple enough, but some rows fall through the query and don't display. Why does this happen?

Approach

Data columns with a DATE datatype have both a date and time component. If your WHERE clause specifies only a date, the time component defaults to 00:00:00. Thus you may think a query reads

```
WHERE begin_date = '20-MAR-97'
```

In fact, however, the condition actually being executed retrieves only those rows where the begin_date is midnight on 20-MAR-97.

You can eliminate this problem in several ways. Figure 3-2 shows two. One uses the TO_CHAR function to format the begin_date; the second uses relational operators. You could also use the LIKE operator to

```
class     begin                    ▼   end
-----     --------------------         --------------------
BX1a      15-JAN-1997 09:30:00         15-JAN-1997 11:45:00
T1A       15-JAN-1997 00:00:00         16-JAN-1997 00:00:00
RT12c     10-FEB-1997 14:30:00         13-FEB-1997 17:00:00
Y1C       31-DEC-1999 22:15:30         01-JAN-2000 08:05:50

SELECT * FROM seminars
WHERE seminar_start_date = '15-JAN-97';    ◀2

class     begin                    end
-----     --------------------     --------------------
T1A       15-JAN-97                16-JAN-97


SELECT * FROM seminars WHERE
TO_CHAR(seminar_start_date, 'dd-MON-yy') = '15-JAN-97';   ◀3

class     begin                    end
-----     --------------------     --------------------
BX1a      15-JAN-97                15-JAN-97
T1A       15-JAN-97                16-JAN-97

SELECT * FROM seminars
WHERE seminar_start_date >= '15-JAN-97'
    AND seminar_start_date < '16-JAN-97';    ◀4
ENTER to continue ...
class     begin                    end
-----     --------------------     --------------------
BX1a      15-JAN-97                15-JAN-97
T1A       15-JAN-97                16-JAN-97
```

Figure 3-3: Two methods for specifying dates in WHERE conditions.

retrieve rows WHERE seminar_start_date LIKE '15-JAN-97%'. Or you could use the TRUNC function: WHERE TRUNC(seminar_start_date) = '15-JAN-97'.

Comments

▶ Two seminar classes begin on 15-JAN-97 but only one of them at midnight.

▶ The query that seems logically correct only returns the class that begins at midnight.

▶ The query works fine if you use TO_CHAR to format the begin date so that it excludes the time component.

▶ Creating a date range with relational operators also works. In this case, the query includes all courses that begin at or later than midnight on 15-JAN-97 and end before midnight on 16-JAN-97. Both courses fall within this range.

See Also

1. Having alternative methods of solving a problem is extremely valuable. Query writers can exercise a range of personal preference and still get out of trouble when problems occur in a query. Of course, not all solutions are equal. Elegance and performance impact are two criteria that should be used to determine which method to employ for a query problem. Later chapters stress the importance of alternative solutions to problems. See, for example, Chapter 7 that discusses several methods for testing and debugging join problems.

2. See page 82 for a example where the TRUNC function is used with dates.

How do I compute duration based on begin and end dates?

I'm trying to write a query to show the duration of training classes in hours and minutes, yet I can't locate an SQL function that provides this information based on starting and end dates. How can I compute duration myself?

Approach

When you subtract two dates, the result is a real number expressed in days (e.g., 1.2 days). The trick lies in formatting the computation to provide duration in more meaningful units than a decimal number of days. Figure 3-4 shows begin and end dates for three hypothetical training classes (including one that runs on New Year's eve 1999). The output formats the duration of the classes in days, hours, minutes, and seconds.

```
class   begin                       end
-----   -------------------         -------------------
BX1a    15-JAN-1997 09:30:00        15-JAN-1997 11:45:00
Y1C     31-DEC-1999 22:15:30        01-JAN-2000 08:05:50
RT12c   10-FEB-1997 14:30:00        13-FEB-1997 17:00:00

COLUMN days FORMAT 9999
COLUMN hhmiss HEADING 'hh24:mi:ss' FORMAT a10
SELECT
▶   FLOOR(seminar_end_date - seminar_start_date) "days",
    TO_CHAR((seminar_end_date - seminar_start_date) +
        TRUNC(SYSDATE),'hh24:mi:ss') "hhmiss"
FROM
    seminars;   ②

days hh24:mi:ss
---- ----------
   0 02:15:00
   0 09:50:20
   3 02:30:00  ◀③
```

Figure 3-4: Calculation of the duration of an event.

Comments

▶ The FLOOR function returns the greatest integer equal to or less than the function's argument. Thus, if the duration is 1.2 days, FLOOR(1.2) returns 1. This provides the days between start and end dates.

▶ The TRUNC function truncates a date to a specified unit (e.g., 'MON' truncates to the first day in the nearest month). If the truncating unit is not specified (as here), the truncation occurs to the nearest day. This makes the time component of the truncated date 00:00:00. The calculation then adds the duration of the training class to the truncated date, producing a new date that is formatted to display only the hours, minutes, and seconds. For example, suppose that TRUNC(SYSDATE) produces 07-APR-97 00:00:00 and that the duration is 1.2 days. Adding the two elements produces the new date 08-APR-97 04:48:00. Formatting the new date with 'HH24:MI:SS' completes the calculation.

▶ Note that the output displays duration as the number of days, hours, minutes, and seconds.

Having gone through the exercise of computing duration, you don't want to reinvent the wheel for each query that requires a similar calculation. Save the expressions as a chunk of SQL (a *segment*, as discussed in Chapter 1) that you can reuse. Generalize the segment by including substitution variables for the begin and end dates. Store this code fragment in a subdirectory devoted to SQL segments. Update your segment inventory (e.g., a list or an Oracle table devoted to the management of SQL segments you've created). Then you can easily retrieve the SQL segment and insert it into your next query that computes event durations.

See Also

1. Chapter 1 on page 15 discusses the usefulness of SQL segments in simplifying the query writer's job. Over time you'll gather an impressive collection of these code fragments, each of which performs a specific task. When that happens, query writing becomes less like programming and more like writing, where you search for the right word or phrase to use.

How do I get counts by week?

I'd like to count the number of sales by week based on a sale date, but I'm having trouble grouping the sales into weeks. How do I group date columns by week?

Approach

Several DATE functions provide ways to group dates by week. Choosing the right function depends on how you want the dates grouped. The NLS_TERRITORY parameter implicitly determines the start day of a week. For example, weeks in the AMERICA territory start by definition on Sunday and run through Saturday. Thus one way to group dates is by the week defined by NLS_TERRITORY. However, you also might choose to group dates by a 7-day period that extends across a Sunday-to-Saturday week. For example, suppose you wanted to count the sales that occurred in the 7-day period ending on a Friday. This defines your week as beginning on Saturday and running through Friday.

Let's examine functions that group dates into both NLS_TERRITORY and user-defined weeks. Figure 3-5 shows sales data for five dates. The figure shows one method to group these sales so that the display date is the Friday in a week defined by NLS_TERRITORY. It also illustrates how to group sales into a week extending from Saturday through Friday.

```
SELECT
    sales_prodid "prod",
    sales_date "salesdate",                          ▼1
    TRUNC(sales_date, 'DAY') + 5 "friday1",
    NEXT_DAY(sales_date, 'SATURDAY') - 1 "friday2"   ◀2
FROM sales
ORDER BY sales_date;

                      Friday      Week
            sales     of week     ending
product     date      (NLS)       Friday
--------    --------  --------    --------
R251        03-JUN-96 07-JUN-96   07-JUN-96
X555        07-JUN-96 07-JUN-96   07-JUN-96
S910        08-JUN-96 07-JUN-96   14-JUN-96   ◀3
R251        12-JUN-96 14-JUN-96   14-JUN-96
X555        14-JUN-96 14-JUN-96   14-JUN-96
```

Figure 3-5: Two methods to group dates by week.

Comments

▶1 Truncating a date using the 'DAY' format yields the first day in a week as defined by NLS_TERRITORY. In this case, the first day of the week is Sunday, so adding 5 days produces Friday dates. Note that this algorithm would differ if the NLS_TERRITORY defined another day of the week as the start date.

▷ The NEXT_DAY function returns the first date that falls on the specified DAY and occurs after the argument date. In this case, the NEXT_DAY function returns the first Saturday after the sale date. If the sales date happens to occur on a Saturday, it returns the next Saturday (i.e., one week later). Subtracting 1 produces Friday dates.

▷ Note that the two grouping procedures differ in their week definitions. One uses a week extending from Sunday to Saturday; the other from Saturday to Friday. The sale that occurred on Saturday 08-JUN-96 illustrates the difference. Using the TRUNC procedure groups this sale with the 07-JUN-96 Friday; using the NEXT_DAY procedure groups this sale with the 14-JUN-96 Friday.

See Also

1. The NLS in NLS_TERRITORY means National Language Support. For related discussions, see the SYS view NLS_SESSION_PARAMETERS and NLS_DATE_FORMAT. The NLS_DATE_FORMAT, for example, featured prominently in the discussion earlier in this chapter on query problems that might arise in the year 2000. See page 77 for this discussion.

How do get a due date that is x business days after an end date?

Faculty members have 14 business days after completion of a seminar to submit final grades for students. How do I determine the due date for grades based on the seminar end date?

Approach

This is a very common question applicable to a variety of situations where one event triggers another event a specified number of business days in the future. Another example is the end of a billing period triggering a payment due date. Let's first deal with the problem without considering holidays and then include holidays as a further complication.

The term *business days* means weekdays as opposed to weekends. What constitutes a weekday varies throughout the world. For purposes of illustration, let's assume that Saturday and Sunday are weekend days. If this is not the case for you, then modify the SQL found below.

SQL Approach

Assuming 5 days in a business week, any N number of business days in the future can be defined by the number of weeks (TRUNC(N/5)) and the remaining number of days (MOD(N,5)). For example, 14 business days is 2 weeks and 4 days. What makes this question so interesting is that a due date depends on two factors: (1) the day that the trigger event occurred and (2) the MOD remaining days. The following table illustrates this.

```
                   Day that trigger event occurs
          Sun       Mon       Tue       Wed       Thu       Fri       Sat
Mod   Day Chg   Day Chg   Day Chg   Day Chg   Day Chg   Day Chg   Day Chg
====================================================================================
 4    Thu  4    Fri  4    Mon  6    Tue  6    Wed  6    Thu  6    Thu  5
 3    Wed  3    Thu  3    Fri  3    Mon  5    Tue  5    Wed  5    Wed  4
 2    Tue  2    Wed  2    Thu  2    Fri  2    Mon  4    Tue  4    Tue  3
 1    Mon  1    Tue  1    Wed  1    Thu  1    Fri  1    Mon  3    Mon  2
 0    Fri -2    Mon  0    Tue  0    Wed  0    Thu  0    Fri  0    Fri -1
```

Table 3-1: Due dates based on business days and day of trigger event.

Comments

▶ First a word about the notation in the table. Consider the cell in the first row (MOD = 4) and the fifth column (Thursday). For example, 14 business days (MOD = 4) after a Thursday trigger date occurs on a Wednesday because of the 2 intervening weekend days. The total number of days between Thursday and the following Wednesday is 6; this number appears in the Chg (Change) column.

▷ Note that the end dates occurring on weekdays are well-behaved and produce easily computed due dates but that end dates falling on weekends provide more problems. For example, 10 business days (MOD = 0) after a Sunday end date occurs on a Friday 2 weeks minus 2 days from the end date.

Any due date can be calculated with the following formula:

```
end_date + 7*TRUNC(N/5) + cell_value_from(MOD(N,5),Day)
```

where cell_value_from is a function that returns a value from Table 3-1 based on the two parameters defined by the rows and columns in the table. Figure 3-6 illustrates an SQL solution.

```
SELECT
      seminar_code "class",
      TO_CHAR(seminar_end_date, 'dd-MON-yyyy, Day') "enddate",
      TO_CHAR(
         seminar_end_date +
         TRUNC(&&days/5)*7 +   ◀①
         DECODE(
            mod(&&days,5),
            4, DECODE(TO_CHAR(seminar_end_date, 'D'),1,4,2,4,7,5,6),
            3, DECODE(TO_CHAR(seminar_end_date, 'D'),1,3,2,3,3,3,7,4,5),
            2, DECODE(TO_CHAR(seminar_end_date, 'D'),5,4,6,4,7,3,2),
            1, DECODE(TO_CHAR(seminar_end_date, 'D'),6,3,7,2,1),
            0, DECODE(TO_CHAR(seminar_end_date, 'D'),1,-2,7,-1,0)   ◀②
            ),
         'dd-MON-yyyy, Day') "duedate"
FROM
      seminars
ORDER BY
      TO_CHAR(seminar_end_date, 'D');

Enter value for days: 14   ◀①

class  enddate                 duedate
-----  --------------------    --------------------
DCx5   16-JUN-1996, Sunday     04-JUL-1996, Thursday
AAx9   24-JUN-1996, Monday     12-JUL-1996, Friday
CD9b   04-JUN-1996, Tuesday    24-JUN-1996, Monday
BX1a   15-JAN-1997, Wednesday  04-FEB-1997, Tuesday
RT12c  13-FEB-1997, Thursday   05-MAR-1997, Wednesday
T1A    17-JAN-1997, Friday     06-FEB-1997, Thursday
R111   01-APR-2000, Saturday   20-APR-2000, Thursday
```

Figure 3-6: SQL calculating due dates from business days and trigger events.

Comments

▷ This element in the algorithm adds 7 days to the event date for each 5-day business week. For example, 14 business days is 2

weeks and 4 days. This element adds 2*7 = 14 days to the event
date to take care of the week component.

▷ The DECODEs consider the day component after breaking the
specified number of business days into weeks and days. The
highlighted DECODE deals with situations where there are no remainder days. Note that if the event date occurs on a Saturday or
Sunday, the DECODE causes the due date to fall on a Friday.

PL/SQL Approach

Procedural languages deal with the problem of due dates much more el-
egantly than SQL. Figure 3-7 shows a PL/SQL function that computes due
dates in a very direct manner.

```
CREATE OR REPLACE FUNCTION due_date
   (event_date IN DATE, business_days IN NUMBER)
RETURN DATE
IS
   due_date DATE := event_date + TRUNC(business_days/5)*7;
   days_left NUMBER := MOD(business_days,5);

BEGIN                                          ▲
   WHILE days_left > 0
   LOOP
      due_date := due_date + 1;

      IF TO_CHAR(due_date, 'D') BETWEEN 2 AND 6 THEN
         days_left := days_left - 1;
      END IF;
   END LOOP;

   RETURN due_date;
END;
/
```

Figure 3-7: PL/SQL function that determines due dates.

Comments

▷ Any number of days can be broken into weeks and remainder
days. For example, 14 business days is 2 weeks and 4 days. The
weeks component gets handled when initializing due_date; the
remainder days get handled in the LOOP by checking to ensure
that the incremented due_date falls on a weekday.

Using a function to retrieve due dates also makes the query much
cleaner, as demonstrated in Figure 3-8.

```
SELECT
      seminar_code "class",
      TO_CHAR(seminar_end_date, 'dd-MON-yyyy, Day') "enddate",
      TO_CHAR(due_date(seminar_end_date, 14), 'dd-MON-yyyy, Day') "duedate"
FROM seminars
ORDER BY                                         ⚠
      TO_CHAR(seminar_end_date, 'D');

class enddate                    duedate
----- ----------------------    ----------------------
DCx5  16-JUN-1996, Sunday       04-JUL-1996, Thursday
AAx9  24-JUN-1996, Monday       12-JUL-1996, Friday
CD9b  04-JUN-1996, Tuesday      24-JUN-1996, Monday
BX1a  15-JAN-1997, Wednesday    04-FEB-1997, Tuesday
RT12c 13-FEB-1997, Thursday     05-MAR-1997, Wednesday
T1A   17-JAN-1997, Friday       06-FEB-1997, Thursday
R111  01-APR-2000, Saturday     20-APR-2000, Thursday
```

Figure 3-8: Query using a PL/SQL function to return due dates.

Comments

▶ All the DECODEs in the SQL solution shown in Figure 3-6 on page 87 get replaced by a simple PL/SQL function. In this case, the due dates returned are 14 business days after the seminars end.

See Also

1. You'd like your queries to be both elegant and fast. Sometimes there's a trade-off that you must make between the two goals. Chapter 9 (Table 9-2 on page 255) shows results of performance comparisons between the SQL and PL/SQL approaches to the due date question.

How do I determine due dates and account for holidays?

Faculty members have 14 business days after a seminar ends to submit grades. How do I compute a due date for grades that also accounts for holidays?

Approach

Holidays differ from location to location even within the same country. If you store holiday dates in a table, there's a convenient variation of the PL/SQL function in Figure 3-7 on page 88 that adjusts for holidays. Figure 3-9 shows the revised algorithm.

```
CREATE OR REPLACE FUNCTION due_date1
   (event_date IN DATE, business_days IN NUMBER)
RETURN DATE
IS
   due_date DATE := event_date + TRUNC(business_days/5)*7;
   days_left NUMBER := MOD(business_days,5);
   extra_days NUMBER;

BEGIN
   WHILE days_left > 0
   LOOP
      due_date := due_date + 1;

      IF TO_CHAR(due_date, 'D') BETWEEN 2 AND 6 THEN
         days_left := days_left - 1;
      END IF;
   END LOOP;

   -- determine holidays between event_date and due_date    ◀①
   SELECT COUNT(*) INTO extra_days FROM holidays
   WHERE holidays_date > event_date
   AND holidays_date <= due_date
   AND TO_CHAR(holidays_date, 'D') BETWEEN 2 AND 6;

   -- recursively call if extra_days contain holidays        ◀②
   IF extra_days > 0 THEN
      due_date := due_date1(due_date, extra_days);
   END IF;

   RETURN due_date;
END;
/
```

Figure 3-9: PL/SQL due date function that accounts for holidays.

Comments

▶ This function, called xdue_date, checks the *HOLIDAY* table to determine how many holidays occurred between the event date and the computed due date. The due date must be adjusted by these extra days.

▶ However, the adjustment to the due date could also contain holidays. Calling the function recursively eliminates this problem.

Let's consider an example. In Figure 3-8 on page 89, one of the seminars had a completion date of 16-JUN-96, making grades due on 04-JUL-96. In the United States this is a national holiday. It happened to fall on a Thursday in 1996. Suppose that the company also gave its employees the Friday after 04-JUL-96 as a holiday, figuring that many employees would take the day anyway to make a long weekend. A *HOLIDAY* table for this company would contain both 04-JUL-96 and 05-JUL-96. Using these holidays, the PL/SQL function in Figure 3-9 produces a new due date for course grades on Monday 08-JUL-96. To arrive at this calculation, the function must adjust the initial due date by one holiday. But because 05-JUL-96 is also a holiday the function gets called recursively until it settles on 08-JUL-96 as the next available weekday that is not also a holiday.

See Also

1. Trying to decide between SQL and PL/SQL approaches to query problems can frequently be difficult. Chapter 9 discusses trade-offs that must sometimes be made between performance and query simplicity. However, there's another component in this trade-off that is often overlooked. The time a query writer must take to write, test, and debug a query should also be considered. If the contortions needed to arrive at a SQL solution reach some ill-defined limit, and the PL/SQL approach saves you time, then factor that into your decision as well.

DECODE Function

The DECODE function is a wonderful addition to Oracle's implementation of SQL because it provides the ability to introduce conditional if . . . then . . . else logic in queries. The traditional DECODE looks for matches — with a syntax that's equivalent to "if x = y, then z, else r". In this section you'll see two variations and extensions of the traditional DECODE.

How can I use DECODE with a greater than (>) operator?

Based on a sales amount, I want to assign a discount rate. I'd like to replicate the if . . . then . . . else functionality in procedural languages. I assume that this needs to be done in the DECODE function, but how?

Approach

Let's assume the following situation: If the sale amount is less than $100, the discount rate is 3%; if the sale amount is greater than or equal to $100 but less than $200, the discount rate is 4%; if the sale amount is greater than or equal to $200 and less than or equal to $350, the discount rate is 5%; and if the sale amount is greater than $350, the discount rate is 6%.

Several techniques produce the desired results.

SQL Approach

The classic solution in SQL uses the DECODE and SIGN functions. The latter function takes the form SIGN(n). If the argument n < 0, the function returns −1; if n > 0, the function returns +1; and if n = 0, the function returns 0. This feature of the SIGN function makes it useful for determining whether one number is larger, smaller, or equal to a second number.

Figure 3-10 shows the DECODE and SIGN functions used to create the discount categories required for the query.

```
SELECT
      sales_total "sales",
      DECODE(SIGN(sales_total - 100), -1, 0.03,   ◀1
            DECODE(SIGN(sales_total - 200), -1, 0.04,
            DECODE(SIGN(sales_total - 350), -1, 0.05, 0, 0.05,
            0.06))) "discount1"                            ◮2
FROM
      sales
ORDER BY 1;
```

Figure 3-10: Relational expressions using DECODE and SIGN functions.

Comments

▶ Pay particular attention to the start and end values in a range of values. Use the format shown here when the ending value (i.e., 100) is not included in the range. If the sales_total is $100, then 100 – 100 = 0, the SIGN is 0, and the value would not be assigned a 3% discount. Note that the same format applies to the next DECODE and SIGN, where the value $200 is not included in the range.

▶ Unlike the preceding example, the value $350 is included in the range of values. Use the format shown here when the ending value (i.e., 350) is included in the range. If the sales_total is $350, then 350 – 350 = 0, the SIGN is 0, and the value does get assigned the discount rate of 5% because the DECODE includes a 0 condition.

PL/SQL Approach

DECODEs quickly become complex. In Figure 3-10 the query nested the DECODE functions three levels deep. It can be very difficult sometimes to figure out exactly what a DECODE does, particularly if you didn't write the expression and it is not well documented. It's far easier to use a procedural language to implement the relational criteria.

Figure 3-11 shows a PL/SQL solution that provides exactly the same functionality as the DECODE and SIGN functions in Figure 3-10. However, it is much easier to understand and to maintain.

```
CREATE OR REPLACE FUNCTION discount
   (sales_total IN NUMBER)
RETURN NUMBER
IS
   discount_rate NUMBER(3,2);

BEGIN
   IF sales_total > 350 THEN
      discount_rate := 0.06;
   ELSIF sales_total >= 200 THEN
      discount_rate := 0.05;
   ELSIF sales_total >= 100 THEN
      discount_rate := 0.04;
   ELSIF sales_total > 0 THEN
      discount_rate := 0.03;
   END IF;

   RETURN discount_rate;
END;
/
```

Figure 3-11: PL/SQL equivalent of the SQL in Figure 3-10.

Comments

▶ The sales ranges that determine discount rates are mutually exclusive. The IF ... THEN ... ELSIF logic ensures exclusive ranges by using a hierarchy of the end value in each range. For example, all sales over $350 qualify for a 6% discount. Rows meeting this criterion will not be considered in the remainder of the IF ... ELSIF structure. This makes it easy to specify the 5% discount as including any remaining sale equal to or greater than $200. For this logic to work correctly, you must order the IF or ELSIF criteria in ascending or descending order based on the sales ranges.

As shown in Figure 3-12, the SQL and PL/SQL approaches return identical results.

```
SELECT
    sales_total "sales",
    DECODE(SIGN(sales_total - 100), -1, 0.03,
        DECODE(SIGN(sales_total - 200), -1, 0.04,
        DECODE(SIGN(sales_total - 350), -1, 0.05, 0, 0.05,
            0.06))) "discount1",
    discount(sales_total) "discount2"  ◀①
FROM sales
ORDER By 1;

      sales    discount1    discount2
   ----------  ----------   ----------
          50        .03          .03
         100        .04          .04
         200        .05          .05
         250        .05          .05
         350        .05          .05   ◀②
         500        .06          .06
```

Figure 3-12: Query using both SQL and PL/SQL sales discounts.

Comments

▶ The PL/SQL function makes the query easier to understand.
▶ If a sale exceeds $350, the appropriate discount is 6%, but a sale of exactly $350 only qualifies for the 5% discount. Both the SQL and the PL/SQL solutions correctly dealt with this value that occurred at the endpoint of one of the specified sales ranges.

See Also

1. Chapter 9 (Table 9-3 on page 257) shows results of performance comparisons between the SQL and PL/SQL approaches to the recode question. Again, you'll be faced with a trade-off.

How do I recode numeric data into categories for frequency reports?

For ease of presentation, I'd like to create sales ranges and then report how many sales fell within each range? Is this possible?

Approach

Actually, this question is very similar to the preceding one. Both situations require that numeric data be grouped into categorical ranges. In the preceding question these ranges determine discount rates to apply to the sales. In this question, however, you only want to code the ranges so that they can be used in a standard frequency distribution report.

The easiest approach uses a PL/SQL function that is nearly identical to the one shown in Figure 3-11 on page 93. Instead of discount rates in the IF statements, however, the new function (called sales_category) merely assigns some dummy code. For completeness, the function appears in Figure 3-13.

```
CREATE OR REPLACE FUNCTION sales_category
    (sales_total IN NUMBER)
RETURN NUMBER
IS
    sales_category NUMBER(2);

BEGIN
    IF sales_total > 350 THEN
        sales_category := 4;    ◄❶
    ELSIF sales_total >= 200 THEN
        sales_category := 3;
    ELSIF sales_total >= 100 THEN
        sales_category := 2;
    ELSIF sales_total > 0 THEN
        sales_category := 1;
    END IF;

    RETURN sales_category;
END;
/
```

Figure 3-13: PL/SQL function recoding numeric sales data in categories.

Comments

▶ Each range of sales is assigned a code. This gets used in the query but has no significance. If you intend to sort the query results by the assigned codes, make sure you assign them in a meaningful way. Here the assignments are consistent with the sales ranges; the highest sales range gets assigned the highest code value and the lowest sales range gets assigned the lowest value.

The query then uses the sales_category function to group numeric sales data into categories. Using the DECODE function provides an easy way to assign descriptive names to the categories. Figure 3-14 shows how this is done.

```
COLUMN category HEADING 'sales|category'
BREAK ON REPORT
COMPUTE SUM OF count ON REPORT
SELECT
    sales_category(sales_total)  "category",
    DECODE(sales_category(sales_total),
        1,  'Less than $100',
        2,  '>= $100 and < $200',
        3,  '>= $200 and <= $350',
        4,  '> $350') "description",
    COUNT(*)  "count"
FROM sales
GROUP BY
    sales_category(sales_total),
    DECODE(sales_category(sales_total),
        1,  'Less than $100',
        2,  '>= $100 and < $200',
        3,  '>= $200 and <= $350',
        4,  '> $350')
ORDER BY 1;


     sales
  category   description                              count
---------- --------------------             ----------
         1   Less than $100                        1
         2   >= $100 and < $200                    1
         3   >= $200 and <= $350                   3
         4   > $350                                1
                                          ----------
sum                                               6
```

Figure 3-14: Frequency report using recoded sales amounts.

Comments

▷ A DECODE function assigns descriptions to each of the dummy sales categories.

See Also

1. DECODE can be a very versatile tool for query writers. The index contains many references to examples where the DECODE function is used in a query, including everything from computing a median to concatenating strings when NULL values exist. See the index under the heading DECODE *function*.

Other Functions

Many useful functions exist besides the DATE and DECODE functions discussed earlier. In this section several of these additional functions appear. Included are CHR, REPLACE, TO_NUMBER, ROUND, and TO_CHAR, which all operate on individual data values. The COUNT function that operates on groups of values is also discussed.

How do I left-justify numeric data?

The identification numbers in my tables are all numeric. I'd like my reports to display these numbers left-justified in a column. Is this possible?

Approach

Oracle includes several conversion functions that convert data values between datatypes — e.g., from character to number, from character to date, from date to character, and so on. One of the functions, TO_CHAR, converts numeric data to character. It accepts as an optional argument a format to use in the conversion.

Displaying numeric data left-justified only requires that TO_CHAR be used to convert the numbers to character data. Do not use the optional conversion format or the characters also will appear right-justified. Figure 3-15 illustrates how the TO_CHAR function works.

```
COLUMN n_id HEADING 'numeric|id'
COLUMN c_id HEADING 'char|id' FORMAT a8     ◀
COLUMN middle FORMAT a6
SELECT
      xname_id "n_id",
 ▶   TO_CHAR(xname_id) "c_id",
      xname_last "last",
      xname_first "first",
      xname_middle "middle"
FROM xname
ORDER BY 3, 4, 5;

    numeric   char
         id   id        last              first       middle
----------    --------  ----------------  ----------  ------
      14907   14907     Carrington        Thomas      J
      51870   51870     Healey            Caroline    V
       2650   2650      O'Leary           Sean
     144972   144972    Sacco             Danielle
                   ▲
                   2
```

Figure 3-15: Left-justifying numeric data.

Comments

▶ Use the COLUMN command to control the display width of the converted numeric data.

▶ Using the TO_CHAR conversion function without the format argument produces a character string that displays left-justified.

See Also

1. For examples of other conversion functions, see the index under *conversion functions*.

2. Chapter 6 (Figure 6-9 on page 186) shows another example where the TO_CHAR function is used to convert a number to a character string.

How do I get COUNT(*) to return a zero?

I'd like to know how many test scores exist for each person in a report population. If no scores exist, I want 0 to appear in the report. But when I use COUNT(*), I get a 1. How can I get zeroes returned if no rows exist?

Approach

COUNT(*) is the only group function that does not ignore NULL values. Since an outer join creates NULL rows if necessary, COUNT(*) will include the NULL rows in counts. Use instead the COUNT function with an argument that is a NOT NULL data column. Figure 3-16 shows how this works.

```
SELECT
    name_id "id",          ▼ 1
    COUNT(*) "count",
    COUNT(tests_id) "count1",   ◀ 2
    SUM(DECODE(tests_id,null,0,1)) "recs"
FROM
    tests,
    name
WHERE
    name_seriesno = name_now(name_id)
    and tests_id(+) = name_id
GROUP BY
    name_id;


                                    number
                          count      tests
id           count(*)   tests_id      rows
-----        --------   --------    -------
a133            1           0          0
a226            1           1          1
a330            2           2          2
a505            1           1          1
                ▲ 1         ▲ 2
```

Figure 3-16: Query illustrating counts that return zeroes.

Comments

▶ 1 COUNT(*) includes NULL rows created by outer joins.
▶ 2 The tests_id column is a NOT NULL column in the *TESTS* table; it could only be NULL if temporarily created by an outer join. COUNT(tests_id) ignores these NULL rows and returns a 0 count.

See Also

1. See Chapter 1 (Figure 1-9 on page 13) for the name_now function.

2. Beginning on page 156, Chapter 5 discusses the special problems that outer joins sometimes present query writers.

How do I remove control characters embedded in data values?

One of my tables has a data column with lengthy values. When the data were input, carriage returns got embedded in the values. I'd like to get rid of the carriage returns. How can I do this?

Approach

In the 7-bit ASCII character set, a carriage return has the decimal value 10. Assuming that you're using the ASCII character set, you could REPLACE all CHR(10) with a NULL or single space. Figure 3-17 shows an example before and after using the REPLACE function.

```
COLUMN class FORMAT a5
COLUMN desc FORMAT a50
SELECT
      seminar_code "class",
      seminar_desc "desc"
FROM
      seminars
WHERE
      seminar_code = 'Y1C';

class  desc
-----  --------------------------------------------------
Y1C    An all-night photo shoot
       at New York City Times Square  ◄1
       as the next millenium arrives


UPDATE seminars SET seminar_desc =
      REPLACE(seminar_desc,chr(10),' ')  ◄2
WHERE seminar_code = 'Y1C';

class  desc
-----  --------------------------------------------------
Y1C    An all-night photo shoot at New York City Times Sq
       uare as the next millenium arrives
```

Figure 3-17: Removing control characters from data values.

Comments

▶ This data value for seminar_desc has two embedded carriage returns.

▶ As used here, the REPLACE function replaces all carriage returns (i.e., CHR(10)) with a single space.

See Also

1. All tables and views used in this book appear in the index under

tables and views. Other examples where the *SEMINARS* table was used include the discussion of due dates that appeared earlier in this chapter (page 86).

2. REPLACE is a character function. Other examples of these functions appear in the index under *character functions*.

How do I determine if character data values are positive integers?

One of my tables has a VARCHAR2 data column that contains mostly positive integers. I want to convert the column to a NUMBER datatype, but first I must identify all values that are not positive integers so that I can update these values. How can I find these data values that are not positive integers?

Approach

Checking that a number is a positive integer is straightforward in SQL. You can use the SIGN function to check that the number is exceeds zero (i.e., SIGN = 1). You can check that the number is an integer using the MOD function (i.e., MOD(n,1) = 0 for integers). However, converting character strings to numbers with the TO_NUMBER function generates an error if the string is not actually a number (e.g., '100a'), so the query fails without identifying data values containing characters.

It's easier to use a PL/SQL function that includes a section to handle any errors that occur when converting character data to numeric data with the TO_NUMBER function. Figure 3-18 shows one possible PL/SQL solution.

```
CREATE OR REPLACE FUNCTION is_pos_integer
    (in_string IN VARCHAR2)
RETURN VARCHAR2
IS
    pos_integer VARCHAR2(1) := 'N';
    num_string NUMBER;

BEGIN
    num_string := TO_NUMBER(in_string, '99999990');
    IF SIGN(num_string) = 1 THEN                        ▲1
        IF MOD(num_string,1) = 0 THEN          ▲2
            pos_integer := 'Y';        ▲3
        END IF;
    END IF;
    RETURN pos_integer;

EXCEPTION
    WHEN OTHERS THEN NULL;
    RETURN pos_integer;

END;                          ▲4
/
```

Figure 3-18: Identifying character strings that are positive integers.

Comments

▶ The format included in the TO_NUMBER function should be

consistent with the definition of the character data column. In this case, xtemp_code is VARCHAR2(8), so a number format of '99999990' was used.

▶ Use the SIGN function to filter only positive numbers.

▶ Use the MOD function to find integers.

▶ The EXCEPTION section traps all errors generated from an invalid TO_NUMBER conversion. It returns the value pos_integer that is declared on initiation to be 'N'.

Figure 3-19 illustrates how the PL/SQL function is_pos_integer can be used to identify character data values that are not positive integers.

```
COLUMN int HEADING 'positive|integer?' FORMAT a8
SELECT
    xtemp_code "char",
    is_pos_integer(xtemp_code) "int"
FROM xtemp;

            positive
char        integer?
--------    --------
100a        N
209         Y
875.1       N
-115        N
```

Figure 3-19: Query identifying character strings that are not positive integers.

See Also

1. The MOD function can be used in other creative ways. Chapter 8 (Figure 8-5 on page 238) shows MOD being used to systematically sample rows from a population.

How do I prevent inaccurate totals when summing rounded values?

One of my queries computes percentages of total sales by product category. I rounded the percentages to two decimal places, but when I add the rounded values, they don't total 100%. How can I prevent this from happening?

Approach

There are two ways to round numeric values in Oracle's implementation of SQL. You can use the ROUND function to explicitly round values based on the scientific method of rounding. If the digit to be dropped is a 0, 1, 2, 3, or 4, the value is rounded down; if the digit to be dropped is 5, 6, 7, 8, or 9, the value is rounded up. You also can rely on the numeric formats available in the COLUMN command, which implicitly round using the scientific method before displaying the value. For example, the format '999.99' rounds to two decimal places.

Used in a summation, the two methods of rounding can produce different results. Figure 3-20 illustrates this difference.

```
BREAK ON REPORT
COMPUTE SUM OF sales ON REPORT
COMPUTE SUM OF pct1 ON REPORT
COMPUTE SUM OF pct2 ON REPORT
COMPUTE SUM OF pct3 ON REPORT
COLUMN pct1 FORMAT 999.999999
COLUMN pct3 FORMAT 999.99         ◀1
SELECT
      sales_prodid "prodid",
      sales_total "sales",
      (sales_total/sales_grand_total)*100 "pct1",
      ROUND((sales_total/sales_grand_total)*100,2) "pct2",   ◀2
      (sales_total/sales_grand_total)*100 "pct3"
FROM totsales, sales;                              ▲1

prodid    ▲4        sales          pct1     pct2     pct3
--------  -----------  ------------  -------  -------
X555               500    33.783784    33.78    33.78
R251               110     7.432432     7.43     7.43
X555               200    13.513514    13.51    13.51
WV24               250    16.891892    16.89    16.89
ACO2               420    28.378378    28.38    28.38
          -----------  ------------  -------  -------
sum               1480   100.000000    99.99   100.00   ◀3
```

Figure 3-20: Rounding with ROUND function or NUMBER formats.

Comments

▶ Round implicitly by applying a NUMBER format in the

COLUMN command. In this case the percentage calculation will be displayed using the format '999.99', which rounds to two decimal places.

▶ Explicitly round by using the ROUND function. In this example, values are again rounded to two decimal places. Note that no column formatting was applied.

▶ Sums of the values rounded with the two methods differ (i.e., 100.00 versus 99.99). In the explicit method, the rounded values are summed to produce 99.99. In the implicit method, the individual (nonrounded) values are summed and then rounded before display. This latter method produces 100.00.

▶ The view *TOTSALES* includes only one data column (sales_grand_total) that contains the total of all sales. This is an instance where a cartesian product created by the absence of join WHERE conditions actually produces the desired result.

Either method of rounding presents problems for the cautious query writer. Using the implicit method, the total appears correct (100.00), but the individually rounded values do not sum to that total. Using the explicit method, the total appears incorrect (99.99), but the individual rounded values do sum to that total. Take your pick; either requires a footnote in a fully documented report.

Note that by both applying the ROUND function and formatting in the COLUMN command, you effectively double round. For example, a ROUND(n,3) rounds to three decimal places. If displayed with a format of '999.99', the rounded three-decimal value is rounded again — this time to two decimal places.

See Also

1. Another example showing the use of the ROUND function appears in Chapter 6 (Figure 6-20 on page 199).

2. Cartesian products occur when you do not join two tables in a query. Frequently this happens by mistake. But occasionally a cartesian product can be put to good use. In Chapter 10 (Figure 10-13 on page 303) a cartesian product is used to distinctly select two objects from *N* objects.

Chapter 4
Select Command

In one form or another the SQL SELECT command lies at the heart of every ad hoc query. It sometimes may seem lost, perhaps buried within an SQL*PLUS shell program or transfigured as a PL/SQL cursor, but it's always there. And if you don't get the SELECT right, your query and report are meaningless at best and dangerously misleading at worst.

The SELECT command is beguilingly simple, consisting of only six clauses in a natural language syntax:

- SELECT lists the items to appear in the report;

- FROM lists the tables needed;

- WHERE defines the report population and describes how to join the tables in the FROM clause;

- GROUP BY identifies criteria for grouping rows before performing group summaries such as counts, sums, and averages;

- HAVING limits the groups appearing in the final report; and

- ORDER BY sorts the query results.

In any given query, only the SELECT and FROM clauses are mandatory. You would be wrong, however, to assume that the SELECT command is simple. A single SELECT may consist of hundreds of lines of programming, with the most critical and most obtuse portions generally occurring in the WHERE clause that defines the report population and constructs the join relationships between tables. Reducing the complexity of SELECT commands with the appropriate use of SQL*PLUS and PL/SQL makes ad hoc queries much more accessible to nonprogrammers.

SELECT **Clause**

In the SELECT clause you list the data columns, expressions, pseudocolumns, literals, and other items that you want to appear in the report. Most questions about the SELECT clause concern expressions and how to build them properly to achieve certain effects. These have been discussed previously in Chapter 3 (Functions). This section examines only a single question concerning ROWID.

How do I display all data columns in a table and the ROWID*?*

I'd like to query all data columns in a table and also include the ROWID. When I do a "SELECT *, ROWID FROM tablename", I get an error message. I know I could explicitly name each data column in the SELECT clause, but is there a simpler method?

Approach

Make a minor modification in the query so that instead of SELECT * you use SELECT tablename.*. Figure 4-1 shows how this works.

```
SELECT name.*, ROWID FROM name;

         last     ▲      first     middle    name
id       name            name      name      seqnum ROWID
-----    ---------------  ---------- ------    ------- -------------------
a505     Carrington      Thomas     J              1 000001F0.0000.0002
a330     Vincent         Caroline                  1 000001F0.0001.0002
a133     O'Leary         Vincent                   1 000001F0.0002.0002
a330     Healey          Caroline   V              2 000001F0.0003.0002
a226     Sacco           Danielle                  1 000001F0.0004.0002
```

Figure 4-1: Selecting ROWID and all data columns in a table.

Comments

▷ Using NAME.* selects all columns from the *NAME* table and allows you to also include literals, pseudocolumns like ROWID, or data columns from other tables listed in the FROM clause.

See Also

1. ROWID is another tool that serves query writers well. You can use ROWID, for example, to help optimize performance (see Figure 4-6 on page 113) or to debug queries (see Chapter 7, Figure 7-9 on page 229).

WHERE **Clause**

If the SQL SELECT command is the heart of each ad hoc query, then the WHERE clause is the heart of each SQL SELECT. Because all testing and debugging is predicated on a stable report population, it's here where you must consciously and carefully identify the report population. For example, once a population gets defined, the query should not lose population items — a process known as *falling through the joins*. Similarly, the query should not pick up population items — a process known as *multiplying through the joins*. Being rock solid about what constitutes the report population and constructing the joins so that they prevent population loss or gain and yet simultaneously return results in a reasonable time provide the major challenges in the WHERE clause. The WHERE clause also can significantly affect query performance and thus the cost of the query.

How do I create an address hierarchy?

A user requested a basic name and address report with a slight twist. She'd like a person's permanent address displayed if it exists; if not, she wants the business address displayed. How can I write a query to do this?

Approach

The user is essentially asking for addresses displayed in a hierarchy with permanent addresses as the highest priority and then business addresses as a second-level priority. In this case the hierarchy only includes two priorities, but the idea easily could be extended to three or more.

Figure 4-2 shows a few rows of data from an address table where the primary key is address_id, address_type, and address_seriesno. Assume that the status indicator (A = active and I = inactive) identifies a valid address. The data include each of the four situations that could occur in a two-level hierarchy. A single person could have

- One or more valid permanent addresses and no valid business address;

- One or more valid business addresses but no valid permanent address;

- One or more valid permanent addresses and one or more valid business addresses; or

- Neither a valid permanent or business address.

This question did not specify what action to take for people who have neither a permanent nor a business address. For now, let's assume that these people will not be included in the report. The next section extends the discussion to include situations where no valid data exist but the person must still appear in the report.

```
id      type seq status
-----   ---- --- ------
@133    PR     1 A
@226    BU     1 A
@330    BU     1 A
@330    PR     1 I      ◀①
@330    PR     2 A
@505    PR     1 I
```

Figure 4-2: Sample address data.

Comments

▶ The person with ID @330 has two permanent addresses, but only one is active. She also has one business address. This person represents one of the four situations that can occur in a two-level hierarchy — where the person has valid data for each priority.

Note that other people in the figure represent the other three situations. That is, @133 has a valid permanent address but no valid business address; @226 has the reverse — a valid business address but no valid permanent address; and @505 has neither a valid permanent address nor a valid business address.

SQL Approach

Figure 4-3 shows an SQL query that displays address information in a (PR:1, BU:2) hierarchy. Note the complex WHERE clause that uses OR and a NOT EXISTS correlated subquery to enforce the hierarchy. Also note that the query uses a PL/SQL function called max_address that returns the most recent address of a given type.

Comments

▶ The WHERE clause that selects the most recent active permanent address begins at this point. Both @133 and @330 meet these criteria.

▶ The WHERE clause that selects the most recent active business address begins here. Both @226 and @330 meet these criteria. Note that @330 meets both criteria at this point.

```
SELECT
    name_id AS id,
    address_type AS type,
    address_seriesno AS seq,
    address_status AS status
FROM
    address a1,
    name
WHERE
    name_seriesno = name_now(name_id)
    AND a1.address_id = name_id
        AND
        (
▶1      (a1.address_type = 'PR'
        AND a1.address_status = 'A'
        AND a1.address_seriesno =
            max_address(name_id, a1.address_type))
▶2      OR
        (a1.address_type = 'BU'
        AND a1.address_status = 'A'
        AND a1.address_seriesno =
            max_address(name_id, a1.address_type)
▶3          AND NOT EXISTS
            (SELECT 'x' FROM address a2
            WHERE a2.address_id = name_id
            AND a2.address_type = 'PR'
            AND a2.address_status = 'A'))
        )
ORDER BY 1;


id      type seq status
-----   ---- --- ------
a133    PR     1 A
a226    BU     1 A            ◀4
a330    PR     2 A
```

Figure 4-3: SQL query that returns an address hierarchy.

▶3 The NOT EXISTS clause deals with people like @330 who have both an active permanent address and an active business address by excluding the active business address.

▶4 The query correctly returns the three rows expected.

For completeness, the PL/SQL function that returns the most recent active address of a specified type is shown in Figure 4-4.

Comments

▶1 The function gets passed an identification number and an address type. The cursor retrieves the most recent active address for that ID number and address type.

```
CREATE OR REPLACE FUNCTION max_address
    (id VARCHAR2, type VARCHAR2)
RETURN NUMBER
AS
max_seriesno NUMBER(2);

CURSOR main_cursor (p_id VARCHAR2, p_type VARCHAR2) IS
    SELECT MAX(address_seriesno)
    FROM address
    WHERE address_id = p_id            ◄1
      AND address_type = p_type
      AND address_status = 'A';

BEGIN
    OPEN main_cursor(id, type);
    FETCH main_cursor INTO max_seriesno;

    IF main_cursor%NOTFOUND THEN
        max_seriesno := NULL;
    END IF;

    CLOSE main_cursor;
    RETURN max_seriesno;
END;
/
```

Figure 4-4: PL/SQL function that identifies the most recent address.

PL/SQL Approach

The SQL query shown in Figure 4-3 provided accurate results but required a fairly complex WHERE clause. Extending the hierarchy to three priority classifications would complicate the query even further. Constructing a PL/SQL function that returns the correct address in a hierarchy greatly simplifies the query. Figure 4-5 illustrates this simplification.

Comments

▶ A single PL/SQL function replaces the complex WHERE clause that produced the address hierarchy in Figure 4-3. Note that the function gets passed an ID number and the hierarchy (i.e., PR addresses as first choice and BU addresses otherwise). Note, too, that the function returns a ROWID that uniquely identifies a single row.

Figure 4-6 shows the PL/SQL function that enforces the address hierarchy. Note that even this is simpler than the SQL solution.

```
SELECT
    name_id AS id,
    address_type AS type,
    address_seriesno AS seq,
    address_status AS status
FROM
    address a1,
    name
WHERE
    name_seriesno = name_now(name_id)
    AND a1.address_id = name_id
        AND a1.ROWID =
                address_hierarchy(name_id, 'PR', 'BU')
ORDER BY 1;                                               ▲1


id     type seq status
-----  ---- --- ------
@133   PR     1 A
@226   BU     1 A
@330   PR     2 A
```

Figure 4-5: Query using a PL/SQL function to return an address hierarchy.

```
CREATE OR REPLACE FUNCTION address_hierarchy
    (id VARCHAR2, type1 VARCHAR2, type2 VARCHAR2)
RETURN ROWID
AS
hierarchy_row ROWID;

CURSOR address_cursor
(p_id VARCHAR2, p_type1 VARCHAR2, p_type2 VARCHAR2) IS
    SELECT ROWID  ◀1
    FROM address
    WHERE address_id = p_id
        AND address_type IN (p_type1, p_type2)  ◀2
        AND address_status = 'A'
        AND address_seriesno = max_address(p_id, address_type)
        ORDER BY DECODE(address_type, p_type1, 0, p_type2, 1);

BEGIN                                                    ▲3
    OPEN address_cursor(id, type1, type2);
    FETCH address_cursor INTO hierarchy_row;

    IF address_cursor%NOTFOUND THEN
        hierarchy_row := NULL;
    END IF;

    CLOSE address_cursor;
    RETURN hierarchy_row;
END;
/
```

Figure 4-6: PL/SQL function that retrieves an address hierarchy.

Comments

▶ Queries that utilize ROWIDs generally optimize performance.

▶ The cursor selects active addresses of the two types passed as arguments in the function.

▶ Eligible address rows get sorted based on their type, with the highest-priority classification (i.e., type1) appearing first. In the execution section, the FETCH retrieves only the first row. In cases where someone had both a valid permanent address and a valid business address, the ORDER BY ensures that the permanent address appears first, gets FETCHed, and subsequently gets returned.

See Also

1. Chapter 9 (Table 9-4 on page 259) shows results of performance comparisons for the SQL and PL/SQL approaches to address hierarchies. These results again indicate a trade-off between query elegance and performance.

How do I create an address hierarchy (continued)?

The user would like to see addresses displayed in a permanent-then-business hierarchy, but if neither a permanent nor a business address exists, she still wants the person to appear in the report. How can I do this?

Approach

The problem has both SQL and PL/SQL solutions. The curious among you can revise the SQL in Figure 4-3 on page 111 to display the correct report. Note that in this query the person (i.e., ID = @505) without a valid permanent or a valid business address must appear in the report.

The PL/SQL solution only requires that an outer join be added to the query in Figure 4-5 on page 113. Figure 4-7 shows the results.

```
SELECT
    name_id AS id,
    address_type AS type,
    address_seriesno AS seq,
    address_status AS status
FROM
    address a1,
    NAME
WHERE
    name_seriesno = name_now(name_id)
    AND a1.address_id(+) = name_id
        AND a1.ROWID(+) =
            address_hierarchy(name_id, 'PR', 'BU')
ORDER BY 1;


id     type seq status
-----  ---- --- ------
@133   PR     1 A
@226   BU     1 A
@330   PR     2 A
@505
```

Figure 4-7: Preserving population using outer joins with an address hierarchy.

Comments

▶ The outer joins retain the person (@505) without a valid permanent or a valid business address. They also would retain anyone without any address information.

See Also

1. Outer joins can pose special problems for query writers. Beginning on page 156, Chapter 5 discusses several of these problems.

GROUP BY **Clause**

The GROUP BY and HAVING clauses tend to be the black sheep of the SELECT command clauses. They're seen less frequently and are subject to more misunderstanding than other clauses. But both play a vital role, GROUP BY to specify the criteria used to group rows in the result set so that summaries of those groups can be made and HAVING to limit which groups actually display in the report (i.e., a kind of WHERE clause but applied to groups).

How do I GROUP BY *a date?*

I'm trying to count the number of seminars by their starting date, but the count is always 1 even though some of the dates are clearly the same. What's going on here?

Approach

The problem occurs because of a misunderstanding about the GROUP BY criterion. Dates include information on hours, minutes, and seconds. Grouping by a date also uses this time information. Consequently, two seminars that start on the same day but at different times will be grouped separately and each will receive a count of 1 in a frequency distribution report. The trick is to format the date column. Figure 4-8 uses the TRUNC function to truncate dates to the nearest day with a time of midnight. Other techniques could accomplish the same thing.

Comments

▶ Using TRUNC without a format truncates to the nearest day. You could apply a format to truncate to another unit such as month, quarter, or year if you wanted counts by these more aggregate units.

▶ In this example, two seminars start on 15-JAN-1997.

See Also

1. This problem is very similar to one discussed in Chapter 3 on page 80 where the query specified a date in a WHERE condition but returned the wrong results. All dates include a time component and require care when used without formatting functions like TRUNC or TO_CHAR.

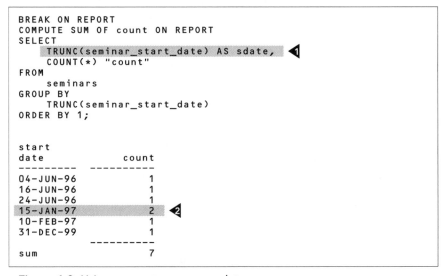

```
BREAK ON REPORT
COMPUTE SUM OF count ON REPORT
SELECT
    TRUNC(seminar_start_date) AS sdate,   ◀①
    COUNT(*) "count"
FROM
    seminars
GROUP BY
    TRUNC(seminar_start_date)
ORDER BY 1;


start
date              count
---------      ----------
04-JUN-96               1
16-JUN-96               1
24-JUN-96               1
15-JAN-97               2    ◀②
10-FEB-97               1
31-DEC-99               1
               ----------
sum                     7
```

Figure 4-8: Using TRUNC to GROUP BY dates.

When does a GROUP BY also ORDER BY?

I'd like to create a sorted view of data, but the ORDER BY clause cannot appear in a view. I've noticed that a GROUP BY seems to sort query results. But is this always the case? Is it possible to use a GROUP BY to accomplish the sort?

Approach

The ORDER BY clause cannot appear in a subquery. Thus commands that use subqueries, such as CREATE VIEW or INSERT, cannot include sorting criteria. A later section discusses sorted inserts (see Figure 4-16 on page 131). The approach used in that section also will work for the CREATE VIEW problem in this question. However, the question here has an interesting dimension aside from the immediate problem of creating a sorted view. Many times a GROUP BY will sort a report, but sometimes it will not. Let's explore the issue a little more deeply.

There is a fundamental difference between GROUP BY and ORDER BY that may be underappreciated. If you ORDER BY col1 and col2 (i.e., ORDER BY col1, col2), the result set is sorted on col1 and, in case of ties, then sorted on col2. However, if you group on the same two columns (i.e., GROUP BY col1, col2), the order of the columns in the GROUP BY clause can sometimes have absolutely no effect on the result set. You could reverse the column order (i.e., GROUP BY col2, col1) and get exactly the same result. Clearly, therefore, something other than a simple sorting occurs with GROUP BY. It's complicated by the presence of indexes.

Consider Figure 4-9 that retrieves an identification number and last name using an index where the leading edge of the index is last name. The report is not sorted by the GROUP BY criteria; that is, the sort order is not by ID and then last name.

Comments

▶ If the GROUP BY also sorted this query, then the order of the result set should be name_id and then name_last.

▶ Note that the name_id column is not sorted. Apparently in building the intermediate results, a sort on name_id was not necessary.

▶ Furthermore, note that not even the two rows for person @330 appear next to each other in the report. The result set is definitely grouped by the combined name_id and name_last columns, but not in a way analogous to the ORDER BY procedure.

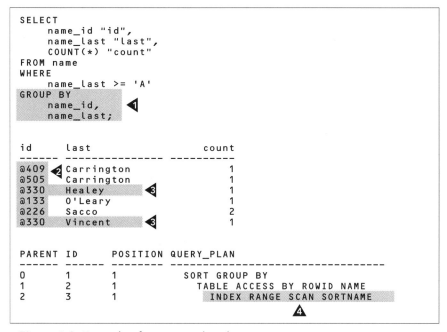

Figure 4-9: Example of GROUP BY that does not ORDER BY.

4▶ The EXPLAIN PLAN shows that the query used the sortname index to retrieve rows. The leading edge of this index is name_last — meaning rows got retrieved based on last name. Examine the report; it appears sorted on last name.

If you remove the complications provided by indexes by forcing a full table scan, for example, then the query results appear much different. Figure 4-10 shows exactly the same query without the WHERE clause condition that caused the Oracle optimizer in Figure 4-9 to utilize the sortname index. Note the changes in the results.

Comments
1▶ In this query the GROUP BY did sort the result set by name_id.
2▶ It also sorted by name_last.
3▶ Note that a full table scan of the name table occurred. The GROUP BY effectively sorted first by name_id and then by name_last when building its intermediate results. If you reverse the order of the two columns in the GROUP BY (i.e., GROUP BY

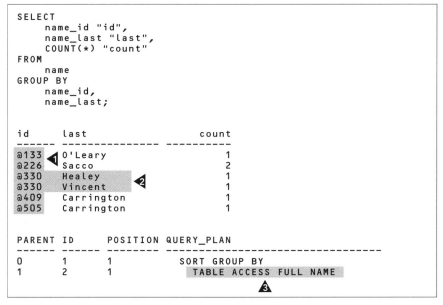

```
SELECT
     name_id "id",
     name_last "last",
     COUNT(*) "count"
FROM
     name
GROUP BY
     name_id,
     name_last;


id      last                    count
------  ----------------        ----------
a133    O'Leary                 1
a226    Sacco                   2
a330    Healey                  1
a330    Vincent                 1
a409    Carrington              1
a505    Carrington              1


PARENT ID      POSITION QUERY_PLAN
------ ------  -------- -------------------------------
0      1       1                SORT GROUP BY
1      2       1                TABLE ACCESS FULL NAME
```

Figure 4-10: Full table scan and GROUP BY results.

name_last, name_id), the report is sorted first by last name and then by ID.

Here's some advice on using GROUP BY to ORDER BY: be careful. If used on only a single data column, GROUP BY and ORDER BY do produce the same results. But if two or more data columns are involved, then the table indexes must be consistent with the ordering you hope to achieve, or you must structure the query to disable indexes and force a full table scan (or use the optimizer hint FULL).

See Also

1. With EXPLAIN PLAN you can better understand the logic applied by the Oracle optimizer as it interprets your query. EXPLAIN PLAN is particularly useful when a query takes an unacceptably long time to complete. Beginning on page 136, Chapter 5 shows examples of EXPLAIN PLAN and how you can display its results graphically.

ORDER BY **Clause**

With the ORDER BY clause you can sort query results by data columns and expressions that may or may not appear in the SELECT clause. It sounds pretty simple, yet the questions generated by ORDER BY provide some surprisingly interesting problems. Some deal with limitations imposed on queries because the ORDER BY may not appear in subqueries; others deal with novel ways to sort items.

How do I ORDER BY when the sort key is too long?

A data column in one of my tables contains lengthy descriptions of training courses. In some cases the length of the column was not sufficient to store the entire description, so I created another column that contains a sequence number. Then I store the course descriptions in a series of rows with different sequence numbers. The text column is VARCHAR2(2000). But when I try to ORDER BY the sequence number, I get an error message ORA-01467 (sort key too long). How can I avoid this error?

Approach

The sort key used in this query exceeds the length supported by Oracle. This normally results from too many columns or group functions in the SELECT clause. To solve the problem, Oracle recommends that the number of columns or group functions be reduced. This error also can be caused by other operations that sort, including GROUP BY and DISTINCT.

In this case, it's pretty difficult to take the recommended action because the query only contains one column. Two possibilities exist, neither one particularly attractive because they both require you to recreate the table using different datatype definitions.

First, you could reduce the length of data column, which is now VARCHAR2(2000) — choosing instead something like VARCHAR2(1800). This might require a fishing expedition to determine a column length small enough so that it does not generate the error. Second, you could make the data column LONG and store the entire course description in one column. Then the ORDER BY is not necessary.

See Also

1. LONG datatypes can cause problems when you want to display them in reports. Chapter 5 on page 168 discusses these problems.

How do I get an EBCDIC sort?

For one of my queries I'd prefer to sort alpha strings before numbers — as occurs when the character set is EBCDIC. Is this possible?

Approach

Character sets use encoding schemes that assign each character a numeric value. Sorting is normally based on these numeric values. In the ASCII character set, for example, the numeric codes 48 to 57 represent the symbols 0 to 9, codes 65 to 90 represent uppercase letters A to Z, and codes 97 to 122 represent lowercase letters a to z. Reports sorted in ascending order using the 7-bit U.S. ASCII character set will sort numbers, uppercase letters, and lowercase letters in that order.

An EBCDIC character set uses numeric codes that differ from the ASCII character set. EBCDIC numbers use the codes 240 to 249; uppercase letters use codes 193 to 201, 209 to 217, and 226 to 233; lowercase letters use the codes 129 to 137, 145 to 153, and 162 to 169. Reports sorted in ascending order using an EBCDIC character set will sort lowercase letters, uppercase letters, and numbers in that order — the reverse of a sort using the ASCII character set.

Oracle SQL includes a function called CONVERT that lets you convert between character sets. The general form of the function is CONVERT(CHAR, destination_set, [source_set]). The destination_set is the character set to convert to; and the optional source_set is the character set to convert from, defaulting to the database character set.

Figure 4-11 illustrates how you can use the CONVERT function to sort according to an EBCDIC character set. In this case, the destination character set is WE8EBCDIC500 (IBM West European EBCDIC Code Page 500). For more information on the character sets supported by Oracle, consult the *Oracle7 Server Reference* manual.

Comments

▶ An ORDER BY using an ASCII character set sorts numbers, uppercase letters, and lowercase letters in that order.

▶ Use the NOPRINT option in the COLUMN command to suppress the printing of the CONVERT expression. You could also achieve the same effect by removing the CONVERT expression from the SELECT clause and placing it in the ORDER BY clause.

▶ Here the IBM West European EBCDIC Code Page 500 character set was used in the conversion.

```
SELECT
      sorttest_code "char"
FROM sorttest
ORDER BY 1;

char
-----
419
A419  ◀❶
c419


COLUMN ebcdic NOPRINT  ◀❷
SELECT
      sorttest_code "char",
      CONVERT(sorttest_code, 'WE8EBCDIC500') "ebcdic"
FROM sorttest
ORDER BY 2;                                 ▲❸

char
-----
c419
A419  ◀❹
419
```

Figure 4-11: Using the CONVERT function to perform an EBCDIC sort.

❹ An ORDER BY using an EBCDIC character set sorts lower-case letters, uppercase letters, and numbers in that order. This reverses the sort order obtained with the ASCII character set.

See Also

1. CONVERT and some of the other conversion functions like CHARTOROWID and ROWIDTOCHAR don't find much use in ad hoc queries. But occasionally they prove useful. For examples where some of these uncommon conversion functions can be helpful, check the index under *conversion functions*.

How can I sort query results based on a user's runtime preference?

Because users run one report sorted in different ways, I presently maintain several versions of a single query that differ only in the ORDER BY clause. Can I maintain just a single query and have users specify the sorting criteria at runtime?

Approach

If a query includes substitution variables in the ORDER BY clause, users can specify different sort criteria each time they run the query. Only the way they specify the criteria presents an issue. Two easy options exist. First, allow users to choose among aliases assigned to columns or expressions in the SELECT clause. Second, allow users to choose the positional locations of columns or expressions in the SELECT clause.

Figure 4-12 shows a query that allows users to sort by an identification number or a name. The PROMPT command provides instructions on how to use either aliases or positional notations to specify the sort order.

```
SET VERIFY OFF
SET ECHO OFF
COLUMN name FORMAT A25
PROMPT To sort by:
PROMPT ID:    enter 1 or id.
PROMPT Name: enter 2 or sortname.
PROMPT ◀1
ACCEPT sort_selection PROMPT 'Enter selection: '
SELECT
     name_id AS id, ◀2
     name_last||', '||name_first||' '||name_middle AS sortname
FROM                                                    ▲2
     name
ORDER BY &sort_selection;


To sort by:
ID:    enter 1 or id.
Name: enter 2 or sortname.

Enter selection: sortname ◀3

ID     SORTNAME
-----  -----------------------------
@505   Carrington, Thomas J
@133   O'Leary, Vincent
@226   Sacco, Danielle
@330   Vincent, Caroline
```

Figure 4-12: Specifying runtime sort criteria.

Comments

▶ The query uses a series of PROMPT and ACCEPT commands to provide instructions to the user. In this case, for example, the user can sort the report by name if he enters an alias (sortname) or the number 2 that locates the name expression in the SELECT clause.

▶ Both the identification number and the name expression are assigned aliases by using AS. This allows you to use the alias in an ORDER BY clause.

▶ In this case the user entered the sortname alias at runtime and the report got sorted by name.

See Also

1. Chapter 2 (Figure 2-9 on page 50) shows another use of PROMPT and ACCEPT commands when interacting with query users at run-time.

How do I sort the UNION of two queries?

When I use UNION to create a compound query, the result rows are sorted automatically. How can I change this sort order?

Approach

UNION works by combining the result sets from two queries and eliminating any duplicates. In the process, the two result sets get sorted by the data columns requested in the queries — column 1 first, then column 2, and so on. Data columns in the queries UNIONed need not be the same, but they must be of the same datatype. For example, if column 1 in the first query is numeric, then column 1 in each UNIONed query also must be numeric.

Sorting UNIONed queries is fairly straightforward. Simply use a positional locator or alias in an ORDER BY clause in the last query. Figure 4-13 illustrates how this works.

```
SELECT
      name_id AS id,
      '1' AS ordercol,      ◀①
      name_last AS col3,
      name_first AS col4
FROM name
WHERE name_seriesno = name_now(name_id)
UNION
SELECT
      person_id AS id,
      '2' AS ordercol,
      person_gender AS col3,
      TO_CHAR(person_birthdate) AS col4
FROM person
ORDER BY 1, ordercol;     ◀②


id      seq col3              col4
-----   --- ---------------   -----------
@133    1   O'Leary           Vincent
@226    1   Sacco             Danielle
@226    2   F            ◀①   24-APR-70
@330    1   Healey            Caroline    ◀③
@330    2                     15-JAN-57
@505    1   Carrington        Thomas
@505    2   M                 22-NOV-67
```

Figure 4-13: Sorting a compound UNION query.

Comments

▶ A literal (i.e., '1' or '2') was used to help sort rows so that name information appeared before gender and birthdate for each person. Without using the literals, for example, the gender/birthdate row for @226 would appear before the name row — because the 'F' gender sorts before the 'S' in 'Sacco.'

▶ Note that the report is sorted by column with position 1 in the SELECT clause and then sorted by the column with alias ordercol.

▶ Columns from two UNIONed queries need not contain the same data columns, but they must use the same datatype. In this case a DATE column (person_birthdate) was converted to a character expression using the TO_CHAR function. The datatype of the expression then matches the datatype for the last name. Both appear in the fourth column in the query.

See Also

1. The fact that UNION compound queries do an implicit sort can be exploited when you'd like to sort but are prevented from doing so because the ORDER BY clause cannot be used (e.g., in subqueries). This side-effect of the UNION operation gets used in Chapter 6 (Figure 6-24 on page 203) to produce a top *N* report when you want to display only those *N* rows with the highest values for a data column.

How do I sort by sequence instead of numeric order?

Sections in our training manuals use a sequential numbering scheme. For example, 1.10 refers to item 10 in section 1. I want to sort the section numbers so that they appear in sequential order (i.e., 1, 1.1, 1.2, . . ., 1.9, 1.10, . . .). But when I do an ORDER BY, the sorting occurs in numeric order (i.e., 1, 1.1, 1.10, 1.11, . . ., 1.19, 1.2, . . .). How can I get a sequential sort? The data column is called section_item and is VARCHAR2(5).

Approach

The trick here is to realize that the section numbering scheme actually contains two pieces of information. The integer portion of the value indicates the section number; the decimal portion of the value indicates the item number within a section. If the table had been created with two NUMBER data columns, one for the section number and a second for the item number, then the sorting would be simple — just ORDER BY section_number, item_number.

But since we're dealing with a single VARCHAR2 column instead of two NUMBER columns, the task becomes one of creating two numeric expressions that can be used to do the sorting. Figure 4-14 illustrates one possibility.

```
SELECT
    section_item "item",
    TRUNC(TO_NUMBER(section_item)) "integer",      ◀①
    TO_NUMBER(
        DECODE(INSTR(section_item,'.'),
        0,0,
        SUBSTR(section_item,INSTR(section_item,'.')+1)      ◀②
        )
    ) "decimal"
FROM sections
ORDER BY 2, 3;

item     integer  decimal
-----    -------- --------
1            1        0
1.1          1        1
1.2          1        2
1.3          1        3
1.10    ◀③   1       10
1.11         1       11
1.12         1       12
1.13         1       13
2            2        0
12          12        0
```

Figure 4-14: Sorting a sequential rather than numeric numbering scheme.

Comments

▶ The integer portion of the section numbering scheme is easily obtained by converting section_item to a number and then truncating that number to zero decimal places.

▶ The decimal portion of the numbering scheme requires a bit more work. The heart of the solution shown in Figure 4-14 relies on the INSTR function to search for a decimal point. If none exists, then a 0 is returned. If a decimal does exist, then the string of digits to the right of the decimal is returned. Converting the character string to a number completes the expression.

▶ Note that sorting on the integer expression and then the decimal expression produces the desired sorting order.

See Also

1. Whenever one data column contains two or more conceptually separate elements, potential query problems arise. The problem in this section is analogous to questions that occur when misusing dates because they contain both a date and time component. See, for example, discussions on page 116 in this chapter and on page 80 in Chapter 3.

2. For another example where the INSTR function gets used in a query, see Chapter 6 (Figure 6-31 on page 210).

How can I do a sorted INSERT?

I'd like to copy data from one table into a temporary table, but to do the copy after first sorting the data. The INSERT command does not permit an ORDER BY in a SELECT subquery. Is there any way to get around this problem?

Approach

There are work-arounds to this problem using SQL and more direct and logically appealing solutions in PL/SQL. Let's examine both. For purposes of illustration, suppose you have a *NAME* table ordered as shown in Figure 4-15, and you want to insert the rows into a new table ordered by last, first, and middle names.

```
SQL> SELECT * FROM name;

id      last              first      middle  seq
-----   ---------------   ----------  ------  ----
ə505    Carrington        Thomas      J       1
ə330    Vincent           Caroline            1
ə133    O'Leary         ◄ Vincent             1
ə330    Healey            Caroline    V       2
ə226    Sacco             Danielle            1
```

Figure 4-15: Unsorted data from a *NAME* table.

Comments

▶ Note that the original data are not in alphabetical order. The task becomes one sorting the data by last, first, and middle names before doing an INSERT to a new table.

SQL Approach

The trick using SQL requires a SELECT subquery in the INSERT command that retrieves rows in the correct order without using the ORDER BY clause. There are a couple of approaches you can take. You could, for example, create an index on the data columns you want sorted and then force the use of that index by structuring the query appropriately and providing hints to the Oracle optimizer.

In our example, we'd want to create a compound index on name_last, name_first, and name_middle. Suppose the index is called sortname_ind. Figure 4-16 shows how you can use this index and the hint INDEX_ASC to retrieve and then insert data in the desired sort order.

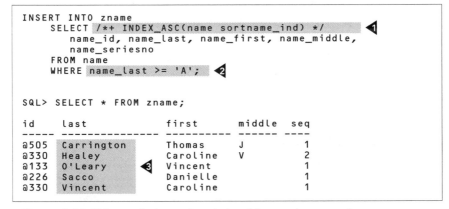

```
INSERT INTO zname
    SELECT /*+ INDEX_ASC(name sortname_ind) */          ◀1
        name_id, name_last, name_first, name_middle,
        name_seriesno
    FROM name
    WHERE name_last >= 'A';          ◀2


SQL> SELECT * FROM zname;

id      last                first       middle  seq
-----   ----------------    ----------  ------  ----
@505    Carrington          Thomas      J       1
@330    Healey              Caroline    V       2
@133    O'Leary        ◀3   Vincent             1
@226    Sacco               Danielle            1
@330    Vincent             Caroline            1
```

Figure 4-16: Using an index and optimizer hints to do a sorted INSERT.

Comments

▶ The INDEX_ASC hint causes the Oracle optimizer to use an
index scan (with the index sortname_ind) on the *NAME* table.
The scan occurs in ascending order of the indexed values. That
is, you have implicitly ordered row retrieval.

▶ Include the leading edge of the index in the WHERE clause to
ensure that the index gets used.

▶ Note that the inserted rows now appear in alphabetical order.

Using a second approach (see Figure 4-17), you can get the same effect with the implicit sort that occurs in UNION compound queries.

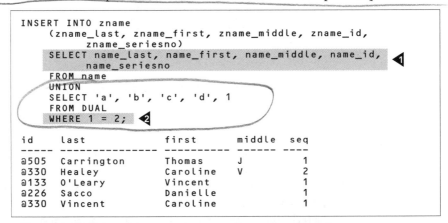

```
INSERT INTO zname
    (zname_last, zname_first, zname_middle, zname_id,
        zname_seriesno)
    SELECT name_last, name_first, name_middle, name_id,     ◀1
        name_seriesno
    FROM name
    UNION
    SELECT 'a', 'b', 'c', 'd', 1
    FROM DUAL
    WHERE 1 = 2;     ◀2

id      last                first       middle  seq
-----   ----------------    ----------  ------  ----
@505    Carrington          Thomas      J       1
@330    Healey              Caroline    V       2
@133    O'Leary             Vincent             1
@226    Sacco               Danielle            1
@330    Vincent             Caroline            1
```

Figure 4-17: Using the UNION set operation to do a sorted INSERT.

Comments

▶ In the first SELECT of the UNION query, put the data columns in the order in which you want them sorted. Here sorting will occur by last, first, and middle names.

▶ The second SELECT in the UNION query is a dummy. Note that the WHERE conditions never equate to TRUE. This SELECT only gets included so you can use UNION to force a sort.

PL/SQL Approach

PL/SQL solutions to the ordered insert problem require no such shenanigans as special indexes, optimizer hints, and appropriately structured subqueries. You simply declare a cursor that contains the ORDER BY statement and then loop through the cursor to do the inserts. Figure 4-18 illustrates one possible PL/SQL procedure to do this. When you EXECUTE the insert_sorted_names procedure, it does the same sorted insert as shown in Figure 4-16.

```
CREATE OR REPLACE PROCEDURE insert_sorted_names
IS
   CURSOR sorted_name_cursor IS
     SELECT *
     FROM name
     ORDER BY name_last, name_first, name_middle;   ◀1
   sorted_name_rec sorted_name_cursor%ROWTYPE;

BEGIN
   FOR sorted_name_rec IN sorted_name_cursor   ◀2
   LOOP
        INSERT INTO sname VALUES
           (sorted_name_rec.name_id,
            sorted_name_rec.name_last,
            sorted_name_rec.name_first,
            sorted_name_rec.name_middle,
            sorted_name_rec.name_seriesno);
   END LOOP;
END;
/
```

Figure 4-18: PL/SQL procedure to do a sorted INSERT.

Comments

▶ The cursor sorted_name_cursor contains an ORDER BY that performs the desired sort.

▶ Using a cursor FOR loop allows you to INSERT one cursor record at a time into the new table. Because the cursor records are sorted, the INSERT also occurs in the correct sequence.

See Also

1. For examples that use the implicit sorting of the UNION operation to work around restrictions on ORDER BY in subqueries, see Chapter 6 (Figure 6-24 on page 203) and Chapter 8 (Figure 8-4 on page 236). Both examples illustrate the use of a dummy query against the DUAL table in the UNION operation.

Chapter 5
Special Problems

Some aspects of SQL and SQL*PLUS generate more problems for query writers than others and elicit an "oh, no, not one of those queries." Often the problems occur because the SQL element gets used infrequently or it contains subtle aspects that require experience to learn.

This chapter discusses several of the prominent problems that most query writers face at one time or another. It includes:

- Hierarchical data relationships;

- NULL values;

- Subqueries;

- Set operations such as UNION, INTERSECT, and MINUS;

- Outer joins;

- LONG datatypes; and

- DISTINCT

One theme this chapter emphasizes is alternative methods of achieving the same effect. Sometimes you get stuck writing a query with one approach; in these situations, it's nice to have alternatives that accomplish the same thing. For example, the result from an outer join also can be duplicated with set operations. Choosing between the two approaches often depends on personal preference, but sometimes circumstances in the query or data tip the scale the other way.

It probably doesn't pay to read this chapter straight through. Use it whenever you encounter a specific problem; otherwise count your blessings.

Hierarchies

In the nonrelational database world, one common way to organize data is hierarchically in a parent-child relationship. The classic example is the manager-employee relationship, where any given employee may report to a manager and also may manage other employees. For querying data that contain hierarchical links, Oracle provides a clause in the SELECT command to specify a starting point in the hierarchy and to identify how the data are linked. The result is called a *hierarchical query*.

How do I sort a hierarchical query?

I've written a query that displays employees in a hierarchy based on their job reporting relationships, much like the classic hierarchical query supplied by Oracle in the scott/tiger database. But I can't figure out a way to order the report so that within a given level the employee names are alphabetical. How can I do this?

Approach

Figure 5-1 shows the scott/tiger example with an additional data column showing the default sort key. Note that this sort key is a string of employee identification numbers that traces a reporting arrangement from the top level (i.e., the president) down to a specific employee. The default sort is essentially an ORDER BY sort_key ASC.

Comments

▶ The sort key used for the default ORDER BY contains a string of employee identification numbers that shows the job hierarchy. For example, the employee named Smith (7369) is managed by 7902, who is managed by 7566, who in turn reports to the president (7839). The sort key for this row is the top-down string of these four employee identification numbers.

Note that the employee names are not arranged in alphabetical order.

By explicitly including an ORDER BY in the query, you can sort the report in some other fashion than the default. In hierarchical queries you also have a pseudocolumn called LEVEL that displays the level of the hierarchy, with the top level being 1 for the president, level 2 including the three employees who report to the president, and so on.

```
SELECT
    LPAD(' ', 2*(LEVEL-1))||ename "org_chart",
    empno,
    mgr,
    job,
    get_sort_key(empno) "sortkey"
FROM
    emp
START WITH mgr IS NULL
CONNECT BY PRIOR empno = mgr;

org_chart       empno    mgr  job         sortkey
-------------   ------   ------ ---------  -----------------
KING             7839           PRESIDENT  7839
  JONES          7566    7839   MANAGER    78397566
    SCOTT        7788    7566   ANALYST    783975667788
      ADAMS      7876    7788   CLERK      7839756677887876
    FORD         7902    7566   ANALYST    783975667902
      SMITH      7369    7902   CLERK      7839756679027369   ◀
  BLAKE          7698    7839   MANAGER    78397698
    ALLEN        7499    7698   SALESMAN   783976987499
    WARD         7521    7698   SALESMAN   783976987521
    MARTIN       7654    7698   SALESMAN   783976987654
    TURNER       7844    7698   SALESMAN   783976987844
    JAMES        7900    7698   CLERK      783976987900
  CLARK          7782    7839   MANAGER    78397782
    MILLER       7934    7782   CLERK      783977827934
```

Figure 5-1: Hierarchical query with the default sort.

The problem with including a simple ORDER BY is that you lose the hierarchical nature of the report. For example, if you ORDER BY the employee's name (ename), you'll just get a straight alpha sort based on last name. This question poses a different problem — to keep the hierarchical nature of the report but to do an alpha sort within a LEVEL. The three people at LEVEL 2 (Jones, Blake, and Clark), for example, should appear in the order Blake, Clark, and Jones with the appropriate job hierarchy underneath each.

Figure 5-2 shows the desired report. It also includes the sort key used to accomplish the ORDER BY. Note that instead of a string of employee identification numbers, the sort key now includes employee names as well.

Comments

▶ The sort key now contains names as well as employee identification numbers. Using an ORDER BY on the sort key retains the hierarchy but produces an alpha sort within a level (even though these rows may not appear next to each other in the report).

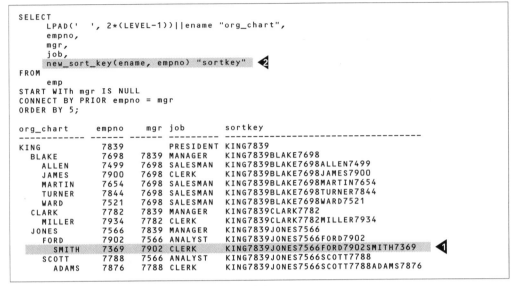

```
SELECT
      LPAD(' ', 2*(LEVEL-1))||ename "org_chart",
      empno,
      mgr,
      job,
      new_sort_key(ename, empno) "sortkey"     ◀2
FROM
      emp
START WITh mgr IS NULL
CONNECT BY PRIOR empno = mgr
ORDER BY 5;

org_chart        empno    mgr job        sortkey
-------------   ------  ------ ---------   ------------------------------------
KING             7839          PRESIDENT  KING7839
  BLAKE          7698    7839  MANAGER    KING7839BLAKE7698
    ALLEN        7499    7698  SALESMAN   KING7839BLAKE7698ALLEN7499
    JAMES        7900    7698  CLERK      KING7839BLAKE7698JAMES7900
    MARTIN       7654    7698  SALESMAN   KING7839BLAKE7698MARTIN7654
    TURNER       7844    7698  SALESMAN   KING7839BLAKE7698TURNER7844
    WARD         7521    7698  SALESMAN   KING7839BLAKE7698WARD7521
  CLARK          7782    7839  MANAGER    KING7839CLARK7782
    MILLER       7934    7782  CLERK      KING7839CLARK7782MILLER7934
  JONES          7566    7839  MANAGER    KING7839JONES7566
    FORD         7902    7566  ANALYST    KING7839JONES7566FORD7902
      SMITH      7369    7902  CLERK      KING7839JONES7566FORD7902SMITH7369    ◀1
    SCOTT        7788    7566  ANALYST    KING7839JONES7566SCOTT7788
      ADAMS      7876    7788  CLERK      KING7839JONES7566SCOTT7788ADAMS7876
```

Figure 5-2: Hierarchical report including an alpha sort.

▶2   A PL/SQL function called new_sort_key generated the sort
keys used to do the ORDER BY.

For completeness, Figure 5-3 shows the PL/SQL function
new_sort_key that produces the sort key used in Figure 5-2. It contains
a loop that builds the sort key by tracing from a given employee up to the
president through the manager relationships. Needless to say, you must
have a compelling reason for wanting to sort a hierarchical report in
some way other than the default.

See Also

1. CONNECT BY . . . START WITH is actually another clause in the
SELECT command, seldom seen among the other more common
clauses. Yet, for returning rows in hierarchical order, the CONNECT
BY . . . START WITH clause is crucial. Query writers frequently use hi-
erarchical data when they debug their queries with EXPLAIN PLAN.
Figure 5-7 on page 142 shows another example of CONNECT BY . . .
START WITH used with EXPLAIN PLAN.

```
CREATE OR REPLACE FUNCTION new_sort_key
  (in_name VARCHAR2, in_empno NUMBER)
RETURN VARCHAR2
AS
  empno_to_check NUMBER(8);
  top_level VARCHAR2(1) := 'N';
  sort_key VARCHAR2(100) := in_name||in_empno;
  CURSOR mgr_cursor IS
    SELECT e1.ename, e1.empno
    FROM emp e1
    WHERE e1.empno =
    (SELECT e2.mgr FROM emp e2 WHERE e2.empno = empno_to_check);
  mgr_rec mgr_cursor%ROWTYPE;

BEGIN
  empno_to_check := in_empno;
  WHILE top_level = 'N'
  LOOP
    OPEN mgr_cursor;
    FETCH mgr_cursor INTO mgr_rec;
    IF mgr_cursor%NOTFOUND THEN
      top_level := 'Y';
    ELSE
      sort_key := mgr_rec.ename||TO_CHAR(mgr_rec.empno)||sort_key;
      empno_to_check := mgr_rec.empno;
    END IF;
    CLOSE mgr_cursor;
  END LOOP;
  RETURN sort_key;
END;
/
```

Figure 5-3: PL/SQL function new_sort_key used in Figure 5-2.

How do I select only the leaves in hierarchical data?

One of my tables contains hierarchical data. I'd like to write a query that selects only the leaves of the hierarchy. How can I do this?

Approach

Hierarchical data can be arranged in an inverted tree structure. The top level is called the *root node*. Each node below the root is a *child*. If a node has children, it is also a *parent*. A node without children is a *leaf*.

Query writers commonly encounter hierarchical data when performing an EXPLAIN PLAN to describe the query execution plan. Figure 5-4 shows a simple query and its execution plan.

```
SELECT
      name_id "id", name_last "last",
      student_regseq "seq", student_sponsor "sponsor"
FROM
      student s1, name
WHERE
      name_seriesno = name_now(name_id)
      AND s1.student_id(+) = name_id
            AND
            (
            s1.ROWID IS NULL
            OR
            s1.student_regseq =
            (SELECT MAX(s2.student_regseq)
            FROM student s2
            WHERE s2.student_id = name_id)
            )
ORDER BY 2;

      id parent position query_plan
   ------ ------ -------- ------------------------------------------
       1      0        1    SORT ORDER BY
       2      1        1      FILTER
       3      2        1        NESTED LOOPS OUTER
       4      3        1          TABLE ACCESS FULL NAME
       5      3        2          TABLE ACCESS BY ROWID STUDENT
       6      5        1            INDEX RANGE SCAN PK_STUDENT
       7      2        2        SORT AGGREGATE
       8      7        1          INDEX RANGE SCAN PK_STUDENT
```

Figure 5-4: Example of hierarchical data in an EXPLAIN PLAN.

Comments

▶ The list of parents does not include nodes 4, 6, or 8. These are the leaves in the query.

Figure 5-5 displays the hierarchical data appearing in the EXPLAIN PLAN. Using this format, the leaves are immediately evident.

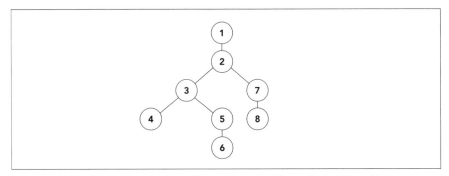

Figure 5-5: Alternative display of EXPLAIN PLAN hierarchy in Figure 5-4.

You can use several methods to find the leaves in hierarchical data. Figure 5-6 uses a correlated subquery and NOT EXISTS to return only those rows which do not serve as a parent.

```
SELECT
      id "id",
      parent_id "parent",
      position "position",
      operation||' '||options||' '||object_name "query_plan"
FROM
      plan_table p1
WHERE NOT EXISTS
      (SELECT 'x'
      FROM plan_table p2
      WHERE p2.parent_id = p1.id);       ◀

      id parent postion query_plan
   ------ ------ ------- ------------------------------------
       4      3       1 TABLE ACCESS FULL NAME
       6      5       1 INDEX RANGE SCAN PK_STUDENT
       8      7       1 INDEX RANGE SCAN PK_STUDENT
```

Figure 5-6: Leaves in the hierarchical data from EXPLAIN PLAN in Figure 5-4.

Comments

▶ This correlated subquery retains only those rows where no other row includes the ID as a parent (i.e., the leaves).

See Also

1. Figure 5-7 on page 142 uses the MINUS operation to find leaves.

2. The PL/SQL for the name_now function used in Figure 5-4 appears in Chapter 1 (Figure 1-9 on page 13).

How can I do a bottom-up hierarchical query?

I find the typical EXPLAIN PLAN results to be somewhat confusing, because to interpret the graphic display you need to read left to right, bottom to top. For example, the query in Figure 5-4 and Figure 5-5 shows node 1 (the ORDER BY) as the root when it's actually the last step performed in executing the query. How can I do a bottom-up EXPLAIN PLAN that might more easily convey the order in which the query steps actually get performed?

Approach

A hierarchical query need not start with just a single root. Suppose we started with the leaves of the EXPLAIN PLAN data from Figure 5-4 on page 140 and follow the lineage of each leaf. Figure 5-7 shows the results.

```
SELECT
     id "id",
     parent_id "parent",
     position "pos",
     LPAD(' ',2*(LEVEL-1))||operation||' '||
          options||' '||object_name "query_plan"
FROM
     plan_table p1
CONNECT BY id = PRIOR parent_id AND id != 0
START WITH id in
     (SELECT id FROM plan_table
     MINUS                                        ◀
     SELECT parent_id FROM plan_table);


     id parent postion query_plan
    ------ ------ ------- ------------------------------------------
       4      3        1 TABLE ACCESS FULL NAME                     ◀
       3      2        1   NESTED LOOPS OUTER
       2      1        1     FILTER
       1      0        1       SORT ORDER BY
       6      5        1 INDEX RANGE SCAN PK_STUDENT
       5      3        2   TABLE ACCESS BY ROWID STUDENT
       3      2        1     NESTED LOOPS OUTER
       2      1        1       FILTER
       1      0        1         SORT ORDER BY
       8      7        1 INDEX RANGE SCAN PK_STUDENT
       7      2        2   SORT AGGREGATE
       2      1        1     FILTER
       1      0        1       SORT ORDER BY
```

Figure 5-7: Hierarchical query starting from leaves of EXPLAIN PLAN.

Comments

▶ This subquery uses the MINUS operation to identify leaves in the hierarchical data. This structure produces the same results as

the correlated subquery shown in Figure 5-6 on page 141.
▶ Note that the nodes 4, 6, and 8 appear at the top level in this
query.

Using the bottom-up approach produces a straight lineage from
child to parent to grandparent and so on, without the branching present
when tracing down from the common ancestor. To understand the query
using the bottom-up approach, you really need to graphically display the
results. Figure 5-8 shows the three lineages combined so as to eliminate
the redundancies present in Figure 5-7. It does allow the query to be interpreted by reading from left to right, top to bottom, but you'll have to
be the judge whether it adds any value over the traditional EXPLAIN PLAN
results.

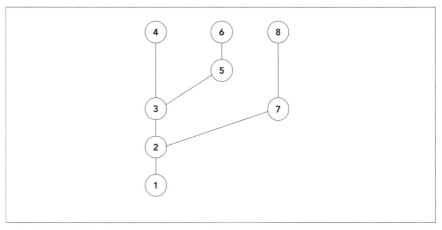

Figure 5-8: Alternate display of bottom-up hierarchical query in Figure 5-7.

See Also

1. The CONNECT BY . . . START WITH clause used in Figure 5-7 returns rows in hierarchical order. Another example of its use appears
in Figure 5-1 on page 137, when displaying employee reporting relationships in a hierarchical fashion.

NULL **Values**

NULL values seem simple enough — a data value that is NULL doesn't exist; we just don't have any information about it. But rest assured, you'll pay lots of attention in your queries to the special problems that NULL values present. Whether they appear naturally in the data or get generated temporarily with outer joins, NULL values often demand their due.

How do I use != with NULL *values?*

I've written a query that's losing population items. I traced the problem to one condition in the WHERE clause that specifies that the state is not equal to NY. What could be simpler than this?

Approach

Using the != operator requires some care whenever the data column in question can contain NULL values. For example, WHERE state != 'NY' excludes all rows where the state is NY, but it also excludes all rows where the state is NULL. Since NULL is not a value, it cannot equal or not equal anything else.

If you want rows containing NULL values to remain in the report, you must modify the != condition slightly. Figure 5-9 shows one way to do this.

```
SELECT
    name_id "id",
    address_loc "state"
FROM address, name
WHERE
    name_seriesno = name_now(name_id)
    AND address_id = name_id
        AND address_type = 'PR'
        AND (address_loc != 'NY' OR address_loc IS NULL)
ORDER BY 1;


id     state
-----  -----
a133   MA
a330   CO
a409
a925
```

Figure 5-9: Using != when NULL values exist.

Comments

▶ If you want to exclude some rows based on the address state but also want to include rows containing NULL values for the state (as might occur with foreign addresses), then use an OR structure with IS NULL to explicitly include NULL values.

Another common but related error occurs when you try to use NULL with IN. For example, WHERE state IN ('NY', NULL) only includes states with the value NY. NULL values are again excluded, for the same reason that NULL values cannot equal or not equal anything.

See Also

1. You also could use the NVL or DECODE functions to solve this problem. For example, WHERE NVL(address_loc, 'MA') != 'NY' would work. Several examples of NVL and DECODE appear in this book. Check the index under NVL *function* or DECODE *function* for specific references.

2. The PL/SQL for the name_now function used in Figure 5-9 appears in Chapter 1 (Figure 1-9 on page 13).

How do I count NULL values?

Figure 5-10 shows a query I wrote to count addresses by state. I know that some of the rows have NULL values for the state, and I used an NVL function to display 'null' when this occurs. But the count indicates zero rows with NULL values. I know this is wrong. What's happening?

```
SELECT
    NVL(address_loc,'null') "state",
    COUNT(address_loc) "count"  ◀
FROM address, name
WHERE
    name_seriesno = name_now(name_id)
    AND address_id = name_id
GROUP BY
    address_loc
ORDER BY 1;


state       count
-----  ----------
CO            2
IL            1
MA            1
NY            2
null          0   ◀
```

Figure 5-10: COUNT that ignores NULL values.

Comments

▶ Counting the address_loc data column produced a count of zero even though some NULL values exist.

Approach

All group functions except one ignore NULL values. The exception is one flavor of the COUNT function. When used as COUNT(*), the count includes all rows meeting the query conditions regardless of whether they contain NULL values in the data column of particular interest. On the other hand, when used as COUNT(column_name) as done in Figure 5-10, the count ignores NULL values, hence the zero that appears in the report.

The solution to the problem is straightforward. You can either replace COUNT(address_loc) with COUNT(*) or with COUNT(expression) where the expression explicitly assigns a value to NULL. For example, COUNT(NVL(address_loc, 'null')) or COUNT(DECODE(address_loc, NULL, 'null')) would work.

See Also

1. For discussion of the same confusion that sometimes occurs between COUNT(*) and COUNT, see Chapter 3 on page 99.

2. Figure 5-10 uses the name_now function. The PL/SQL for this function appears in Chapter 1 (Figure 1-9 on page 13).

Subqueries

Subqueries abound in ad hoc queries. They are wonderful inventions with great flexibility. One form in particular appears frequently in queries. The correlated subquery acting as predicate to an EXISTS or NOT EXISTS finds considerable use in defining report populations when you need to check for the presence or absence of a characteristic but don't actually need to see the value in the report. This section includes a question about correlated subqueries.

Often the function of a subquery can be replaced conveniently with a PL/SQL function. This makes your query writing much cleaner; instead of a messy looking subquery, you simply employ a PL/SQL function conveniently named so as to convey intent. This section also discusses these alternatives to subqueries.

How do I get a maximum value for each population item?

To display the most recent student-related information for people attending our training classes, I need to retrieve only the last row pertaining to each student. In this case a sequential number is used as each new row of data is input for a student. What's the easiest way to retrieve the most recent information for each student?

Approach

The SQL structure normally used to solve this type of problem is the correlated subquery. For each item in the report population, the subquery searches other rows for that item and returns the row or rows meeting the subquery conditions. In this case, for each student in the report population, the subquery identifies the single row containing the maximum sequential number for that student (i.e., the row with the most recent data).

Figure 5-11 shows a simple example of two students, one registered at two separate times for training classes and the other at three separate times. Note that the column student_regseq identifies the most recent registration. The column student_sponsor identifies who paid for the training.

Comments

▶ Selecting the maximum student_regseq for each student returns the most recent training registration information.

```
id        seq   sponsor          fee   regdate
-----     ----  ----------    ------   --------
a226       1    Mixed          1200    23-APR-97
a226       2    Self            200    11-JUL-97
a226       3    Self            400    02-DEC-97   ◀
a505       1    Self            500    19-JUN-97
a505       2    Employer       1500    04-NOV-97
```

Figure 5-11: Sample training registration data.

Constructing a subquery to return the row with the maximum student_regseq for each student is straightforward. Figure 5-12 illustrates such a subquery.

```
SELECT
    s1.student_id "id",
    s1.student_regseq "seq",
    s1.student_sponsor "sponsor",
    s1.student_total_fee "fee"
FROM
    student s1, name
WHERE
    name_seriesno = name_now(name_id)
        AND name_id IN ('a226','a505')
    AND s1.student_id = name_id
        AND s1.student_regseq =
        (SELECT max(s2.student_regseq)
        FROM student s2                    ◀
        WHERE s2.student_id = name_id)
ORDER BY 1;

id        seq   sponsor          fee
-----     ----  ----------    ------
a226       3    Self            400
a505       2    Employer       1500
```

Figure 5-12: Correlated subquery that retrieves most recent training data.

Comments

▶ The subquery correlates with the main query through the student_id. It uses the group function MAX to retrieve the maximum student_regseq (i.e., the most recent training registration).

The interesting aspect of this question appears only when you begin adding WHERE conditions from the correlating table. Then you must be conscious of the symmetry between the main query and the subquery. For example, what would happen if we added a condition to the main query that student_sponsor = 'Self'? Figure 5-13 provides the results.

```
SELECT
    s1.student_id "id",
    s1.student_regseq "seq",
    s1.student_sponsor "sponsor",
    s1.student_total_fee "fee"
FROM
    student s1,
    name
WHERE
    name_seriesno = name_now(name_id)
        AND name_id IN ('@226','@505')
    AND s1.student_id = name_id
        AND s1.student_sponsor = 'Self'   ◀1
        AND s1.student_regseq =
        (SELECT MAX(s2.student_regseq)
        FROM student s2
        WHERE s2.student_id = name_id)
ORDER BY 1;


id        seq  sponsor        fee
-----    ----  ----------    ------
@226       3   Self            400   ◀1
```

Figure 5-13: Unbalanced subquery and main query (version 1).

Comments

▶ Note that the main query contains the condition student_sponsor = 'Self' but that the subquery does not. The results of this query differ from those in Figure 5-12 (no row appears for @505). Think for a moment about what the query requests. The translation is: Consider only those rows where student_sponsor = 'Self' and from these display only those where the student_regseq is the maximum among all registrations for that student. In slightly different words: Retrieve the most recent training data for a student but display them only if the student paid for the course herself.

Consider the situation with @505 (see Figure 5-11 on page 149). This person does have one row meeting the main query condition that student_sponsor = 'Self.' But the student_regseq for this row is 1, which is not the most recent registration for the student. The subquery condition is not met, and no row for this student displays.

Whenever you add a WHERE condition from the correlating table, several situations can occur. These are:

- In a balanced structure, the main query and the subquery both contain the condition;

- In one unbalanced structure, the main query contains the condition and the subquery does not; or

- In a second unbalanced structure, the subquery contains the condition but the main query does not.

Each of the three structures produces a query whose meaning differs slightly from the others. The first unbalanced structure we've already discussed (see Figure 5-13). Here's what the other two structures yield:

- The balanced structure returns the most recent training data where the student paid for the courses. This report includes two rows: student_regseq = 3 for @226 and student_regseq = 1 for @505.

- The unbalanced structure with the condition in the subquery returns the same results as the balanced structure but does so in a less efficient manner because the main query does not filter the rows for consideration.

The take-home message here is that WHERE conditions in correlating tables should pose a caution flag for query writers. Often, balancing the main query and the subquery provides the desired result, but this may not always be the case. There may be situations where you deliberately choose to unbalance the main query and the subquery.

See Also

1. Correlated subqueries are wonderful when defining report populations. Used with EXISTS or NOT EXISTS they qualify a population much like an adjective qualifies a noun, identifying the presence or absence of some characteristic (e.g., whether any overdue balances exist). As such, they're good candidates for SQL segments that you can later reuse. See Chapter 7 (Figure 7-4 on page 223) for an example of a correlated subquery used to define a population.

2. The name_now function is used in Figure 5-12. Chapter 1 (Figure 1-9 on page 13) shows the PL/SQL for this function.

Are there alternatives to correlated subqueries?

How could I write the query in Figure 5-12 on page 149 without using a correlated subquery?

Approach

As we'll see shortly with outer joins, it's always helpful to have a variety of ways to achieve the same effect. When one approach proves difficult to implement or degrades system performance, you have a fallback.

Often you can easily replace a correlated subquery with a PL/SQL function. This approach has the added feature that it simplifies the SQL query and makes it easier to read and maintain. Figure 5-14 shows how this works.

```
SELECT
    student_id "id",
    student_regseq "seq",
    student_sponsor "sponsor",
    student_total_fee "fee"
FROM
    student,
    name
WHERE
    name_seriesno = name_now(name_id)
        AND name_id IN ('a226','a505')
    AND student_id = name_id
        AND student_regseq = max_regseq(name_id)   ◀
ORDER BY 1;


id      seq  sponsor        fee
-----   ---- ----------    ------
a226       3 Self             400
a505       2 Employer        1500
```

Figure 5-14: PL/SQL function that replaces a correlated subquery.

Comments

▶ The PL/SQL function max_regseq returns the maximum student_regseq for each person in the report population. This single line replaces the correlated subquery shown in Figure 5-12 on page 149.

Figure 5-15 shows the PL/SQL function max_regseq.

See Also

1. Chapter 9 (Table 9-5 on page 261) shows the performance

```
CREATE OR REPLACE FUNCTION max_regseq
   (id VARCHAR2)
RETURN NUMBER
AS
   CURSOR student_cursor (p_id VARCHAR2) IS
     SELECT MAX(student_regseq)
     FROM student
     WHERE student_id = p_id;
   max_regseq NUMBER(2);


BEGIN
   OPEN student_cursor(id);
   FETCH student_cursor INTO max_regseq;

   IF student_cursor%NOTFOUND THEN
      max_regseq := NULL;
   END IF;

   CLOSE student_cursor;
   RETURN max_regseq;
END;
/
```

Figure 5-15: PL/SQL function max_regseq used in Figure 5-14.

implications of using a PL/SQL function or a correlated subquery. Again, you'll be faced with a trade-off between query simplicity and performance.

2. The PL/SQL for the name_now function used in Figure 5-14 appears in Chapter 1 (Figure 1-9 on page 13).

Set Operations

Oracle includes four set operations — UNION, UNION ALL, INTERSECT, and MINUS. Each operation allows you to combine two or more queries into what's called a *compound query*, but with different effects:

- UNION selects all rows in either query and eliminates duplicates;

- UNION ALL selects all rows in either query but does not eliminate duplicates;

- INTERSECT selects all distinct rows in both queries; and

- MINUS selects all rows in the first query that are not in the second query.

The set operations are really wonderful tools to have available in your query writer's toolkit. Often you can duplicate the function of set operations with joins and subqueries, but sometimes the set operations are indispensable as alternatives. And some effects can only be achieved with set operations, as this section discusses.

Is there a join structure equivalent to UNION?

If I have two tables, call them A and B, how can I write a join between the tables so that the result set is equivalent to performing a UNION?

Approach

At present you can't. This requires something called a *full outer join* in which the outer join symbol appears on both sides of the join criteria (i.e., A(+) = B(+)). The full outer join was introduced in the ANSI/ISO SQL-92 standards but has not yet been implemented in most versions of SQL. If you attempt a full outer join in Oracle SQL, you presently receive error ORA-01468 (a predicate may reference only one outer-joined table).

There are times when set operations equivalent to outer joins are useful. Several examples appear in the next section on outer joins. Let's use a simple example to explore these equivalents.

Suppose we have two tables A and B. Table A contains three identification numbers — 101, 102, and 103. Table B contains two identification numbers — 103 and 104. Figure 5-16 shows several joins, their equivalent set operation, pseudo-SQL that you can use to implement the set operation in a query, and the query results.

```
Join                    Set equivalent     Pseudo-SQL              Results
=================================================================================
A.id = B.id             A INTERSECT B      q1:A = B                103

A.id(+) = B.id          (A INTERSECT B)    q1:A = B                103,104
                        UNION              UNION
                        (B MINUS A)        q2:B NOT EXISTS A

A.id = B.id(+)          (A INTERSECT B)    q1:A = B        ⚠       101,102,103
                        UNION              UNION
                        (A MINUS B)        q2:A NOT EXISTS B

A.id(+) = B.id(+)       A UNION B          q1:A                    101,102,103,104
(not available)                            UNION
                                           q2:B
```

Figure 5-16: Table joins and their set operation equivalents.

Comments

▶ The outer join A.id(+) = B.id can be implemented with set operations by constructing two queries and UNIONing them. The first query contains a straight join between the two tables (i.e., A.id = B.id). The second query includes a main query against table B and a correlated subquery as a NOT EXISTS predicate (i.e., NOT EXISTS (SELECT 'x' FROM A WHERE A.id = B.id)).

See Also

1. Set operations can be quite useful when debugging queries, particularly when trying to find rows that unexpectedly fail join criteria. In such situations, you often need to identify the rows and examine the data to determine the exact problem. See Chapter 7 (Figure 7-10 on page 229) for an example of the MINUS operation used in this fashion.

Outer Joins

Outer joins confuse many query writers. The confusion starts with the (+) sign — when you're faced with the issue of where to put it. Let's see; does it go to the left or right of the equal sign? From this start, things only get worse when you throw in rules to follow, NULL values as complications, and limitations on the use of outer joins. No wonder so many frequently asked questions concern outer joins.

How do I prevent population loss when using outer joins?

I'm working with two tables, one a master and the second a detail. Some people who appear in the master table have no data in the detail table. I want the report to include everyone I select from the master table regardless of whether they have detail information. I know I should use an outer join, but it isn't working properly.

Figure 5-17 illustrates the problem for four people from my report population. For each of the four, I want to display all training registrations where the student paid for the class himself. The figure shows that I'm only getting one of the four people in the report even though I'm using an outer join. What's going on here?

```
id       last              seq  sponsor        fee
-----    ----------------  ---  ----------     -----
a133     O'Leary             1  Self            325   ◀1
a330     Healey              1                  740
a409     Alvarez
a925     Carrington          1  Employer        610

SELECT
      name_id "id",
      name_last "last",
      student_regseq "seq",
      student_sponsor "sponsor",
      student_total_fee "fee"
FROM
      student,
      name
WHERE name_seriesno = name_now(name_id)
            AND name_id IN ('a133','a925','a409','a330')
         AND student_id(+) = name_id   ◀2
         AND student_sponsor = 'Self'
ORDER BY 1;

id       last              seq  sponsor        fee
-----    ----------------  ---  ----------     -----
a133     O'Leary             1  Self            325   ◀2
```

Figure 5-17: Outer join that doesn't produce desired results.

Comments

▶ Given the query criteria, only one person (@133) of the four has well-behaved data. This person has training registration data and paid for classes himself. Note that each of the other three people presents a problem for the query. One person (@409) has no training information at all; another (@925) has training data but the employer paid for the course; and the third (@330) has training data but the student_sponsor column is NULL.

▶ The query includes an outer join between the *STUDENT* and *NAME* tables, but only the well-behaved data appear in the report.

Approach

For outer joins to work properly, you must follow two simple rules:

- Use the outer join on *all* conditions that join two tables. In this example the *STUDENT* and *NAME* tables are joined through only a single condition, and the outer join appears correctly in this condition. But if two or more join conditions occurred, then the outer join must appear in each of the conditions.

- Because outer joins produce NULL rows if necessary, any WHERE condition that compares a NULL data value to a literal also must include an outer join on the data column in question. You can ignore this rule if you explicitly deal with NULL values using a function such as NVL.

The query in Figure 5-17 falters by using student_sponsor = 'Self'. Rows created through the outer join student_id(+) = name_id are entirely NULL. Consequently, none of them contain the value 'Self' in student_sponsor. The remedy is straightforward; simply use an outer join so that student_sponsor(+) = 'Self'. You also can use an alternative structure to achieve the same effect; for example, NVL(student_sponsor, 'Self') = 'Self' would work.

If you want the NULL rows to display in the report in special ways, you may also need to use a function like NVL in the SELECT clause. The query in Figure 5-11 lists several data columns. But suppose instead you wanted to sum on a NUMBER column and wanted the NULL values created with outer joins to be considered zeroes. Then NVL(numeric_column, 0) would appear in the SUM.

The second rule listed above also applies when the data column containing NULL values appears in an expression. Figure 5-18 illustrates the use of an outer join in an expression that's compared with a literal.

```
SELECT
    name_id "id",
    name_last "last",
    student_regseq "seq",
    student_sponsor "sponsor",
    student_total_fee "fee",
    student_regdate "regdate"
FROM
    student,
    name
WHERE name_seriesno = name_now(name_id)
        AND name_id in ('@133','@925','@409','@330')
    AND student_id(+) = name_id
            AND TO_CHAR(student_regdate(+),'YYYY') = '1997'
ORDER BY 1;                                          ⚠

id      last               seq  sponsor         fee   regdate
-----   ---------------    ---  ----------      -----  ---------
@133    O'Leary              1  Self            325   17-SEP-97
@330    Healey               1                  740   03-FEB-97
@409    Alvarez
@925    Carrington           1  Employer        610   10-MAY-97
```

Figure 5-18: Outer join on data column in an expression.

Comments

▶ The outer join in student_id(+) = name_id creates a NULL row for @409 who has no student data. To include this person in the report, you'll need an outer join on the student_regdate column that appears in the expression specifying the year is 1997. You also could use an alternative structure that dealt explicitly with NULL values (e.g., using the NVL or DECODE functions).

See Also

1. Query problems from outer joins and those from NULL values frequently appear together like a matched set. For questions on NULL values, see the discussion that begins on page 144.

2. Figure 5-17 and Figure 5-18 used the name_now function. The PL/SQL for this function appears in Chapter 1 (Figure 1-9 on page 13).

How can I do an outer join to a subquery?

With one of my queries I'm getting error message ORA-01799 (a column may not be outer-joined to a subquery). The situation is simple. I've got a population of people and all of them should appear in the report. If they have training registration data, I want to see their most recent information. Clearly, an outer join is required for people without training data. It's also clear that I need a subquery to return the most recent training data for people who have those data. Figure 5-19 shows the query I thought would work. Is there a solution to this problem?

```
id      last              seq  sponsor        fee  regdate
-----   ---------------   ---  ----------    ----- ----------
a133    O'Leary            1   Self           325  17-SEP-97
a226    Sacco              1   Mixed         1200  23-APR-97
a226    Sacco              2   Self           200  11-JUL-97
a226    Sacco              3   Self           400  02-DEC-97
a330    Healey             1                  740  03-FEB-97
a409    Alvarez
a505    Carrington         1   Self           500  19-JUN-97
a505    Carrington         2   Employer      1500  04-NOV-97
a925    Appiah             1   Employer       610  10-MAY-96
                       ❶

SELECT
      name_id "id",
      name_last "last",
      s1.student_regseq "seq",
      s1.student_sponsor "sponsor",
      s1.student_total_fee "fee"
FROM
      student s1,
      name
WHERE name_seriesno = name_now(name_id)
      AND s1.student_id(+) = name_id            ❷
           AND s2.student_regseq(+) =
           (SELECT max(s2.student_regseq)
           FROM student s2
           WHERE s2.student_id = name_id)
ORDER BY 1;
```

Figure 5-19: Outer join to a subquery produces an error.

Comments

▶ The query should return the highlighted rows.

▶ The outer join student_id(+) = name_id retains people in the query even if they don't have student data. The second outer join, between student_regseq and a subquery, produces an error.

Approach 1

You'll have to remove the second outer join between student_regseq and the subquery yet still find a way to include the rows generated as a result of the first outer join. One way to accomplish this uses the fact that outer joins produce NULL rows. Figure 5-20 illustrates this approach.

```
SELECT
    name_id "id",
    name_last "last",
    s1.student_regseq "seq",
    s1.student_sponsor "sponsor",
    s1.student_total_fee "fee"
FROM
    student s1,
    name
WHERE name_seriesno = name_now(name_id)
    AND s1.student_id(+) = name_id
        and
        (
        s1.rowid IS NULL          ◄
        OR
        s1.student_regseq =
            (SELECT MAX(s2.student_regseq)
            FROM student s2
            WHERE s2.student_id = name_id)
        )
ORDER BY 1;


id     last               seq sponsor      fee
-----  ----------------   --- ----------   -----
a133   O'Leary              1 Self          325
a226   Sacco                3 Self          400
a330   Healey               1                740
a409   Alvarez                             ◄
a505   Carrington           2 Employer     1500
a925   Appiah               1 Employer      610
```

Figure 5-20: Subquery structure that retains rows created with outer joins.

Comments

▶ The only rows that meet the criteria 'WHERE s1.rowid IS NULL' are those created by the outer join. This query returns all rows created with the outer join or uses the subquery to return the most recent training registration data.

Approach 2

The UNION set operator provides another way to achieve the same effect as an outer join. One query includes rows from the report population that do not exist in the *STUDENT* table. A second query includes rows that do exist in the *STUDENT* table. In this second query, joins and subqueries can be used without recourse to outer joins. Doing a UNION of the two queries is equivalent to doing an outer join (see Figure 5-16 on page 155). Figure 5-21 illustrates how this works.

```
SELECT
      name_id "id",
      name_last "last",
      TO_NUMBER('') "seq",
      '' "sponsor",
      TO_NUMBER('') "fee"
FROM
      name
WHERE name_seriesno = name_now(name_id)
      AND NOT EXISTS
      (SELECT 'x'
      FROM student                            ◀①
      WHERE student_id = name_id)
UNION       ◀②
SELECT
      name_id "id",
      name_last "last",
      s1.student_regseq "seq",
      s1.student_sponsor "sponsor",
      s1.student_total_fee "fee"
FROM
      student s1,
      name
WHERE name_seriesno = name_now(name_id)
      AND s1.student_id = name_id
          AND s1.student_regseq =        ◀③
          (SELECT MAX(s2.student_regseq)
          FROM student s2
          WHERE s2.student_id = name_id)
ORDER BY 1;


id     last                seq sponsor        fee
-----  ----------------    --- ----------     -----
a133   O'Leary               1 Self           325
a226   Sacco                 3 Self           400
a330   Healey                1 Mixed          740
a409   Alvarez
a505   Carrington            2 Employer      1500
a925   Appiah                1 Employer       610
```

Figure 5-21: UNION set operation equivalent to an outer join.

Comments

▶① The first query selects everyone from the report population who does not have *STUDENT* data.

▶② The UNION operation used with queries structured in this manner produces the equivalent of an outer join.

▶③ The second query selects everyone from the report population who does have *STUDENT* data. The subquery returns the most recent information.

Approach 3

You also can use a PL/SQL function that removes the messiness existing in the two previous approaches. Figure 5-22 shows a query that uses a PL/SQL function called max_regseq.

```
SELECT
    name_id "id",
    name_last "last",
    s1.student_regseq "seq",
    s1.student_sponsor "sponsor",
    s1.student_total_fee "fee",
    s1.student_regdate "regdate"
FROM
    student s1,
    name
WHERE name_seriesno = name_now(name_id)
    AND s1.student_id(+) = name_id
        AND s1.student_regseq(+) = max_regseq(name_id)
ORDER BY 1, 3;                                    ▲

id      last              seq  sponsor       fee  regdate
-----   ---------------   ---  ----------   -----  ---------
a133    O'Leary            1   Self          325   17-SEP-97
a226    Sacco              3   Self          400   02-DEC-97
a330    Healey             1   Mixed         740   03-FEB-97
a409    Alvarez
a505    Carrington         2   Employer     1500   04-NOV-97
a925    Appiah             1   Employer      610   10-MAY-96
```

Figure 5-22: PL/SQL function equivalent to outer join to a subquery.

Comments

▶ This one line replaces the complex UNION or OR structures required in the previous SQL solutions. For each name_id, the function max_regseq returns the maximum student_regseq. If none exists, it returns NULL. The outer join s1.student_regseq(+) retains NULL rows for display. This simple structure is equivalent to an outer join to a subquery.

The PL/SQL that created the function max_regseq was shown earlier in Figure 5-15 on page 153.

See Also

1. Chapter 9 (Table 9-6 on page 263) shows results from performance comparisons of the three approaches to this outer join problem.

2. Several figures in this section use the name_now function. The PL/SQL for this function appears in Chapter 1 (Figure 1-9 on page 13).

How can I do an outer join with an IN or OR?

One of my queries that worked with Version 6 of Oracle now returns the error message ORA-01719 (outer join operator not allowed in operand of OR or IN). Figure 5-23 shows the query. Is there another way of writing the query that's equivalent to performing an outer join with IN?

```
id      last              seq  sponsor       fee
-----   ----------------  ---  ----------    -----
@133    O'Leary             1  Self            325
@330    Healey              1                  740
@409    Alvarez
@925    Appiah              1  Employer        610


SELECT
      name_id "id",
      name_last "last",
      s1.student_regseq "seq",
      s1.student_sponsor "sponsor",
      s1.student_total_fee "fee"
FROM
      student s1,
      name
WHERE name_seriesno = name_now(name_id)
            AND name_id IN ('@133','@330','@409','@925')
      AND s1.student_id(+) = name_id
            AND s1.student_sponsor(+) IN ('Self','Employer')
ORDER BY 1;                                              ⚠1
```

Figure 5-23: Query using an outer join with IN produces an error.

Comments

▶ An outer join with IN or OR now produces error ORA-01719.

Approach 1

Figure 5-23 includes data for the report population. Note there are three different categories that the data fall into:

- No *STUDENT* data exist (@409);

- *STUDENT* data meeting the criteria exist (@133 and @925); and

- *STUDENT* data exist, but they do not meet the query criteria (@330).

The query must accommodate all three types of data. Figure 5-24 shows one alternative that uses an outer join, a fairly complex OR condition, and DECODEs in the SELECT. It's not a pretty sight, but it does produce the desired results.

```
SELECT
    name_id "id",
    name_last "last",
    DECODE(s1.student_sponsor,
            'Self', s1.student_regseq,
            'Employer', s1.student_regseq, NULL) "seq",      ◀1
    DECODE(s1.student_sponsor,
            'Self', s1.student_sponsor,
            'Employer', s1.student_sponsor, NULL) "sponsor",
    DECODE(s1.student_sponsor,
            'Self', s1.student_total_fee,
            'Employer', s1.student_total_fee, NULL) "fee"
FROM
    student s1,
    name
WHERE name_seriesno = name_now(name_id)
    AND s1.student_id(+) = name_id
            AND
            (
            s1.ROWID IS NULL  ◀2
            OR
            s1.student_sponsor IN ('Self','Employer')       ◀3
                    AND s1.student_regseq =
                    (SELECT MAX(s2.student_regseq)
                    FROM student s2
                    WHERE s2.student_id = name_id
                    AND s2.student_sponsor IN ('Self','Employer'))
            OR
            s1.ROWID =
            (SELECT MAX(s2.ROWID)      ◀4
            FROM student s2
            WHERE s2.student_id = name_id
                    AND NOT EXISTS   ◀4
                    (SELECT 'x'
                    FROM student s3
                    WHERE s3.student_id = name_id
                    AND s3.student_sponsor IN
                            ('Self','Employer')))
            )
ORDER BY 1;

id      last              seq  sponsor      fee
-----   ---------------   ---  ----------   -----
@133    O'Leary            1   Self         325
@330    Healey
@409    Alvarez
@925    Appiah             1   Employer     610
```

Figure 5-24: SQL query displaying results expected from an outer join and IN.

Comments

▶ The DECODEs on the *STUDENT* data columns only display data if student_sponsor is one of the two values (i.e., 'Self' or 'Employer') specified in the WHERE conditions. Why this is necessary is explained below.

▶ This condition retains people like @409 who have no

STUDENT data.

▶ This condition returns the well-behaved data situations (i.e., @133 and @925) where student_sponsor is either 'Self' or 'Employer'.

▶ This condition returns one row for each person who has *STUDENT* data but no rows where student_sponsor is 'Self' or 'Employer' (i.e., @330). The DECODEs in the SELECT clause display NULL values for these rows when they appear in the report.

Approach 2

By contrast to the solution shown in Figure 5-24, constructing the UNION equivalent to an outer join provides a more appealing approach to the problem. Figure 5-25 illustrates this approach.

```
SELECT
     name_id "id", name_last "last", s1.student_regseq "seq",
     s1.student_sponsor "sponsor", s1.student_total_fee "fee"
FROM
     student s1, name
WHERE
     name_seriesno = name_now(name_id)
     AND s1.student_id = name_id
          AND s1.student_sponsor IN ('Self','Employer')     ◀❶
          AND s1.student_regseq =
          (SELECT MAX(s2.student_regseq)
          FROM student s2
          where s2.student_id = name_id
          and s2.student_sponsor in ('Self','Employer'))
UNION
SELECT
     name_id "id", name_last "last", TO_NUMBER('') "seq",
     '' "sponsor", TO_NUMBER('') "fee"
FROM
     name
WHERE
     name_seriesno = name_now(name_id)
     AND NOT EXISTS
     (SELECT 'x'
     FROM student
     WHERE student_id = name_id                             ◀❷
     AND student_sponsor IN ('Self','Employer'));

id      last              seq   sponsor         fee
-----   ---------------   ---   ----------    -----
@133    O'Leary            1    Self            325
@330    Healey
@409    Alvarez
@925    Appiah             1    Employer        610
```

Figure 5-25: SQL query using UNION equivalent to an outer join with IN.

Comments

▶ The first query selects all rows with the well-behaved data where student data exist with student_sponsor of 'Self' or 'Employer' (i.e., @133 and @925).

▶ The second query creates rows for members of the report population who do not have a student_sponsor of 'Self' or 'Employer' (i.e., @330 and @409). When UNIONed, the two queries produce the desired report.

Approach 3

By contrast to both the previous solutions, a PL/SQL function provides the most appealing solution to the problem. Figure 5-26 illustrates this approach.

```
SELECT
     name_id "id",
     name_last "last",
     s1.student_regseq "seq",
     s1.student_sponsor "sponsor",
     s1.student_total_fee "fee"
FROM
     student s1,
     name
WHERE name_seriesno = name_now(name_id)
     AND s1.student_id(+) = name_id
          and s1.ROWID(+) =
               sponsor_exist(name_id, 'Self', 'Employer')
ORDER BY 1;                                                    ▲

id      last              seq  sponsor          fee
-----   ----------------  ---  ----------       -----
@133    O'Leary            1   Self             325
@330    Healey
@409    Alvarez
@925    Appiah             1   Employer         610
```

Figure 5-26: PL/SQL function equivalent to an outer join used with IN.

Comments

▶ The PL/SQL function sponsor_exist returns ROWIDs for each person where student data exist with student_sponsor of 'Self' or 'Employer'. Whenever no such data exist, the function returns a NULL. The outer join s1.ROWID(+) retains these rows for display in the report.

Figure 5-27 shows the PL/SQL function itself.

```
CREATE OR REPLACE FUNCTION sponsor_exist
   (id VARCHAR2, sponsor1 VARCHAR2, sponsor2 VARCHAR2)
RETURN ROWID
AS
   student_rowid ROWID;
   CURSOR main_cursor
   (p_id VARCHAR2, p_sponsor1 VARCHAR2, p_sponsor2 VARCHAR2) IS
     SELECT ROWID
     FROM student
     WHERE student_id = p_id
     AND student_sponsor IN (p_sponsor1, p_sponsor2)
     ORDER BY student_regseq desc;

BEGIN
   OPEN main_cursor(id, sponsor1, sponsor2);
   FETCH main_cursor INTO student_rowid;

   IF main_cursor%NOTFOUND THEN
      student_rowid := NULL;
   END IF;

   CLOSE main_cursor;
   RETURN student_rowid;
END;
/
```

Figure 5-27: PL/SQL function sponsor_exist used in Figure 5-26.

See Also

1. The three approaches to this problem exact different performance costs. Chapter 9 (Table 9-7 on page 267) shows results from performance comparisons among the three approaches. Once again, your choice of an approach will require compromises.

2. Chapter 1 (Figure 1-9 on page 13) shows the PL/SQL for the name_now function used in several figures in this section.

LONG **Datatypes**

Query writers frequently look for information that they or others can use to make decisions and take action. This gives the query writer a printed-page orientation to the database, because the printed page is usually the format in which database information gets presented. LONG datatypes, which in Oracle7 can contain up to 2 gigabytes of information, don't fit well with a printed report that might only be 80 or 130 characters wide. Thus LONG datatypes pose special query problems.

How do I format a LONG *column for display?*

I created a table to store the SQL queries I write. The data column containing the SQL has a LONG datatype. When I use the COLUMN command to format the display width of this column in reports, it doesn't seem to have any effect. For example, COLUMN query_sql FORMAT A100 only displays the first 80 characters and then stops. What's happening here?

Approach

Three factors interact to affect the display of LONG data columns in reports. Two of these factors are the SQL*PLUS system variables LONG and LONGCHUNKSIZE. The third factor is the FORMAT assigned in the COLUMN command, if any.

The LONG system variable sets the maximum display width for columns with LONG datatypes. By default, this value is 80, meaning that only 80 characters appear in the report unless you change the system setting. The maximum setting in Oracle7 is 2 gigabytes. You'll want to SET LONG big enough to display the largest value that will appear in the report.

The LONGCHUNKSIZE system variable sets the character size of increments used to retrieve LONG values. By default, the system setting is 80. You can increase this value up to a system-dependent maximum determined by MAXDATA.

Without a COLUMN command, the default display width of LONG data columns is the smaller of the two system variables LONG and LONGCHUNKSIZE. If you do use a COLUMN command, the display width is the smaller of LONGCHUNKSIZE and the format provided in the COLUMN command. Therefore, if LONGCHUNKSIZE is 80 and you use a format of A100 in a COLUMN command, the display width will be 80 characters.

Figure 5-28 shows the use of LONG, LONGCHUNKSIZE, and FORMAT to display a LONG data column in a report.

```
SET LONG 1000
SET LONGCHUNKSIZE 100
COLUMN sql FORMAT a60 WORD_WRAPPED
SELECT
      query_code "id",
      query_create_date "create",
      query_sql "sql"
FROM
      queries
WHERE
      query_code = 102;

    id create     sql
------ ---------- ------------------------------------------------------------
   102 09-JUL-96 select name_id id, name_last last, s1.student_regseq seq,
                 s1.student_sponsor sponsor, s1.student_total_fee fee from
                 student s1, name where name_seriesno = name_now(name_id) and
                 name_id in ('a133','a330','a409','a925') and
                 s1.student_id(+) = name_id and s1.rowid(+) =
                 sponsor_exist(name_id, 'Self','Employer') order by 1;
```

Figure 5-28: Formatting a LONG data column for display.

Comments

▶ By setting the system variable LONG to 1000, you can display up to 1000 characters in a LONG column.

▶ Retrieval of LONG data columns will occur in increments of 100 characters. The default is 80.

▶ The COLUMN command uses a FORMAT of A60 for the LONG column. Because this value is smaller than the LONGCHUNKSIZE setting, the display width in the report will be 60.

See Also

1. For a related discussion of LONG and LONGCHUNKSIZE, see the section in Chapter 2 on page 54 that describes how to compress report columns when the physical line size of the report is limited.

DISTINCT **Keyword**

The DISTINCT keyword is a curious beast. It finds considerable use when
testing and debugging queries to ensure the integrity of the report population (see Chapter 7). But it also can act as a crutch to a sloppy query,
allowing you to display the desired results without writing a tight query.
Try to avoid using DISTINCT as you construct queries.

How do I display only those rows where one data column is distinct?

I need to select a complete row whenever one of the columns is distinct.
SELECT DISTINCT does not produce the desired result. For example,
SELECT DISTINCT colA, colB, colC returns all rows when the combination of colA, colB, and colC is distinct. I want the query to return colA,
colB, and colC but only when colA is distinct. Is there a way to do this?

Approach

Let's deal with a specific example using the training registration data
shown in previous figures. Suppose we want to identify all students who
have only registered once for training classes. That is, student_id must
be distinct. Further, suppose that the report should display the three columns student_id, student_regseq, and student_sponsor.

Figure 5-29 shows one approach to the problem. Note that it uses a
subquery to return a count grouped by the column that must be distinct.
The main query retains only those rows where the count is 1 (i.e., the
column is distinct).

Comments

▶ The data include three rows for people who each registered
only once for training classes.

▶ The DISTINCT feature is captured here by requiring the
count returned by the subquery to be 1. The GROUP BY in the
subquery groups rows by the column that must be distinct.

Other SQL structures produce the same effect. For example, you
could use a correlated subquery where the correlating column is the one
that must be distinct. In general, the solution is WHERE 1 = (SELECT
COUNT(*) FROM SameTable t2 WHERE t2.ColDistinct = t1.ColDistinct).
In the example in Figure 5-29, this becomes WHERE 1 = (SELECT
COUNT(*) FROM student s2 WHERE s2.student_id = s1.student_id).

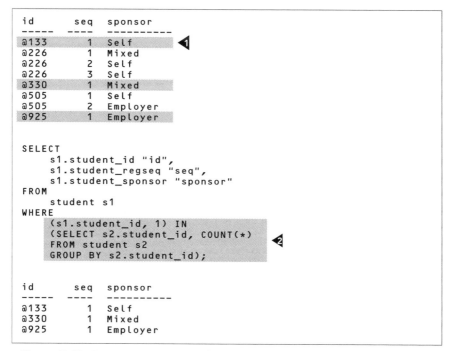

```
id        seq    sponsor
-----     ----   ----------
a133       1     Self          ◀ 1
a226       1     Mixed
a226       2     Self
a226       3     Self
a330       1     Mixed
a505       1     Self
a505       2     Employer
a925       1     Employer


SELECT
    s1.student_id "id",
    s1.student_regseq "seq",
    s1.student_sponsor "sponsor"
FROM
    student s1
WHERE
    (s1.student_id, 1) IN
    (SELECT s2.student_id, COUNT(*)       ◀ 2
    FROM student s2
    GROUP BY s2.student_id);


id        seq    sponsor
-----     ----   ----------
a133       1     Self
a330       1     Mixed
a925       1     Employer
```

Figure 5-29: Query returning rows for distinct values in one column.

See Also

1. When testing a query to determine if join problems exist, DISTINCT plays an important role. Beginning on page 218, Chapter 7 discusses the special uses of DISTINCT when finding and correcting join errors.

Chapter 6
Reports

Most people learn SQL by writing queries that produce simple lists. These reports appear in a row-and-column format, where the columns refer to characteristics of items in the report population (i.e., the rows).

One of the more frustrating struggles in learning SQL occurs when query writers try to prepare reports that do not fit the basic list format. How, for example, should you construct a simple frequency distribution that displays counts by some population characteristic like gender or color code or product number? It sounds simple enough, but trying to do this presents a challenge for many query writers.

To go beyond the basic list report, you'll find that queries often require considerable coordination between SQL, SQL*PLUS, and PL/SQL. Sometimes they even require tricks. For example, people frequently ask how to prepare a report that shows the top 5 (or 10 or whatever) items in the population based on some numeric characteristic like salary or test score. There are several ways to approach this problem and the chapter discusses each, but one approach relies on a feature of UNIONed compound queries that is not intuitive but nonetheless gets the job done.

When learning most things that are complex, it's better to copy what others have already done and to adapt that to your own purpose. This chapter provides several report types that you can use in your queries. Consider the queries you see in this chapter as templates, as SQL *segments* that you can use to prepare similar reports. Save them for later reuse. The next time you prepare a cross-tabulation, for example, you'll only need to retrieve your cross-tabulation template and dust if off for the present query. This way you'll never need to remember the tricks or how you coordinate SQL, SQL*PLUS, and PL/SQL to produce a desired effect.

Enjoy the variety of reports this chapter discusses.

Major Types

Ad hoc queries tend to be quite specific and the reports themselves fairly simple. For complex reports based on multiple populations or requiring statistical analysis, you'll need to use full-fledged report writers (e.g., SQR) or comprehensive report and analysis packages (e.g., SAS). But for many purposes, SQL, SQL*PLUS, and PL/SQL serve admirably as reporting tools.

This section discusses several major categories of reports that frequently cause query writers problems.

How can I do a frequency distribution report?

I'd like to prepare a simple report that counts population items by a single characteristic. In this case I want to count people by their gender. I'd also like a total count included. How can I do this?

Approach

You can produce a basic frequency distribution using the COUNT function and a GROUP BY. To get a grand total, you'll need to coordinate the two SQL*PLUS commands BREAK and COMPUTE. Figure 6-1 shows how this works.

```
BREAK ON REPORT
COMPUTE SUM OF count ON REPORT      ◀❶
COLUMN sex FORMAT a3
COLUMN count FORMAT 99999
SELECT
      person_gender "sex",
      COUNT(*) "count"            ◀❷
FROM
      person,
      name
WHERE
      name_seriesno = name_now(name_id)
      AND person_id = name_id
GROUP BY
      person_gender              ◀❷
ORDER BY 1;

sex    count
---    ------
F         3
M         2
          1          ◀❸
       ------
sum       6
```

Figure 6-1: Example of a frequency distribution report.

Comments

▶ Coordinating the BREAK and COMPUTE commands in this way produces the grand total.

▶ The SELECT clause contains a COUNT(*) or COUNT(column_name) and the characteristic you wish to count by. The GROUP BY also must include this data column.

▶ Note that NULL values sort at the end of the report. You might prefer to include an NVL(person_gender, 'na') in the SELECT and GROUP BY clauses to deal explicitly with NULL values.

The SQL and SQL*PLUS commands that produce a frequency distribution report are very simple. Save the structure as an SQL segment and you can reuse it whenever you have a need for this type of report.

See Also

1. Frequency distributions are commonly requested reports. An example showing counts of database tables by their owners appears in Chapter 1 (Figure 1-1 on page 2). The SQL that produced this frequency distribution is shown in Appendix A on page 320.

2. Report templates repeatedly prove their worth when you write queries. Save the basic frequency distribution report after first removing everything specific to an individual query (e.g., SELECT clause columns). You'll be left with the structure common to all frequency distribution reports. The next time you need to prepare such a report, pull out this template and reuse it. Report templates are just one type of SQL segment. For a discussion about SQL segments, see Chapter 1 on page 15.

3. The PL/SQL for the name_now function used in Figure 6-1 appears in Chapter 1 (Figure 1-9 on page 13).

How do I include code descriptions in a frequency distribution report?

People who read my frequency distributions may not know the coded values that appear in the report. How can I include code descriptions in a frequency distribution?

Approach

You'll need an extra data column in the SELECT and GROUP BY clauses and one extra join, but other than this the report is identical to the basic frequency distribution.

Figure 6-2 shows an example of a frequency distribution that includes code descriptions.

```
BREAK ON REPORT
COMPUTE SUM OF count ON REPORT
COLUMN sex FORMAT a3
COLUMN description FORMAT a12
COLUMN count FORMAT 99999
SELECT
    person_gender "sex",
    cgender_desc "description",     ◀1
    COUNT(*) "count"
FROM
    cgender,
    person,
    name
WHERE
    name_seriesno = name_now(name_id)
    AND person_id = name_id
    AND cgender_code(+) = person_gender   ◀2
GROUP BY
    person_gender,
    cgender_desc     ◀1
ORDER BY 1;

sex    description      count
---    ------------    ------
F      Female              3
M      Male                2
                          1
                       ------
sum                        6
```

Figure 6-2: Frequency distribution that includes code descriptions.

Comments

▶ The data column containing the code description appears in the SELECT and GROUP BY clauses.

▶ The table containing the code descriptions must, of course, be joined in the main query. Here an outer join is used. This retains population items that have NULL values in the coded data column. It also retains population items that have invalid codes should you be operating in a database without constraints that ensure that codes are valid before they're committed.

See Also

1. For a discussion of outer joins and some of the problems they sometimes pose for query writers, see the discussion beginning in Chapter 5 on page 156.

2. Figure 6-2 uses the name_now function. Chapter 1 (Figure 1-9 on page 13) shows the PL/SQL for this function.

How can I do a cross-tabulation report?

I'd like to prepare a table that shows counts by two characteristics of the report population. In this case I'd like a count of students by gender and the form of payment they made during their last training registration. I'd like a grand total and subtotals as well. How can I do this?

Approach

A two-way cross-tabulation merely extends the basic frequency distribution by one dimension. The BREAK and COMPUTE commands needed to produce totals and subtotals are a little more complicated, but basically it's just the same report as shown in Figure 6-1.

Figure 6-3 shows a simple two-way cross-tabulation.

```
BREAK ON REPORT ON sex SKIP 1
COMPUTE SUM OF count ON REPORT sex  ◀
COLUMN sex FORMAT a3
COLUMN count FORMAT 99999
SELECT
        person_gender "sex",
        student_sponsor "sponsor",
        COUNT(*) "count"
FROM
        person,
        student
WHERE
        student_regseq = max_regseq(student_id)
        AND person_id = student_id
GROUP BY
        person_gender,
        student_sponsor
ORDER BY 1, 2;

sex   sponsor        count
---   ----------     ------
F     Employer          1
      Self              1
                        1
***                  ------
sum                     3

M     Employer          1
      Self              1
***                  ------
sum                     2

                     ------
sum                     5
```

Figure 6-3: Example of a two-way cross-tabulation report.

Comments

▶ Both the BREAK and COMPUTE commands include references to the alias for person_gender (i.e., sex). This produces the sub-totals for the report.

Two-way cross-tabulation reports get requested frequently. Save the structure in Figure 6-3 as an SQL segment so that you'll have it available for reuse. This way you'll never need to remember how the BREAK and COMPUTE commands should be coordinated. You'll just cut and paste to construct the new query.

See Also

1. The PL/SQL for the max_regseq function used in Figure 6-3 appears in Chapter 5 (Figure 5-15 on page 153).

2. Chapter 1 on page 15 discusses the use of SQL segments to simplify the crafting of ad hoc queries.

How do I prepare a traditional cross-tabulated report?

I'd like to present users with a cross-tabulation in the traditional table format, where the values in one data column appear in rows and the values in the second data column appear as columns in the report. Is this possible?

Approach 1

There are two problems with the cross-tabulation in Figure 6-3 on page 178. First, no marginal totals appear for the student_sponsor column, and second, most people expect cross-tabulations in a table format with counts in the table cells.

Assuming that you know what values exist in the data for one of the two cross-tabulated variables, there's a fairly simple way to create a traditional cross-tabulation. Figure 6-4 illustrates how this is done.

```
BREAK ON REPORT
COMPUTE SUM OF col1 col2 count ON REPORT    ◀1
COLUMN sex FORMAT a3
COLUMN col1 HEADING 'Male' FORMAT 99999
COLUMN col2 HEADING 'Female' FORMAT 99999
COLUMN count FORMAT 99999
SELECT
    NVL(student_sponsor, 'Unknown') "sponsor",
    SUM(DECODE(person_gender,'M',1,0)) "col1",
    SUM(DECODE(person_gender,'F',1,0)) "col2",    ◀2
    COUNT(*) "count"
FROM
    person,
    student
WHERE
    student_regseq = max_regseq(student_id)
    AND person_id = student_id
GROUP BY
    NVL(student_sponsor, 'Unknown')
ORDER BY 1;


sponsor        Male Female   count
----------     ------ ------  ------
Employer         1      1       2
Self             1      1       2
Unknown          0      1       1
               ------ ------  ------
sum              2      3       5
```

Figure 6-4: Example of a traditional cross-tabulation report.

Comments

▶ The COMPUTE and BREAK commands coordinate to produce

the totals by gender.

▶ Note that the query explicitly identifies the gender codes that will appear as report columns. In this case, only the values of M or F for person_gender will appear in the report. This means that you must have run a prior report to identify each of the values that could appear as report columns. Otherwise, you run the risk that population items will not be counted. The cross-tabulated report in Figure 6-3 on page 178 does not require any prior knowledge about possible data values.

The report in Figure 6-4 is an example of a more general class of *rotated table* reports, in which the values of one data column display as columns in the report. Each data value that will act as a report column appears in an appropriate DECODE expression in the SELECT clause of the query. This requires prior knowledge of the data values, although if you're eager for a challenge, you could build a dynamic SQL query that would add a DECODEd expression to the SELECT clause for each value that appeared in one of the two cross-tabulated columns.

Approach 2

Another way to produce a traditional spreadsheet uses a special table that looks like an identity matrix with 1s along the diagonal and 0s elsewhere. Here's how it works.

Figure 6-5 describes a table called *SEXIDEN* and lists its values. The table contains one data column for each row that will populate it. In the case of person_gender, there are only two codes possible — M for male and F for female — so the table includes a sexiden_male and a sexiden_female column. Note the occurrences of 1s and 0s.

```
SQL> DESC sexiden
  Name                                       Null?     Type
  ---------------------------------------- --------  ----
  SEXIDEN_CODE                             NOT NULL  VARCHAR2(1)
  SEXIDEN_MALE                             NOT NULL  NUMBER(1)
  SEXIDEN_FEMALE                           NOT NULL  NUMBER(1)

SQL> SELECT * FROM sexiden;

code          male        female
----     ----------    ----------
M                 1             0  ◀
F                 0             1
```

Figure 6-5: Identity table for use in cross-tabulated reports.

Comments

▶ Note the diagonal placement of the 1s, as you would find in an identity matrix. In this case, only two valid codes can appear in person_gender. However, in a cross-tabulation that used a data column with five valid codes, the table you construct would have six columns (including one for the code) and five rows.

Figure 6-6 illustrates how an identity table produces a cross-tabulated report.

```
BREAK ON REPORT
COMPUTE SUM OF col1 col2 count ON REPORT
COLUMN sex FORMAT a3
COLUMN col1 HEADING 'male' FORMAT 99999
COLUMN col2 HEADING 'female' FORMAT 99999
COLUMN count FORMAT 99999
SELECT
    NVL(student_sponsor, 'Unknown') "sponsor",
    SUM(sexiden_male) "col1",
    SUM(sexiden_female) "col2",        ◀ 1
    COUNT(*) "count"
FROM
    sexiden,
    person,
    student
WHERE
    student_regseq = max_regseq(student_id)
    AND person_id = student_id
    AND sexiden_code = person_gender   ◀ 1
GROUP BY
    NVL(student_sponsor, 'Unknown')
ORDER BY 1;


sponsor          male female   count
----------      ------ ------  ------
Employer            1      1       2
Self                1      1       2
Unknown             0      1       1
                ------ ------  ------
sum                 2      3       5
```

Figure 6-6: Identity table used to produce a cross-tabulated report.

Comments

▶ The join to the identity table occurs through person_gender. If, for example, person_gender = F, then sexiden_male = 0 and sexiden_female = 1. For this row the sums that appear in the SELECT clause leave the number of males unchanged and add 1 to the number of females.

See Also

1. Chapter 9 (Table 9-8 on page 269) shows that there are no performance differences between the two methods that produce traditional cross-tabulations.

2. The DECODE function is a very useful tool for query writers. See the discussion that begins in Chapter 3 on page 92 for examples.

3. Chapter 5 (Figure 5-15 on page 153) shows the PL/SQL for the max_regseq function used in Figure 6-4 and Figure 6-6.

4. For another example where the *SEXIDEN* table is used, see Figure 6-8 on page 185.

How can I do a cross-tabulation of sums?

I'd like to prepare a cross-tabulation showing sums and counts. In this
case I'd like to show total training fees by gender and by the type of sponsorship (i.e., who paid for the training). How can I do this?

Approach

This requires only a minor modification to the basic cross-tabulation report. Figure 6-7 a query with the sum of student training fees.

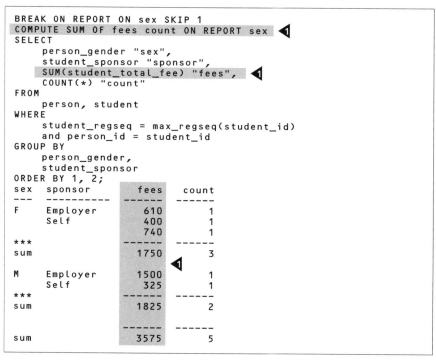

```
BREAK ON REPORT ON sex SKIP 1
COMPUTE SUM OF fees count ON REPORT sex   ◀1
SELECT
     person_gender "sex",
     student_sponsor "sponsor",
     SUM(student_total_fee) "fees",   ◀1
     COUNT(*) "count"
FROM
     person, student
WHERE
     student_regseq = max_regseq(student_id)
     and person_id = student_id
GROUP BY
     person_gender,
     student_sponsor
ORDER BY 1, 2;
sex   sponsor          fees     count
---   ----------      -----    ------
F     Employer          610       1
      Self              400       1
                        740       1
***                   -----    ------
sum                    1750       3
                             ◀1
M     Employer         1500       1
      Self              325       1
***                   -----    ------
sum                    1825       2

                      -----    ------
sum                    3575       5
```

Figure 6-7: Example of a cross-tabulation with sums and counts.

Comments

▶ Cross-tabulated sums require only that the SUM is added to
the SELECT clause of the basic cross-tabulation report and that
the alias is added to the COMPUTE command.

See Also

1. See Chapter 5 (Figure 5-15 on page 153) for max_regseq.

How do I prepare a traditional cross-tabulation of sums?

I'd like to prepare a cross-tabulation of sums in a traditional table format, showing marginals and a grand total. How can I do this?

Approach

By using the identity matrix table introduced in Figure 6-5 on page 181, it's easy to prepare a traditional cross-tabulation of sums. Figure 6-8 shows sums of training fees by type of sponsorship and gender.

```
BREAK ON REPORT ON sex SKIP 1
COMPUTE SUM OF fee1 fee2 fee3 ON REPORT
COLUMN fee1 HEADING 'male|fees' FORMAT 99999
COLUMN fee2 HEADING 'female|fees' FORMAT 99999
COLUMN fee3 HEADING 'total|fees' FORMAT 99999
SELECT
    NVL(student_sponsor, 'Unknown') "sponsor",
    SUM(student_total_fee * sexiden_male) "fee1",      ◀1
    SUM(student_total_fee * sexiden_female) "fee2",
    SUM(student_total_fee) "fee3"
FROM
    sexiden, person, student
WHERE
    student_regseq = max_regseq(student_id)
    and person_id = student_id
    and sexiden_code = person_gender
GROUP BY
    NVL(student_sponsor, 'Unknown')
ORDER BY 1;

            male  female   total
sponsor     fees    fees    fees
----------  ------  ------  ------
Employer     1500     610    2110
Self          325     400     725
Unknown         0     740     740
            ------  ------  ------
sum          1825    1750    3575
```

Figure 6-8: Identity table used to produce a cross-tabulation of sums.

Comments

▶ Consider a row where person_gender = F, so that sexiden_male = 0 and sexiden_female = 1 (see Figure 6-5 on page 181). The multiplications by sexiden_male and sexiden_female that occur in the SELECT expressions add the registration fee to the female total and not to the male total.

See Also

1. See Chapter 5 (Figure 5-15 on page 153) for max_regseq.

How do I block a report?

I have too much information to fit into a spreadsheet report of rows and columns. I'd like to block the report so that each row appears as a single column with the data values for the various data columns underneath each other. How can I do this?

Approach

Blocking a report can be accomplished using the NEWLINE option in the COLUMN command, which inserts a carriage return before the value displays. Column headings should be set off because there is only one display column in a blocked report. However, by including literals in the SELECT clause you can label the data values so that you know what you're looking at.

Figure 6-9 illustrates a simple blocked report.

```
SET HEADING OFF          ◀①
COLUMN label NEWLINE
SELECT
     'id:      ',    ②
     name_id "id",
     'name:     ' label,   ◀③
     name_last||', '||name_first||' '||name_middle "name",
     'sex:      ' label,
     person_gender "sex",
     'fees:     ' label,
     TO_CHAR(student_total_fee) "fee"
FROM
     student,
     person,
     name
WHERE
     name_seriesno = name_now(name_id)
     AND person_id = name_id
     AND student_id = name_id
          and student_regseq = max_regseq(name_id)
ORDER BY 1;


id:        a505
name:      Carrington, Thomas  J
sex:       M                       ◀④
fees:      1500

id:        a330
name:      Healey, Caroline  V
sex:       F
fees:      740
```

Figure 6-9: Example of a blocked report.

Comments

▶ Data values will not appear in columns in this report, so set the column headings off

▶ Include a COLUMN command that inserts a carriage return before each of the labels.

▶ Include labels for each of the data columns so that when the values display, it's clear what they mean. Assign each of the labels the same alias (e.g., here it's ingeniously called 'label') and then use that alias in the COLUMN command with the NEWLINE option.

▶ Note that the report is blocked and the data is labeled.

See Also

1. Blocked reports generally require that you create your own column headings. Beginning on page 206, this chapter demonstrates how to custom build your own headers.

2. Figure 6-9 uses the name_now and the max_regseq functions. The PL/SQL for name_now appears in Chapter 1 (Figure 1-9 on page 13); the PL/SQL for max_reqseq appears in Chapter 5 (Figure 5-15 on page 153).

How can I block only part of a report?

I wrote a name and address query in which I'd like to block only the address data columns so that they appear underneath each other. How can I do this?

Approach

This requires only a minor modification to the basic blocked report. The COLUMN NEWLINE option works a little differently because you're only blocking some of the data columns. You'll also need to explicitly line up the blocked data values so that they appear underneath each other.

Figure 6-10 shows a simple report in which the address is blocked.

```
SET HEADING OFF
COLUMN name FORMAT a25
COLUMN city NEWLINE          ◀1
COLUMN country NEWLINE
SELECT
    name_id "id",
    name_last||', '||name_first||' '||name_middle "name",
    address_street1 "st1",
    LPAD(' ',32)||
  2     get_city_line(address_city, address_loc,      ◀3
          address_pcode) "city",
    LPAD(' ',32)||UPPER(country_name) "country"
FROM
    countries,
    address,
    name
WHERE
    name_seriesno = name_now(name_id)
    AND address_id = name_id
        AND address_type = 'PR'
        AND address_seriesno = max_address(name_id, 'PR')
    AND country_code(+) = address_country
ORDER BY 2;

a409   Alvarez, Xavier M              2095 Elmina Road
                                      Accra              ◀4
                                      GHANA

a505   Carrington, Thomas J           RR4
                                      Saco, ME 04072
```

Figure 6-10: Example of a partially blocked report.

Comments

1▶ Include a COLUMN command with the NEWLINE option for each blocked data column.

2▶ Align the blocked data values using the LPAD function. You'll have to determine the numeric argument manually for this function based on where the blocked data should appear.

▶ The SELECT clause in Figure 6-10 includes a PL/SQL function that builds the city address line from three data columns, which in a U.S. address would contain city, state, and zip code.

▶ Note that only the address lines are blocked in the report.

For completeness, Figure 6-11 shows the PL/SQL function.

```
CREATE OR REPLACE FUNCTION get_city_line
   (city VARCHAR2, location VARCHAR2, postalcode VARCHAR2)
RETURN VARCHAR2
AS
   city_address_line VARCHAR2(30) := NULL;

BEGIN
   IF city IS NULL AND location IS NULL AND postalcode IS NULL THEN
      city_address_line := NULL;
   ELSIF location IS NULL THEN
      city_address_line := city||' '||postalcode;
   ELSE
      city_address_line := city||', '||location||' '||postalcode;
   END IF;

   RETURN city_address_line;
END;
/
```

Figure 6-11: PL/SQL function that builds a city, state, and zip code address line.

See Also

1. Sometimes partially blocked reports suffer from blank lines that detract from the appearance of the report and can, at times, even be misleading. This happens, for example, when blocking multiple line addresses. If the table allows three street address lines, but the address for a specific person only requires one line, then blocking the address produces two blank lines between the street and the city lines. For a discussion of the problem, see page 208 in this chapter.

2. Figure 6-10 used two PL/SQL functions — name_now and max_address. For name_now, see Chapter 1 (Figure 1-9 on page 13); for max_address, see Chapter 4 (Figure 4-4 on page 112).

How can I do a report on a preprinted form?

When they call customers, our telemarketers use a preprinted form containing biographical data. Can I prepare a report to print on the form?

Approach

This is both tricky and a bit laborious. So long as the form is not too complex and you don't need to locate data values precisely on the form, you can use a variation of the blocked report.

Figure 6-12 illustrates how this works for a simple report. You'll have to be the judge of whether the time you spend preparing the query to fit your form is actually worth the effort.

```
SET HEADING OFF
BREAK ON id SKIP PAGE
COLUMN NextLine NEWLINE
COLUMN id NEWLINE
SELECT
        ' ',
        name_id id,
        name_last||', '||name_first||' '||name_middle NextLine,
        ' ' NextLine,
        ' ' NextLine,     ◀1
        ' ' NextLine,
        ' ' NextLine,
        LPAD(' ',3)||person_gender||
            DECODE(person_gender, NULL, LPAD(' ', 19),     ◀2
            LPAD(' ',18))||student_sponsor NextLine,
        LPAD(' ',3)||TO_CHAR(person_birthdate)||
            DECODE(person_birthdate, NULL, LPAD(' ', 19),
            LPAD(' ',10))||TO_CHAR(student_total_fee)
FROM
        student,
        person,
        name
WHERE
        name_seriesno = name_now(name_id)
        AND person_id = name_id
        AND student_id = name_id
            AND student_regseq = max_regseq(name_id)
ORDER BY 2;
```

Figure 6-12: Blocked query formatted to fit a preprinted form.

Comments

▶ Create blank lines in the report using this expression. A column command for NextLine assigns it the NEWLINE option, meaning that the expression (i.e., the single blank space) gets displayed on the next line.

▶ Note how complex the formatting can become. In particular, you'll need to consider what happens when data values are NULL or their length can vary.

Figure 6-13 aligns a preprinted form and one page of the report side-by-side. When printed on the form, the report will display values in appropriate places.

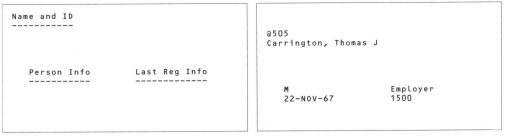

Figure 6-13: Results of the query in Figure 6-12.

See Also

1. For another example of a query that uses the DECODE function to control NULL values, see Chapter 2 (Figure 2-14 on page 60).

2. The name_now and max_regseq functions were used in Figure 6-12. For the PL/SQL of these two functions, see Chapter 1 (Figure 1-9 on page 13) and Chapter 5 (Figure 5-15 on page 153) respectively.

How can I do a master-detail report?

I'd like to prepare a report in which there may be a one-to-many relationship between the population items and detail present in another table. In this case, I'd like a report for students showing detail about each of the times they registered for training classes. How can I do this?

Approach

In appearance, a partially blocked report and a master-detail report look similar. In fact, however, the structure of a master-detail query is more similar to that of the traditional spreadsheet row-and-column query than it is to the partially blocked query.

Figure 6-14 illustrates a simple master-detail report.

```
BREAK ON id ON name ON sex SKIP 1 ◀
SELECT
     name_id "id",
     name_last||', '||name_first||' '||name_middle "name",
     person_gender "sex",
     student_regseq "regseq",
     student_sponsor "sponsor",
     student_total_fee "fee"
FROM
     student,
     person,
     name
WHERE
     name_seriesno = name_now(name_id)
          AND name_id IN ('@133','@226','@505')
     AND person_id = name_id
     AND student_id = name_id
ORDER BY 1, 4;

id      name                               sex  regseq  sponsor      fee
-----   ------------------------------     ---  ------  ----------   ------
@133    O'Leary, Vincent                   M         1  Self            325

@226    Sacco, Beth                        F         1  Mixed          1200
                         ◢2◣                          2  Self            200
                                                      3  Self            400

@505    Carrington, Thomas J               M         1  Self    ◢3◣     500
                                                      2  Employer       1500
```

Figure 6-14: Example of a master-detail report.

Comments

▶ Use the BREAK command to eliminate redundant master information that would be repeated for each detail row.

▶ In this report, master information on people in the

population appears.

▶ Detail information on training registrations also appears.

See Also

1. Chapter 2 on page 44 provides more detail about using the BREAK command to suppress redundant information in reports.

2. The PL/SQL for the name_now function used in Figure 6-14 appears in Chapter 1 (Figure 1-9 on page 13).

How can I do a running total report?

I'd like to prepare a report that displays a numeric data column and running totals for this column. Is this possible?

Approach 1

Yes, but the degree of difficulty varies with the complexity of the data. Let's start out with well-behaved data and then make things messier.

Figure 6-15 shows an SQL solution that produces a running total of student training fees when each student in the report population only has one fee. Note that the SQL uses a non-equijoin of the *STUDENT* table to itself. With a large *STUDENT* table, this approach may create performance problems.

```
BREAK ON report
COMPUTE SUM OF fee1 ON REPORT
COLUMN fee1 HEADING 'fee' FORMAT 999999
COLUMN fee2 HEADING 'running|fee' FORMAT 999999
SELECT
     s1.student_id "id",
     s1.student_total_fee "fee1",
     SUM(s2.student_total_fee) "fee2"       ◀3
FROM
     student s2,
     student s1
WHERE
     s1.student_id IN ('a133','a330','a925')    ◀2
 ▶   AND s2.student_id <= s1.student_id
          AND s2.student_id IN ('a133','a330','a925')   ◀2
GROUP BY
     s1.student_id,
     s1.student_total_fee
ORDER BY 1;

          ▲                running
id             fee            fee
-----      -------        -------
a133           325            325
a330           740           1065
a925           610           1675
               -------
sum           1675
```

Figure 6-15: SQL query that produces running totals.

Comments

▶ The query includes a self-join of the *STUDENT* table to itself. The join is also a non-equijoin that works because it's coordinated with the ORDER BY clause. If the rows were not sorted by student_id, then the join criteria would not produce the correct running totals.

▷ Any WHERE conditions that apply to one *STUDENT* table must also apply to the second *STUDENT* table. Without this symmetry, the query will not produce the correct running totals.

▷ The running totals get computed in this expression.

Approach 2

Let's continue with the well-behaved data from Figure 6-15, but use a PL/SQL function to produce the running totals. Figure 6-16 shows a query using the function running_fee that accepts a student_id as an argument and returns the appropriate running total.

```
BREAK ON REPORT
COMPUTE SUM OF fee1 ON REPORT
COLUMN fee1 HEADING 'fee' FORMAT 999999
COLUMN fee2 HEADING 'running|fee' FORMAT 999999
SELECT
     student_id "id",
     student_total_fee "fee1",
     running_fee(student_id) "fee2"     ◀①
FROM
     student
WHERE
     student_id IN ('a133','a330','a925')     ◀②
ORDER BY 1;

              running
id         fee      fee
-----  -------  -------
a133       325      325
a330       740     1065
a925       610     1675
           -------
sum       1675
```

Figure 6-16: Query that uses a PL/SQL function to produce running totals.

Comments

▷ The PL/SQL function simplifies this query by removing the self-join.

▷ The running_fee function must be coordinated with the ORDER BY clause and any WHERE conditions that pertain to the *STUDENT* table.

Figure 6-17 shows the PL/SQL that produces the running totals.

```
CREATE OR REPLACE FUNCTION running_fee
    (id VARCHAR2)
RETURN NUMBER
AS
    running_fee NUMBER(8);
    CURSOR main_cursor (p_id VARCHAR2) IS
        SELECT SUM(student_total_fee)
        FROM student
        WHERE student_id <= p_id
        AND student_id in ('a133','a330','a925');    ◀①

BEGIN
    OPEN main_cursor(id);
    FETCH main_cursor INTO running_fee;

    IF main_cursor%NOTFOUND THEN
        running_fee := NULL;
    end if;

    CLOSE main_cursor;
    RETURN running_fee;
END;
/
```

Figure 6-17: PL/SQL function running_fee used in Figure 6-16.

Comments

▶① Note that the WHERE conditions in the cursor coordinate with the WHERE conditions in the main query in Figure 6-16. The cursor condition student_id <= id mirrors the ORDER BY clause in the main query.

Approach 3

Let's now consider the general situation and allow each population item to have more than one training registration. In the previous example the ORDER BY student_id allowed us to write a self-join or a PL/SQL function to compute the correct running total. But when one person may have more than one training fee, you need a way to identify not only the student involved but also the specific fee involved before computing running totals.

There are several ways this could be done. For example, you could ORDER BY student_id and the date the registration took place. Figure 6-18 takes a slightly different approach and sorts by student_id and the ROWID. The ROWID, of course, is unique and allows you to identify a specific fee when computing the running totals.

```
BREAK ON REPORT ON id
COMPUTE SUM OF fee1 ON REPORT
COLUMN row_id NOPRINT  ◀1
COLUMN fee1 HEADING 'fee' FORMAT 999999
COLUMN fee2 HEADING 'running|fee' FORMAT 999999
SELECT
      student_id "id",
      student.rowid "row_id",
      student_total_fee "fee1",
      running_fee3(student_id, student.rowid) "fee2"  ◀1
FROM
      student
WHERE
      student_id between '@133' and '@925'
ORDER BY 1, 2;

             2      running
id         fee         fee
-----   -------    -------
@133       325        325
@226      1200       1525
           200       1725
           400       2125
@330       740       2865
@505      1500       4365
           500       4865
@925       610       5475
*****   -------
sum       5475
```

Figure 6-18: Query using a second PL/SQL function to produce running totals.

Comments

▶1 The query includes ROWID but does not print this pseudocolumn in the report. The ROWID gets passed to the PL/SQL function and is used there to determine the items to include in the running total.

▶2 The ORDER BY must be mirrored in the PL/SQL function to produce the correct running total.

For completeness, Figure 6-19 shows the PL/SQL function used in Figure 6-18.

Comments

▶1 This WHERE condition mirrors the ORDER BY clause in the main query and ensures that the correct running total gets computed. Note, too, that the other WHERE condition in the cursor is exactly identical again to the WHERE condition in the main query (see Figure 6-18). This coordination is also necessary.

```
CREATE OR REPLACE FUNCTION running_fee3
    (id VARCHAR2, row_id ROWID)
RETURN NUMBER
AS
    running_fee NUMBER(5);
    CURSOR main_cursor (p_id VARCHAR2, p_row_id ROWID) IS
        SELECT SUM(student_total_fee)
        FROM student
        WHERE student_id||ROWIDTOCHAR(student.rowid) <=     ◀
            p_id||ROWIDTOCHAR(p_row_id)
        AND student_id BETWEEN 'a133' and 'a925';

BEGIN
    OPEN main_cursor(id, row_id);
    FETCH main_cursor INTO running_fee;

    IF main_cursor%NOTFOUND THEN
        running_fee := NULL;
    END IF;

    CLOSE main_cursor;
    RETURN running_fee;
END;
/
```

Figure 6-19: PL/SQL function running_fee3 used in Figure 6-18.

See Also

1. Chapter 9 (Table 9-9 on page 271) compares performance tests for the SQL and PL/SQL approaches to running totals. It does so for the simple case where each member of the population only appears once.

2. Another example of a non-equijoin appears in Figure 6-25 on page 204 that shows how to construct a top *N* report.

3. The discussion about the symmetry required between WHERE conditions in PL/SQL cursors and WHERE conditions in the main query is very similar to the discussion about balanced correlated subqueries. The discussion about balanced and unbalanced subqueries begins on page 148 in Chapter 5.

How can I do a percentage distribution report?

I'd like to prepare a frequency distribution report but also include the percentage distribution. How can I construct a report like this?

Approach 1

Whatever approach you take, you'll need essentially two passes at the data — one pass to find the total count to use as the denominator in the percentage calculations and a second pass to prepare the actual report.

One attractive way to do this utilizes a view that provides the grand total needed to calculate the percentages. Figure 6-20 shows a simple percentage distribution report using a view.

```
BREAK ON REPORT
COMPUTE SUM OF count pct ON REPORT
COLUMN sex FORMAT A3
SELECT
      person_gender "sex",
      COUNT(*) "count",
      ROUND(100*COUNT(*)/totname_total,0) "pct"    ◀1
FROM
      person,
      name,
      totname    ◀2
WHERE
      name_seriesno = name_now(name_id)
      AND person_id = name_id
GROUP BY
      person_gender,
      totname_total
ORDER BY 1;

sex        count           pct
---   ----------   ----------
F              3            50
M              2            33
               1            17
            ----------   ----------
sum            6           100
```

Figure 6-20: Using a view to prepare a percentage distribution report.

Comments

▶ The query uses a view called ***TOTNAME*** that returns a single value containing the number of items in the report population. This value gets used to compute the percentage distributions.

▶ Since the view ***TOTNAME*** returns only a single value, it is not necessary to include any joins to the view. The placement of the view in the FROM clause, as shown here, is consistent with tuning for the rule-based optimizer.

For completeness, Figure 6-21 shows the SQL that created the *TOTNAME* view. Note that the WHERE conditions must match exactly the conditions used in the main query to define the report population.

```
CREATE OR REPLACE VIEW totname
    (totname_total)
AS
(SELECT
    COUNT(*)
FROM
    name
WHERE
    name_seriesno = name_now(name_id));
```

Figure 6-21: View used to compute percentage distributions in Figure 6-20.

You can easily extend a view to handle percentage distributions for cross-tabulations. For example, suppose you wanted a percentage distribution in a two-way cross-tabulation in which gender was one of the two variables. Instead of a view with only the grand total, you would create a view that included subtotals by gender. These could be used in the query to produce percentage distributions within each gender. You would, of course, need to join the view in the main query (unlike the situation in Figure 6-20, where a cartesian product worked fine).

With Oracle7 Release 7.2 or later, the view that determines the denominator for percentage calculations can be a subquery in the FROM clause, allowing you to duplicate the effect of a view "on the fly."

Approach 2

A second way that also produces percentage distributions uses PL/SQL to compute the grand total, saves this in a bind variable, and then uses the bind variable in the query. Figure 6-22 illustrates this approach.

Comments

▶ The query uses a bind variable called nametot to store the count of population items. This then gets used in the calculation of the percentages.

▶ The WHERE condition in the PL/SQL must be identical to the condition in the main query that identifies the report population. Otherwise, the count in the bind variable will be incorrect.

▶ The bind variable appears in this expression that computes percentages.

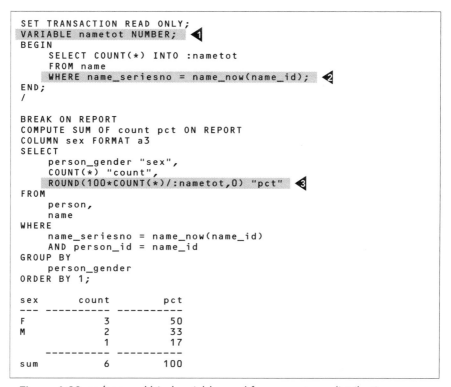

```
SET TRANSACTION READ ONLY;
VARIABLE nametot NUMBER;    ◀1
BEGIN
    SELECT COUNT(*) INTO :nametot
    FROM name
    WHERE name_seriesno = name_now(name_id);   ◀2
END;
/

BREAK ON REPORT
COMPUTE SUM OF count pct ON REPORT
COLUMN sex FORMAT a3
SELECT
    person_gender "sex",
    COUNT(*) "count",
    ROUND(100*COUNT(*)/:nametot,0) "pct"   ◀3
FROM
    person,
    name
WHERE
    name_seriesno = name_now(name_id)
    AND person_id = name_id
GROUP BY
    person_gender
ORDER BY 1;

sex        count         pct
---     ----------   ----------
F              3           50
M              2           33
               1           17
        ----------   ----------
sum            6          100
```

Figure 6-22: PL/SQL and bind variable used for percentage distributions.

See Also

1. Note that Figure 6-22 uses an anonymous PL/SQL block and a SQL SELECT query. To ensure that no database changes affect the query after processing completes in the PL/SQL block, use the SET TRANSACTION command with the READ ONLY option. For discussion about the proper use of this command, see Chapter 2 on page 46.

2. Chapter 9 (Table 9-10 on page 273) compares performance tests of the two approaches used to construct percentage distributions.

3. The PL/SQL for the name_now function used in Figure 6-22 appears in Chapter 1 (Figure 1-9 on page 13).

How can I do a top N report?

I'd like to prepare a report that includes only the top *N* population items based on the rank order of a numeric data column. In this case I want a report that lists the top 3 students based on their training registration fees. How can I do this?

Approach 1

Frequently, you'll see proposed solutions to this problem that use ROWNUM, as in SELECT col_name FROM table_name WHERE ROWNUM <=3 ORDER BY 1. While it looks like this approach should work, unfortunately, it does not. The pseudocolumn ROWNUM is determined before the ORDER BY occurs, so you'll just get the first 3 rows that meet the WHERE conditions. It would be unusual if this produced the correct results, but not impossible. For example, if the first 3 rows also happened to have the highest data values or if the query used a descending index on col_name to return rows, then ROWNUM coincidentally would produce the correct results.

To ensure you get the top *N* rows, other approaches are required. Figure 6-23 presents some training registration data that we'll use throughout this section. The task is to return rows rank ordered by student_total_fee. Note that we'll need to deal with the issue of ties because the value with rank order 3 is 740 and two rows include this value.

id	seq	sponsor	fee	regdate
@505	2	Employer	1500	04-NOV-97
@226	1	Mixed	1200	23-APR-97
@330	1		740	03-FEB-97
@925	2	Self	740	28-JUL-97
@925	1	Employer	610	10-MAY-96
@505	1	Self	500	19-JUN-97
@226	3	Self	400	02-DEC-97
@133	1	Self	325	17-SEP-97
@226	2	Self	200	11-JUL-97

Figure 6-23: Sample data for use in top *N* queries.

This first approach ignores ties but only uses SQL and does allow you to use ROWNUM successfully. It requires a bit of a trick. When you create a compound query with UNION, the results are implicitly sorted. In Figure 6-24, the query uses a subquery and a UNION to order the values of student_total_fee. Applying a ROWNUM condition in the main query works fine. Figure 6-24 illustrates this approach.

```
SELECT
      s1.student_id "id",
      s1.student_total_fee "fee"
FROM
      student s1
WHERE
      -1 * s1.student_total_fee in
               (SELECT -1 * s2.student_total_fee   ◀1
               FROM student s2
               UNION
               SELECT 0
               FROM DUAL
               WHERE 1=2)   ◀2
      AND ROWNUM <=3;
                          ▲3
id          fee
-----      ------
@505        1500
@226        1200
@330         740
```

Figure 6-24: UNION subquery used for a top *N* report.

Comments

▶ The implicit sort generated by the UNION occurs in ascending order. To pick the top *N*, meaning the largest N values, you'll need a descending sort. The equivalent of a descending sort occurs when you sort the negatives of the values of interest.

▶ The WHERE condition in the second query of the compound subquery is never true. This ensures that only rows from the first query appear in the UNIONed set.

▶ Note that ROWNUM now returns the top 3 values. Ties, however, are not considered. Top 3 in this report does not mean the top 3 rankings; it just means 3 rows with the largest fees. A top 3 ranking report would include person @925 who also had 740 for student_total_fee (see Figure 6-23).

Approach 2

Now let's consider a top *N* ranking report where ties should be included. One approach relies solely on SQL. It is, however, subject to performance problems with large tables. Figure 6-25 illustrates this approach.

Comments

▶ Rows ranked in the top 3 get identified in the subquery that counts the DISTINCT number of student_total_fee values greater

```
SELECT
    s1.student_id "id",
    s1.student_total_fee "fee"
FROM
    student s1                              ▼
WHERE
    3 >=
    (SELECT COUNT(DISTINCT s2.student_total_fee)
    FROM
    student s2
    WHERE s2.student_total_fee >= s1.student_total_fee)
ORDER BY 2 DESC;                            ▲

id         fee
-----      ------
a505       1500
a226       1200
a330        740    ◄②
a925        740
```

Figure 6-25: SQL query that produces a top *N* report.

than or equal to the value from the main query. This query relies on a non-equijoin between ***STUDENT*** and itself.

▶ Note that ties do get included properly using this query.

Approach 3

You also can use PL/SQL to produce a top *N* ranked report. The cutoff value is determined using a PL/SQL cursor and is saved in a bind variable that then gets used in an SQL query. Figure 6-26 shows how this works.

Comments

▶ Declare a PL/SQL cursor that sorts in descending order the values to be ranked.

▶ A PL/SQL loop fetches values of student_total_fee into a bind variable (called cutoff) until the *N*th value occurs. Here *N* is 3.

▶ The main query selects all rows where student_total_fee equals or exceeds the value of the bind variable. Note that the query deals properly with ties.

See Also

1. For another example where a dummy query against DUAL gets used to implicitly sort data with a UNION operation, see Chapter 8 (Figure 8-4 on page 236) that discusses how to sample the *N*th row from sorted data.

```
SET TRANSACTION READ ONLY
VARIABLE cutoff NUMBER
DECLARE
    i NUMBER;
    CURSOR main_cursor IS
        SELECT student_total_fee
        FROM student
        ORDER BY 1 DESC;        ◄1
BEGIN
    OPEN main_cursor;
    FOR i IN 1 .. 3
    LOOP
        FETCH main_cursor INTO :cutoff;    ◄2
    END LOOP;
    CLOSE main_cursor;
END;
/
SELECT
    student_id "id",
    student_total_fee "fee"
FROM
    student
WHERE
    student_total_fee >= :cutoff    ◄3
ORDER BY 2 DESC;

id          fee
-----       ------
a505        1500
a226        1200
a330         740
a925         740
```

Figure 6-26: PL/SQL used to produce a top *N* report.

2. For another example of a query using a non-equijoin, see Figure 6-15 on page 194 in this chapter, where a running total appears.

3. Performance comparisons between the two approaches are shown in Chapter 9 (Table 9-11 on page 275). Stay away from non-equijoins!

Formatting

Most queries shown in the preceding section can serve as complete templates for similar reports you may need to prepare. For a few of the queries, however, additional formatting is required to produce a properly polished report. This section discusses two such formatting issues.

How do I build custom headers when headers must be set off?

When I block or partially block a report, I SET HEADING OFF because the report no longer has the row-and-column format where column headings are meaningful. Yet often I'd like to provide some headers to help the user when reading the report. Is it possible to build custom headers?

Approach

The partially blocked report in Figure 6-10 on page 188 did not include headers. Including descriptive headers would add value to the report. Luckily, it's easy to do with the TTITLE command. Figure 6-27 shows a shell program used to run the SQL query for the partially blocked report in Figure 6-10. Customized report headings get built in the TTITLE command.

Comments

▶ Use the COL option in the TTITLE command to create descriptive headers. The line separating the headers from the report gets built in a command file called defheadr.sql called from the shell. Alternatively, you could just include the string (i.e., '====' etc.) in the TTITLE command.

For completeness, Figure 6-28 shows the program defheadr.sql that builds the line separating the header from the report body.

```
COLUMN xline NEW_VALUE xHeaderLine NOPRINT
SELECT LPAD('=',60,'=') xline FROM DUAL;
```

Figure 6-28: Building a heading and report separator line (defheadr.sql).

See Also

1. The TTITLE and BTITLE commands can be used for many things other than top and bottom report titles. Another example appears in

```
SET TERMOUT OFF
START &&object.\clears
START &&object.\printer
START &&object.\date
START &&object.\time
START &&tool.\defheadr

TTITLE LEFT 'Partially blocked report with custom header' SKIP 1 -
      LEFT 'Date: ' xDate '       Time: ' xTime -
      RIGHT 'Page: ' FORMAT 999 SQL.PNO SKIP 1 -
      LEFT 'Report name: test10.lis' -
      RIGHT 'SQL name: test10.sql' SKIP 2 -
         LEFT 'id' COL 7 'name' COL 33 'address' SKIP 1 -
         LEFT xHeaderLine SKIP 1;

SPOOL &&or2.\test10.lis
      START &&or2.\xtest10
SPOOL OFF
START &&object.\clears
START &&object.\screen

Partially blocked report with custom header
Date: 21-JUL-1996     Time: 09:04              Page:    1
Report name: test10.lis             SQL name: test10.sql

id    name                         address
==================================================================
@409  Alvarez, Xavier M            2095 Elmina Road
                                   Accra
                                   GHANA

@505  Carrington, Thomas J         RR4
                                   Saco, ME 04072
```

Figure 6-27: Building custom headers with the TTITLE command.

Chapter 2 on page 64 where TTITLE and BTITLE get used to control an HP laser printer.

2. See Figure 6-9 on page 186 for details about how to produce a blocked report.

How do I get rid of blank lines in blocked reports?

I've written a query that produces a name and address report where the address is blocked. Some people in the report population don't have a second address line. When this happens, a blank line appears in the report. This breaks up the address and makes the report appear awkward. How can I eliminate the display of NULL values in blocked or partially blocked reports?

Approach

Figure 6-29 illustrates the basic problem that occurs when you block data containing NULL values.

```
id      name                       address
================================================================
a133  O'Leary, Vincent             Bayview Rd

                                   Ipswich, MA 01938     ◣

a330  Healey, Caroline V           Greenbriar Estates
                                   1200 Ridgewood Ln
                                   Destrehan, LA 70047

a409  Alvarez, Xavier M            2095 Elmina Road

                                   Accra                 ◣
                                   GHANA
```

Figure 6-29: NULL values can produce blank lines in blocked data.

Comments

▶ In this query, two people have NULL values in the second address line. This produces blank lines in the report that unnecessarily disrupt the address block.

You could SET NULL or use the NULL clause of the COLUMN command to display a value such as 'Not available' whenever a NULL occurs. But this may provide small remedy in situations like addresses where people are used to seeing addresses of differing complexity each nicely blocked with no blank lines or NULL substitutes. If the report is a mailing label, the 'Not available' solution is particularly unacceptable to postal authorities.

Figure 6-30 displays address blocks in the preferred fashion without blank lines. The query relies on a PL/SQL function to build each line of the address depending on the availability of NOT NULL data values.

```
COLUMN name FORMAT a25
COLUMN NextLine NEWLINE
SELECT
      name_id "id",
      name_last||', '||name_first||' '||name_middle "name",
      address_street1 "st1",
      get_address_line(address_street2,
          get_city_line(address_city, address_loc, address_pcode),
          UPPER(country_name), 1, 32) "NextLine",
      get_address_line(address_street2,
          get_city_line(address_city, address_loc, address_pcode),    ◀1
          UPPER(country_name), 2, 32) "NextLine",
      get_address_line(address_street2,
          get_city_line(address_city, address_loc, address_pcode),
          UPPER(country_name), 3, 32) "NextLine"
FROM
      countries,
      address,
      name
WHERE
      name_seriesno = name_now(name_id)
      AND address_id = name_id
              AND address_type = 'PR'
              AND address_seriesno = max_address(name_id, 'PR')
          AND country_code(+) = address_country
ORDER BY 1;

id    name                         address
================================================================
@133  O'Leary, Vincent             Bayview Rd
                                   Ipswich, MA 01938


@330  Healey, Caroline V           Greenbriar Estates
                                   1200 Ridgewood Ln
                                   Destrehan, LA 70047


@409  Alvarez, Xavier M            2095 Elmina Road
                                   Accra
                                   GHANA
```

Figure 6-30: PL/SQL function used to eliminate blank lines from blocked data.

Comments

▶ The PL/SQL function get_address_line has five arguments: a street address line; a city, state, and zip code line; a country name; the line number in the address block being built; and the number of spaces needed to align the address in the report. The concatenated city argument gets build from another PL/SQL function (get_city_line) shown in Figure 6-11 on page 189.

Note that the query includes the get_address_line function three times, once for each line in the address block that's being built.

Figure 6-31 shows the PL/SQL function get_address_line. Note that it builds a specific line in the blocked address based on the availability of NOT NULL data values.

```
CREATE OR REPLACE FUNCTION get_address_line
  (street2 VARCHAR2,
   city_state_zip VARCHAR2,
   country VARCHAR2,
   address_line_number NUMBER,
   left_pad_num NUMBER)
RETURN VARCHAR2
AS
   address_line VARCHAR2(80);
   data_available VARCHAR2(3);
   var_num NUMBER(1);

BEGIN                                                      ▼
  data_available := NVL(SIGN(ASCII(SUBSTR(street2,1,1))),0)||
     NVL(SIGN(ASCII(SUBSTR(city_state_zip,1,1))),0)||
     NVL(SIGN(ASCII(SUBSTR(country,1,1))),0);

  var_num := INSTR(data_available,'1',1,address_line_number);

  IF var_num = 1 THEN                                     ▲
     address_line := street2;
  ELSIF var_num = 2 THEN
     address_line := city_state_zip;
  ELSIF var_num = 3 THEN
     address_line := country;
  END IF;

  address_line := LPAD(' ', left_pad_num)||address_line;

  RETURN address_line;
END;
/
```

Figure 6-31: PL/SQL function get_address_line used in Figure 6-30.

Comments

▶ This statement builds a string based on the availability of NOT NULL data values in the address data. For example, if only the city line is NOT NULL, the data_available string will be '010', where a 1 indicates that data exist and a 0 indicates that the value is NULL.

▶ The INSTR function and the following IF statement identify the address data that will be returned. For example, if the data_available string is 010 and the address_line_number is 1 (i.e., we're trying to build the first line of the blocked address), then the INSTR function and the IF statement identify the city data as the first NOT NULL data value. This then gets returned from the PL/SQL function and used in the report.

Just to make that sure this is clear, let's take another example. Assume that street line 2 is NULL, the city line and country both exist, and that we're trying to build the second line of the blocked address (i.e., address_line_number is 2). The data_available string is 011, the INSTR function returns 3, and the IF statement identifies the country name as the data value to return.

Note that if the INSTR function returns 0, it means the Nth occurrence of NOT NULL data does not exist. The PL/SQL function returns a NULL in this case. In effect, the PL/SQL function forces all NULL values to display at the bottom of the blocked data in the report, where their appearance does not detract from the report.

See Also

1. The discussion about partially blocked reports appears in a preceding section of this chapter on page 188.

2. Figure 6-30 uses three PL/SQL functions — name_now, shown in Chapter 1 (Figure 1-9 on page 13); max_address, shown in Chapter 4 (Figure 4-4 on page 112); and get_city_line, shown in Figure 6-11 on page 189.

3. The INSTR function proves useful when you want to search a string for the presence of a substring. Chapter 4 (Figure 4-14 on page 128) provides another example where this function helps a query work properly.

External Applications

Sometimes the report output from a query is only an intermediate step in preparation for use of the report in another application. When this happens, you'll need to format the report so that the external application can read and process it conveniently. This section discusses two such cases.

How do I construct an ASCII file for mail merges?

I'd like to extract name and address information into a flat file that I can use with the mail merge feature in my word processor. Data columns should be comma-delimited, and the first line should be a header that identifies the data columns. How can I do this?

Approach

Flat file extracts find considerable use as input data for external applications like word processors or statistical packages. Producing a flat file with a header line requires only a minor variation on a technique introduced in Chapter 2.

Figure 6-32 illustrates one way to produce a comma-delimited name and address file that also includes a header line that some word processors require for data identification.

Comments

▶ Disable all SQL*PLUS commands that could produce output.

▶ Set LINESIZE large enough to accommodate your data. Setting PAGESIZE 0 disables all headers, top and bottom titles, page breaks, pausing, and other formatting. You'll still need to specifically disable ECHO, FEEDBACK, and TIMING.

▶ Enabling TRIMSPOOL eliminates trailing blanks that normally pad report output to the length set by LINESIZE. This reduces the file size. You'll need one query to produce the header line and a second query to produce the comma-delimited data. Setting PAGESIZE 0 disables the page breaks between reports, so you won't need to enable EMBEDDED.

▶ Note the extensive use of the concatenation operator that produces the commas in the report output.

▶ The final report consists of a header line and the extracted data.

```
SET ECHO OFF
SET FEEDBACK OFF     ◀1
SET TIMING OFF

SET PAGESIZE 0       ◀2
SET LINESIZE 70

SET TRIMSPOOL ON     ◀3

SPOOL &&or2.\merge.dat
   SELECT
      'id,last,first,middle,st1,city,loc,pcode,natn,eor'
   FROM DUAL;
   SELECT
      name_id||','||
      name_last||','||
      name_first||','||
      name_middle||','||
      address_street1||','||   ◀4
      address_city||','||
      address_loc||','||
      address_pcode||','||
      UPPER(country_name)||','||
      'x'
   FROM
      countries,
      address,
      name
   WHERE
      name_seriesno = name_now(name_id)
      AND address_id = name_id
            AND address_type = 'PR'
            AND address_status = 'A'
            AND address_seriesno = max_address(name_id, 'PR')
      AND country_code(+) = address_country;
SPOOL OFF

id,last,first,middle,st1,city,loc,pcode,natn,eor          ◀5
@409,Alvarez,Xavier,M,2095 Elmina Road,Accra,,,GHANA,x
@505,Carrington,Thomas,J,RR4,Saco,ME,04072,,x
@330,Healey,Caroline,V,Greenbriar Estates,Destrehan,LA,70047,,x
@133,O'Leary,Vincent,,Bayview Rd,Ipswich,MA,01938,,x
```

Figure 6-32: SQL query that produces a comma-delimited flat file.

See Also

1. The header line gets produced in one query; the comma-delimited data from a second query. Producing a single output file from two or more queries sometimes proves indispensable. For more discussion about creating a single report from multiple queries, see Chapter 2 on page 46.

2. The PL/SQL for the name_now function used in Figure 6-32 appears in Chapter 1 (Figure 1-9 on page 13). The max_address function appears in Chapter 4 (Figure 4-4 on page 112).

3. See Chapter 2 on page 62 for additional discussion about formatting an ASCII flat file with an SQL query.

How do I prepare a fixed-format flat file?

I'd like to prepare an ASCII flat file for use with a statistical package and want a fixed format so that each data column begins and ends in a specific location. How can I do this?

Approach

This requires only a minor variation to the comma-delimited query shown in Figure 6-32 on page 213. Figure 6-33 illustrates one way to prepare fixed-format flat files.

```
SET ECHO OFF
SET FEEDBACK OFF
SET TIMING OFF

SET PAGESIZE 0
SET LINESIZE 60

SET COLSEP ''    ◀1

COLUMN id FORMAT a5    ◀2
COLUMN last FORMAT a15
COLUMN fee FORMAT a8
COLUMN rdate FORMAT a11
SPOOL &&or2.\test6.lis
   SELECT                        ▽2
     RPAD(name_id, 5) "id",
     RPAD(name_last, 15) "last",
     RPAD(to_char(student_total_fee), 8) "fee",
     TO_CHAR(student_regdate)||' x' "rdate"
   FROM
     student,
     name
   WHERE
     name_seriesno = name_now(name_id)
     AND student_id = name_id
          AND student_regseq = max_regseq(name_id);
SPOOL OFF


a505 Carrington      1500      04-NOV-97 x
a133 O'Leary          325      17-SEP-97 x
a330 Healey           740      03-FEB-97 x
a226 Sacco            400      02-DEC-97 x
a925 Appiah           740      28-JUL-97 x
```

Figure 6-33: SQL query that produces a fixed-format flat file.

Comments

▶ This command causes report columns to print without separation, giving you total control over data placement.

▶ Include COLUMN command formats consistent with the

padding done in the SELECT clause. For example, if name_id is right-padded to length 5, then the FORMAT option should be A5 in the COLUMN command.

See Also

1. Figure 6-33 uses two PL/SQL functions. The name_now function appears in Chapter 1 (Figure 1-9 on page 13); the max_regseq function appears in Chapter 5 (Figure 5-15 on page 153).

Chapter 7
Utilities

This chapter contains two of the most important discussions in this book. One concerns the importance of the report population, knowing what it is and defining it properly. The second concerns how to fix things when they go wrong.

Let's start with the latter. You should expect problems to occur in ad hoc queries. This is their nature; in fact, if problems don't occur, you must be very skilled or must be doing boring repetitive queries where you've already solved the problems.

Error-free first drafts of queries should not be an important goal. But finding and fixing the errors easily are important. You don't want to be stuck; you want an easy way to identify when errors exist, an easy way to find the source of the errors, and an easy way to fix the problem. This chapter discusses several debugging tools that allow you this flexibility.

When debugging queries, you absolutely *must* have a clear and accurate understanding of the report population. This probably seems obvious and maybe even seems trivial. But populations are neither obvious nor trivial, and if you don't get them right, your query will suffer.

This chapter discusses a very simple name and address report to drive home the choices that you as a query writer must make about report populations. Even in this simple case at least four different populations are possible. No one population is inherently right or wrong; it all depends on the query in question. However, you must explicitly deal with the alternatives before you really understand the report population. Only then can you actually debug the query with assurance.

Debugging

Most query problems originate in the joins. It's here that you define the report population and make available for display items of information about the population. Thus you'll need to start debugging a query with a firm understanding of the report population and tools that let you find and fix join problems easily. This section discusses these tools.

How do I identify join problems?

I've written a fairly complex query with joins to eight tables. The query doesn't return the correct number of population items, however, so one or more of the joins must be the problem. How can I find the error?

Approach

To identify join problems, it is absolutely essential that you know what your population is and how many items it includes. Otherwise, when things go wrong, you may be unable to detect it.

Each query contains a population that is defined by all or some portion of the WHERE conditions. This is the *report population*. You must know exactly what portion of the WHERE clause defines the population because all testing of joins will use this information.

Let's consider a simple situation that hammers home the nuances in population definition. Assume you want a name and address report on 10 people, 1 of whom has no address and 2 of whom have two addresses. What's the report population? How many items does the population include? Is it 9, 10, 13, or 14? Each of these represents a possible population. Take, for example, the population of 10. This is a population of people without regard to their address. The population of 9 is a population of people who have addresses; the population of 13 is a population of addresses for people with at least one address; and the population of 14 is a population of addresses for all 10 people.

Figure 7-1 defines each of these four populations using tables introduced in earlier chapters. Note how the population definitions differ for each of these four populations.

Identifying join problems must start with a clear definition of the report population. If you decide your population includes 10 people, then a query that returns 9 or 14 items means one of two things: (1) it contains an error, or (2) you don't understand the report population.

Here's a test to ensure that you really do understand your report

```
People who have addresses: count = 9
    name_seriesno = name_now(name_id)
    and address_id = name_id
        and address_seriesno = max_address(name_id, 'PR')


People without regard for addresses: count = 10
    name_seriesno = name_now(name_id)
    and address_id(+) = name_id
        and address_type(+) = 'PR'
        and address_seriesno(+) = max_address(name_id, 'PR')


Addresses for people with at least one address: count = 13
    name_seriesno = name_now(name_id)
    and address_id = name_id
        and address_type = 'PR'


Addresses for all 10 people: count = 14
    name_seriesno = name_now(name_id)
    and address_id(+) = name_id
        and address_type(+) = 'PR'
```

Figure 7-1: SQL definitions of four possible populations.

population. Start writing each new query by defining the report popula-
tion in SQL. Test your definition by doing a select COUNT(*) and
COUNT(DISTINCT . . .). The two numbers should be identical.
Figure 7-2 shows an example of this test.

```
SELECT
    COUNT(*) "count",
    COUNT(DISTINCT name_id) "dist"
FROM
    name
WHERE
    name_seriesno = name_now(name_id);


                    count
    count(*)      distinct
    ----------  ----------
            6           6  ◀
```

Figure 7-2: Testing the query population definition.

Comments

▶ When you properly understand the report population, the
two counts will be identical. In this query the population includes
6 people from the *NAME* table.

Consider a situation in which the two counts differ. Suppose the query in Figure 7-2 contained a join to the *ADDRESS* table and that COUNT(*) was 8 and COUNT(DISTINCT name_id) was 6. This means that you either don't understand the report population or that you've defined it incorrectly. If the report population contains 6 people, then the two counts should each be 6. However, if the report population is the 8 addresses, then the two counts should each be 8. Either could be correct depending on what you want the query to do, but you *must* know the difference. If the population is 8, then the correct counts will be COUNT(*) and COUNT(DISTINCT name_id | | address_seriesno). This literally forces you to acknowledge that the population items are addresses and not people.

Once the report population is properly defined, testing the joins is straightforward. Use a procedure called *stepping through the joins*. It works like this:

- Do a COUNT(*) and COUNT(DISTINCT . . .) for the entire query. If the two counts differ from your population counts, you have a problem in the joins.

- Add one join at a time to the basic population definition and perform the COUNT(*) and COUNT(DISTINCT . . .) again. Whenever the counts change from the population values, you've located a join that contains a problem. For example, suppose the query contains 5 joins in addition to those included in the population definition. Include the first join with the population definition and run the counts. If they're the same as the population definitions, then move to the next join. Proceed in this fashion through all the joins until you find the one(s) where the counts differ from the population values.

- Two types of errors can occur in joins: Either you can lose population items (called *falling through a join*), or you can gain population items (called *multiplying through a join*). For example, assume the population COUNT(*) was 6 and the COUNT(DISTINCT . . .) was 6 (designated here as 6/6 for ease of discussion). Also assume that when you add one of the joins, you now get a count of 5/5. In this case you've lost 1 population item. If the counts are 6/7, then you got a multiplication through the join and one population item appears twice. If you got counts of 5/7, it means the join has both types of errors — population loss and population gain.

Sometimes the error in the joins is obvious. But often it is not.

Correcting the join conditions requires that you first identify which rows create the problems. You can then compare the data values in these rows with the join conditions and determine why they either fell through or multiplied through the join. The next sections discuss these topics.

See Also

1. Correlated subqueries as predicates to EXISTS or NOT EXISTS are marvelous adjectives qualifying a population. One reason they're so useful is that falling through a join and multiplying through a join are never a problem with these query structures. You simply look for the existence or absence of a characteristic; they become part of your population definition. For more discussion on this point, see the section on subqueries that begins in Chapter 5 on page 148.

2. Figure 7-1 uses two PL/SQL functions — name_now and max_address. The PL/SQL for name_now appears in Chapter 1 (Figure 1-9 on page 13); the PL/SQL for max_address is in Chapter 4 (Figure 4-4 on page 112).

How do I find rows that fell through a join?

I've written a query that contains a problem in one join. Population items fall through this join, but I can't figure out why. How can I identify the rows that fall through the join so that I can examine their data values and determine why they cause problems with the join logic?

Approach

After you isolate a query problem to a specific join, it's often helpful to examine the rows that fail the join condition. Let's continue with the example from Figure 7-2 where the population included 6 people. Figure 7-3 shows a query where join errors occur.

```
SELECT
     COUNT(*) "count",
     COUNT(DISTINCT name_id) "dist"
FROM
     address,
     person,
     name
WHERE
     name_seriesno = name_now(name_id)
     AND person_id = name_id
     AND address_id = name_id
          AND address_type = 'PR'
          AND address_status = 'A';


                     count
   count(*)        distinct
 ----------       ----------
            5               4   ◀
```

Figure 7-3: Query that contains two types of join failures.

Comments

▶ The counts should be 6 and 6. Apparently, two people fell through the joins and 1 person multiplied through the join.

To find the offending join, use the procedure discussed in the preceding section and step through the joins one-by-one. First, add the *PERSON* join and rerun the counts. Then add the *ADDRESS* join and do the counts again. In the example above, both problems occur in the *ADDRESS* join.

To identify rows that fall through a join, use a simple SQL query with a NOT EXISTS correlated subquery. Figure 7-4 illustrates how this works to identify the two people who fell through the join in Figure 7-3.

```
SELECT
        name_id
FROM
        name
WHERE
        name_seriesno = name_now(name_id)
        AND NOT EXISTS
        (SELECT 'x'
        FROM address
        WHERE address_id = name_id
                AND address_type = 'PR'
                AND address_status = 'A');


id
-----
@226
@925
```

Figure 7-4: SQL structure to identify items that fall through a join.

Comments

▶ Use NOT EXISTS and a correlated subquery with the exact WHERE conditions that you used in the problematic join (e.g., see Figure 7-3 on page 222). This will identify the rows that fell through the join. In this case, the two people affected by the query have ID numbers @226 and @925.

Then examine the data for the rows that fell through the join. You'll find the reasons for the join failures by examining the data values. Occasionally it's a problem with the data, such as invalid codes that were not trapped with referential constraints. Most frequently, however, the problem is query writer error in the join logic. Figure 7-5 shows *ADDRESS* data for the two people who fell through the *ADDRESS* join in our example.

id	type	seq	status	city	loc	postal code	nat
@226	BU	1	A	Charleston	IL	60954	
@925							

Figure 7-5: Data for two people who fell through the *ADDRESS* join.

Comments

▶ This report makes it immediately clear why @226 and @925 fell through the address join. One person (@226) has no PR address; the second (@925) has no address at all.

At this point you're prepared to revise the original query. Both situations in our example can be fixed with outer joins. Figure 7-6 shows COUNT(*) and COUNT(DISTINCT . . .) after including outer joins.

```
SELECT
      COUNT(*) "count",
      COUNT(DISTINCT name_id) "dist"
FROM
      address,
      person,
      name
WHERE
      name_seriesno = name_now(name_id)
      AND person_id = name_id
      AND address_id(+) = name_id
            AND address_type(+) = 'PR'
            AND address_status(+) = 'A';



                      count
    count(*)        distinct
  ----------      ----------
            7               6  ◀
```

Figure 7-6: Query that prevents population loss.

Comments

▶ The query now includes the correct number of people (i.e., six), indicating that we've plugged the join problems that cause population loss. Note, however, that one person still multiplies through a join. The next section discusses this problem.

See Also

1. This section used a correlated subquery to find rows that fell through a join. You also could use other methods to identify these rows. For a discussion of these methods, see the section in this chapter on DBA tools that begins on page 228.

2. You can use correlated subqueries as predicates to EXISTS or NOT EXISTS to help define report populations. They behave very much like adjectives qualifying nouns. For a discussion of this, see Chapter 5 on page 151.

3. Outer joins often pose problems for query writers. For a discussion of some of these problems, see the sections that begin Chapter 5 on page 156

4. The PL/SQL for the name_now function appears in Chapter 1 (Figure 1-9 on page 13).

How do I find rows that multiplied through a join?

I've written a query that contains a problem in one join. Population items multiply through this join, but I can't figure out why. How can I identify the rows that multiply through the join so that I can examine their data values and determine why they cause problems with the join logic?

Approach

Let's continue with our example from preceding sections. You can identify rows that multiply through a join using a distinctive SQL structure with a GROUP BY and a HAVING. Figure 7-7 illustrates how this works.

```
SELECT
    name_id "id",
    COUNT(*) "count"
FROM
    address, name
WHERE
    name_seriesno = name_now(name_id)
    AND address_id(+) = name_id
        AND address_type(+) = 'PR'
        AND address_status(+) = 'A'
GROUP BY
    name_id
HAVING                      ◀1
    COUNT(*) > 1;


id          count(*)
-----       ----------
a330               2    ◀1
```

Figure 7-7: SQL structure that identifies items that multiply through a join.

Comments

▶ GROUP BY and HAVING are the keys to this query, returning all population items that appear more than once in the result set.

Based on this information, you can examine the data for population items that multiplied through the joins. In most cases the problem occurs in the join logic, but occasionally you'll uncover data problems that the database design did not prevent.

In our example the situation is simple; the person has two active permanent addresses. By choosing only one of the two, you can avoid the problem of multiplying through the join. Figure 7-8 shows the final query and it's accompanying COUNT(*) and COUNT(DISTINCT . . .).

```
SELECT
     COUNT(*) "count",
     COUNT(DISTINCT name_id) "dist"
FROM
     address,
     person,
     name
WHERE
     name_seriesno = name_now(name_id)
     AND person_id = name_id
     AND address_id(+) = name_id
          AND address_type(+) = 'PR'
          AND address_status(+) = 'A'
          AND address_seriesno(+) =
               max_address(name_id, 'PR');   ◀

                    count
     count(*)     distinct
     ----------   ----------
            6            6   ◀
```

Figure 7-8: Final query that solves all join problems.

Comments

▶ The PL/SQL function max_address introduced in Chapter 4 (Figure 4-4 on page 112) returns the last active address of a specified type. The outer join preserves the previous fix in Figure 7-6 on page 224 that prevented population loss.

In complicated queries with multiple joins that need debugging, make sure you run the last COUNT(*) and COUNT(DISTINCT . . .) on the entire query. It's possible that by fixing one join at a time you'll get interactions between your join solutions so that the entire query still does not return the correct counts.

See Also

1. Instead of GROUP BY and HAVING, you can also use other methods to identify rows that multiply through joins. For a discussion of these methods, see the section in this chapter on DBA tools that begins on page 230.

2. See Chapter 1 (Figure 1-9 on page 13) for the name_now function and Chapter 4 (Figure 4-4 on page 112) for the max_address function.

DBA Tools

Debugging tools used by query writers to find and fix join problems originate in tools that database administrators use for other purposes. This
section discusses those tools and emphasizes alternative methods of accomplishing the same task. It's important for query writers to have a variety of methods they can employ as needed. Not any one method works
best in all situations.

How do I find foreign key violations?

How can I identify rows in one table that should have corresponding
rows in a second table but do not? For example, I might have a master
table and a detail table and want to delete all rows in the master table
without detail information. Or I might want to find foreign key viola-
tions by identifying all rows in one table where the foreign key references
a primary key that does not exist in a second table. Are there alternative
approaches to this problem?

Approach

This question is of interest to query writers because it's essentially the
same one as finding rows that fall through a join. The solutions to this
question provide query writers with alternative methods to debug their
queries by finding rows that fall through a join.

Frequently it is difficult to classify one approach as the *best*. Generally
speaking, however, as long as two queries both return accurate results,
the query that completes in the shortest time is preferred (this assumes,
of course, that the query writer doesn't spend hours finding the optimal
query when he could have written an acceptable query in minutes).

Figure 7-9 shows four alternative methods that all identify rows from
one table that do not have corresponding information in a second table.
In the figure, the table names are A and B. These tables are joined
through the common column named xid.

Comments

▶ Method 1 uses an outer join to create NULL rows in table B
for items in table A that do not exist in table B. The query then
uses ROWID IS NULL to identify these rows.

▶ Method 2 uses a correlated subquery as a predicate to NOT
EXISTS.

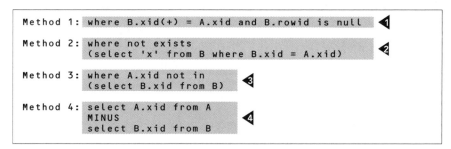

Figure 7-9: Identifying rows in one table not represented in a second table.

> ▶ Method 3 uses a subquery but not a correlated subquery.
> ▶ Method 4 uses a compound query and the MINUS operation.

Method 2, which is the approach used to identify rows that fell through the *ADDRESS* join in Figure 7-4 on page 223, works well when the join columns are the leading edge of indexes in both tables A and B. When indexes do not exist, or you cannot take advantage of the leading edge of available indexes, use the MINUS compound query. Figure 7-10 illustrates this when debugging the *ADDRESS* join from our example.

```
SELECT
      name_id "id"
FROM
      name
MINUS
SELECT
      address_id "id"
FROM
      address
WHERE
      address_type = 'PR'
      AND address_status = 'A';


id
-----
@226
@925
```

Figure 7-10: Identifying rows that fell through the join in Figure 7-3.

See Also

1. Chapter 9 (Table 9-12 on page 278) compares the performance of the four methods for finding rows in one table without corresponding rows in a second table.

How do I find duplicates in a table?

I tried to create a unique index on a combination of several columns yet got error ORA-01452 that duplicate keys existed. How do I find which rows contain duplicates on these columns?

Approach

A DBA might ask this question; query writers never consider duplicate keys. But solutions to the problem do affect query writers, because you can use the same techniques to debug your queries when rows multiply through joins. Figure 7-7 on page 226 found multiple address records when only one was expected. This is very similar to finding duplicates.

Figure 7-11 provides several alternative methods for identifying duplicate keys in a table. The figure presents the simplest situation where the key is only a single column, but the methods can be extended easily to multiple columns. Note that the debugging technique used to find rows that multiplied through the address join in Figure 7-7 relied on Method 1.

```
Method 1:  SELECT col1, COUNT(*)
           FROM table_name A
           WHERE ...
           GROUP BY col1
           HAVING COUNT(*) > 1;        ◀1

Method 2:  SELECT col1
           FROM table_name A
           WHERE ...
               AND 1 <
               (SELECT COUNT(*) FROM table_name B
               WHERE B.col1 = A.col1);   ◀2

Method 3:  SELECT col1
           FROM table_name A
           WHERE ...
               AND EXISTS
               (SELECT 'x'
               FROM table_name B
               WHERE B.col1 = A.col1      ◀3
               AND B.ROWID != A.ROWID);
```

Figure 7-11: Methods to identify duplicate keys in a table.

Comments

▶ Method 1 uses a GROUP BY and HAVING to identify col1 values that appear more than once.

▶ Method 2 uses a correlated subquery to identify col1 values that appear more than once.

▶ Method 3 also uses a correlated subquery, this time as a predicate to an EXISTS. The condition is met when two rows have the same col1 value but their ROWIDs differ.

Chapter 9 discusses the performance implications of these alternative methods for finding duplicates. Figure 7-12 illustrates how Method 2 can be used to debug the address join in our earlier example and find rows that multiplied through this join.

```
SELECT
      name_id "id"
FROM
      name
WHERE
      name_seriesno = name_now(name_id)
      AND 1 <
      (SELECT COUNT(*)
      FROM address
      WHERE address_id = name_id
            AND address_type = 'PR'
            AND address_status = 'A');


id
-----
a330
```

Figure 7-12: Identifying rows that multiplied through the join in Figure 7-3.

See Also

1. Chapter 9 (Table 9-13 on page 280) compares the performance of the three methods for identifying duplicates.

2. The PL/SQL for the name_now function used in Figure 7-12 appears in Chapter 1 (Figure 1-9 on page 13).

Chapter 8
Statistics

SQL was not designed as a statistical analysis tool, and it is generally not equipped to handle this type of analysis. In almost every instance when statistical analysis is required, you should look to other tools. Use SQL as a tool to extract and construct a dataset that can then be used in a statistical package like SAS or SPSS.

Having said this, however, there are some statistically related questions that arise frequently among people writing ad hoc queries. For example, Oracle includes a few tantalizing group functions that perform basic statistical operations such as finding the minimum, maximum, and average. But other measures not included as group functions often would prove useful; measures of central tendency like the median or measures of spread like the interquartile range come to mind. Does this mean that every time you want to find the median of a group of values you must extract a data set to a statistical package? Some basic set of statistical functions would prove extremely useful to query writers. This chapter discusses two additions to the group functions provided by Oracle.

This chapter also discusses several ways of sampling data. You might, for example, be asked to draw samples from a population to receive different types of mailings where later analysis will determine the effectiveness of the various mailings. In some situations, a simple systematic sample (i.e., every Nth row) might work; in other situations, you might need to draw random samples. This chapter discusses how to incorporate both types of samples into your query work. The random number generator included in this chapter improves on most system-supplied generators and should serve adequately for the majority of query applications.

Samples

Sampling in ad hoc queries usually has an applied focus. You can use samples while debugging to limit the result set or to examine selected rows in more depth. Query writers also sample when they provide subsets of data to government agencies or when they're asked to participate in market research studies. This section discusses several sampling techniques.

How do I select the Nth row from a query?

I want to select just one row from a query. If I use WHERE ROWNUM = 1, I get the same row returned each time. How can I vary the row returned?

Approach 1

Let's assume that ordering of the rows is unimportant (the next section relaxes this restriction). Figure 8-1 shows unsorted *NAME* data.

```
id      last                rownum
-----   ---------------     ----------
@505    Carrington              1
@133    O'Leary                 2
@330    Healey                  3
@226    Sacco                   4
@409    Alvarez                 5
@925    Appiah                  6
```

Figure 8-1: Unsorted *NAME* data.

Suppose you want to examine ROWNUM 5. Using WHERE ROWNUM = 5 returns no rows. By including a GROUP BY, however, you can then use HAVING to limit the query to the desired ROWNUM (see Figure 8-2).

```
SELECT name_id "id", name_last "last", ROWNUM "rownum"
FROM name
WHERE name_seriesno = name_now(name_id)
GROUP BY name_id, name_last, ROWNUM
HAVING ROWNUM = 5;

id      last                rownum
-----   ---------------     ----------
@409    Alvarez                 5
```

Figure 8-2: SQL query that samples one row from unsorted data.

Comments

▶ Sample one ROWNUM using GROUP BY and HAVING clauses.

Approach 2

PL/SQL cursors provide a direct solution to this problem. Figure 8-3 illustrates one approach, using a PL/SQL cursor to fetch the *N*th row and a bind variable to save the ROWID. A query then uses this bind variable.

```
SET TRANSACTION READ ONLY
VARIABLE rown VARCHAR2(20)    ◀①
DECLARE
    i NUMBER;
    CURSOR main_cursor IS
        SELECT ROWIDTOCHAR(ROWID)
        FROM name
        WHERE name_seriesno = name_now(name_id);
BEGIN
    OPEN main_cursor;
    FOR i IN 1 .. &&number_of_row          ◀①
    LOOP
        FETCH main_cursor INTO :rown;      ◀①
    END LOOP;
    CLOSE main_cursor;
END;
/
SELECT name_id "id", name_last "last"
FROM name
WHERE name.rowid = CHARTOROWID(:rown);     ◀②

id      last
-----   ----------------
@409    Alvarez
```

Figure 8-3: PL/SQL approach that selects one row from unsorted data.

Comments

▶① A bind variable called rown is created to store the ROWID of the *N*th row fetched from the cursor. The value of *N* is entered by the user at runtime (as &&number_of_row).

▶② The query uses the bind variable to return only one row.

See Also

1. Chapter 9 (Table 9-14 on page 283) shows results of performance tests for the SQL and PL/SQL approaches to sampling the *N*th row.

2. ROWNUM is a beguiling SQL keyword often misued. See, for example, Chapter 6 on page 202.

3. Use the SET TRANSACTION command to prevent database changes that occur between the two queries from affecting the results. For a discussion, see Chapter 2 on page 46.

4. Chapter 1 (Figure 1-9 on page 13) lists the PL/SQL for name_now.

How do I select the Nth row from sorted data?

I'd like to select just one row from a query where the data are first sorted. How can I do this?

Approach

Adding an ORDER BY to the PL/SQL cursor shown in Figure 8-3 on page 235 let's you easily sort and then select a single row. This is definitely the approach to take.

If you insist on a pure SQL solution, however, things become trickier. You cannot simply add an ORDER BY to the SQL shown in Figure 8-2 on page 234 because ROWNUM is computed based on the order that data are retrieved from the table *before* the ORDER BY takes effect. For example, if you added an ORDER BY name_last to the query in Figure 8-2, the query would still return (@409, Alvarez) as ROWNUM 5.

You need some way to retrieve sorted data. Using an appropriate index is one method. Figure 8-4 illustrates a second method that makes use of the fact that a UNION performs an implicit sort.

```
SELECT
     name_id "id",
     name_last "last",
     ROWNUM "rownum"
FROM
     name
WHERE
     name_seriesno = name_now(name_id)
     AND (name_last, name_id) IN
     (SELECT name_last, name_id
     FROM name
     WHERE name_seriesno = name_now(name_id)    ◀1
     UNION
     SELECT 'x', 'y' FROM DUAL WHERE 1=2)
GROUP BY
     name_id,
     name_last,
     ROWNUM
HAVING
     ROWNUM = 5;

id     last                     rownum
-----  ----------------  ----------
a133   O'Leary                       5
```

Figure 8-4: SQL query that samples one row from sorted data.

Comments

▶ Including name_last as the first element in the compound

subquery forces an implicit sort on this column. The portion of the compound subquery that selects from DUAL is a dummy query that never equates to TRUE but allows you to use UNION to force the sort. All very convoluted.

See Also

1. Subqueries may not include the ORDER BY clause. This means that you cannot sort easily under certain circumstances, such as when you create a view or when you do an INSERT. Instead, query writers must fall back on side-effects like the implicit sort available in the UNION operation. For an example of a query that relies on the implicit sort of a UNION operation, see Chapter 6 (Figure 6-24 on page 203) for discussion about the top N report.

2. Figure 8-4 uses the name_now function. For the PL/SQL used to create name_now, see Chapter 1 (Figure 1-9 on page 13).

How can I draw a systematic sample?

I'd like to select every *N*th row from a query. For example, if I want a 10 percent sample, I'd select every tenth row. How can I construct a query that will do this?

Approach 1

By making only a minor modification to the SQL that samples one row from a query (see Figure 8-2 on page 234), you can systematically draw a sample of every *N*th row. Figure 8-5 shows how this works.

```
SELECT
      name_id "id",
      name_last "last",
      ROWNUM "rownum"
FROM
      name
WHERE
      name_seriesno = name_now(name_id)
GROUP BY
      name_id,
      name_last,
      ROWNUM
HAVING
      MOD(ROWNUM,2) = 0;   ◀

id      last                    rownum
-----   ----------------   ----------
@133    O'Leary                      2
@226    Sacco                        4
@925    Appiah                       6
```

Figure 8-5: SQL query that systematically samples every second row.

Comments

▶ The MOD function used in the HAVING clause retains every second row. You can select every *N*th row with MOD(ROWNUM, *N*) = 0; just substitute a value of your choice for *N*.

Approach 2

PL/SQL provides a simple, direct approach to systematic sampling. You merely open a cursor and output every *N*th row that's fetched.
Figure 8-6 illustrates the general approach. In this case a report is prepared using the PL/SQL package called DBMS_OUTPUT that sends output to the terminal. You also could modify the PL/SQL to insert data to a temporary table rather than output them to a report.

```
SET SERVEROUTPUT ON  ◀1
DECLARE
     CURSOR main_cursor IS
         SELECT name_id, name_last, ROWNUM
         FROM name
         WHERE name_seriesno = name_now(name_id);
BEGIN
     DBMS_OUTPUT.PUT_LINE('id      last                    rownum');  ◀2
     DBMS_OUTPUT.PUT_LINE('----- --------------- ----------');
     FOR name_rec IN main_cursor
     LOOP
         IF MOD(name_rec.ROWNUM, &&every_nth_row) = 0 THEN  ◀3
             DBMS_OUTPUT.PUT(RPAD(name_rec.name_id,6));
             DBMS_OUTPUT.PUT(RPAD(name_rec.name_last,16));
             DBMS_OUTPUT.PUT_LINE(LPAD(TO_CHAR(name_rec.ROWNUM,'999'),10));
         END IF;
     END LOOP;
END;
/

id    last              rownum
----- --------------- ----------
a133  O'Leary              2
a226  Sacco                4
a925  Appiah               6
```

Figure 8-6: PL/SQL that systematically samples every Nth row.

Comments

1▶ Enable the SERVEROUTPUT system variable to display output from the built-in PL/SQL package DBMS_OUTPUT.

2▶ The PUT and PUT_LINE procedures from DBMS_OUTPUT are used to prepare the report.

3▶ Every Nth row is selected with a MOD function. You can vary N at runtime by specifying a value for the substitution variable &&every_nth_row.

See Also

1. Performance comparisons for the SQL and PL/SQL approaches to systematic sampling appear in Chapter 9 (Table 9-15 on page 285).

2. The PL/SQL for the name_now function appears in Chapter 1 (Figure 1-9 on page 13).

How do I randomly sample rows?

I'd like to randomly sample rows from a query. How can I construct a query that provides this kind of sampling?

Approach

Oracle doesn't supply a function that produces uniform random deviates, which is a prerequisite for random sampling. Thus it's first necessary to create a random number generator. Figure 8-7 implements the so-called minimal standard random number generator of Park and Miller. This generator improves on the technique (called the *linear congruential method*) employed in many system-supplied random generators by reducing the sequential correlation possible on successive calls. Since it was first proposed in 1969, the minimal standard generator has passed all new theoretical tests and has become increasingly used. More complex generators exist, but Press et al. (1992) call the minimal standard generator "satisfactory for the majority of applications."

```
-- Implements the Park and Miller minimal standard random number
-- generator. See William H. Press et.al., Numerical Recipes in C:
-- The Art of Scientific Computing (Cambridge University Press, 1992).
--
-- Note: assumes that the first time getrand is called, you seed it
-- by setting previous_random_number to a positive integer
-- eg, to_number(to_char(sysdate,'dddhhsssss'))
--
-- Sample usage: execute getrand (:prev_random, :rnddev)
--

CREATE OR REPLACE PROCEDURE getrand
  (previous_random_number IN OUT NUMBER, random_deviate OUT NUMBER)
AS
  a NUMBER := 16807;         -- POWER(7,5)
  m NUMBER := 2147483647;    -- POWER(2,31) - 1
  q NUMBER := 127773;        -- from Schrage algorithm
  r NUMBER := 2836;          -- from Schrage algorithm
  k NUMBER := NULL;
  rnd NUMBER := previous_random_number;

BEGIN
  -- generate uniform random deviate between 0.0 and 1.0
  --
  k := TRUNC(rnd/q);
  rnd := a*(rnd - k*q) - r*k;
  IF rnd < 0 THEN
    rnd := rnd + m;
  END IF;
  random_deviate := rnd/m;
  previous_random_number := rnd;
END;
/
```

Figure 8-7: Minimal standard random number generator.

Once you have a random number generator, it can be used to randomly select rows from a query. Figure 8-8 illustrates how to randomly select a single row from a query.

```
SET TRANSACTION READ ONLY;
VARIABLE prev_random NUMBER
VARIABLE rnddev NUMBER            ◄1
VARIABLE maxrownum NUMBER

DECLARE
    CURSOR main_cursor IS
      SELECT COUNT(*) FROM name
      WHERE name_seriesno = name_now(name_id);        ▼2
BEGIN
    :prev_random := TO_NUMBER(TO_CHAR(SYSDATE,'dddhhsssss'));
    OPEN main_cursor;
    FETCH main_cursor INTO :maxrownum;
    CLOSE main_cursor;
END;
/

EXECUTE getrand(:prev_random, :rnddev)   ◄3

SELECT
      name_id "id",
      name_last "last",
      ROWNUM "rownum"
FROM
      name
WHERE
      name_seriesno = name_now(name_id)
GROUP BY
      name_id,
      name_last,
      rownum
HAVING
      ROWNUM = TRUNC(:rnddev * :maxrownum) + 1;   ◄4

id    last                     rownum
----- ---------------- ----------
@226  Sacco                        4
```

Figure 8-8: Randomly selecting one row from an SQL query.

Comments

▶ The first time in a single session that you use the random number procedure, you'll need to declare two bind variables that will hold a random number and the random deviate (i.e., the random number constrained to the range 0.0 to 1.0). Also declare a bind variable maxrownum to contain the number of rows returned by the query. The value of this variable gets determined in the PL/SQL block.

▶ The first time in a single session that you use the random number generator you'll also need to seed the generator. Here the date and time are formatted to produce this seed.

▶ The minimal standard random number generator uses :prev_random as input. It produces a uniform random deviate output as :rnddev. It also produces a new random number that's output as :prev_random for use in subsequent calls to getrand.

▶ The query uses the random deviate :rnddev and the number of rows in the query (:maxrownum) to select a single row for display.

You also can use the random number procedure to randomly select a sample for statistical analysis or other research uses. For example, you might want to randomly select 10% of your customers to receive a newly redesigned promotional piece so that you can compare its effectiveness against the previous promotion.

Figure 8-9 illustrates how to use the getrand procedure to produce a random sample. The output in this case is a report, but it could just as easily be an ASCII flat file suitable for mail merges or statistical analysis.

Comments

▶ This PL/SQL program uses a temporary table called *SAMPLE* that includes only the single data column sample_rownum. The table gets populated with randomly generated numbers in the range from 1 to max_number_rows (i.e., COUNT(*) from the query in question). The program later loops through the report_cursor and retains for display only those rows whose ROWNUM exists in the *SAMPLE* table.

See Also

1. Chapter 6 on page 212 describes how to produce an ASCII flat file from a query.

2. The name_now function used in this section appears in Chapter 1 (Figure 1-9 on page 13).

```
SET SERVEROUTPUT ON
DECLARE
    i NUMBER;
    max_number_rows NUMBER;
    sample_size NUMBER := 2;
    get_rownum NUMBER;
    CURSOR maxrow_cursor IS
        SELECT COUNT(*) FROM name
        WHERE name_seriesno = name_now(name_id);
    CURSOR report_cursor IS
        SELECT name_id, name_last, ROWNUM
        FROM name
        WHERE name_seriesno = name_now(name_id);
    CURSOR sample_cursor IS
        SELECT sample_rownum FROM sample ORDER BY 1;         ◀

BEGIN
    -- get number of rows in query
    OPEN maxrow_cursor;
    FETCH maxrow_cursor INTO max_number_rows;
    CLOSE maxrow_cursor;

    -- draw sample
    FOR i IN 1 .. sample_size
    LOOP
        getrand(:prev_random, :rnddev);
        INSERT INTO sample VALUES (TRUNC(:rnddev * max_number_rows)+1);  ◀
    END LOOP;

    -- prepare report
    DBMS_OUTPUT.PUT_LINE('id     last                    rownum');
    DBMS_OUTPUT.PUT_LINE('----- --------------- ----------');

    OPEN sample_cursor;
    FETCH sample_cursor INTO get_rownum;

    FOR report_rec IN report_cursor
    LOOP
        IF report_rec.ROWNUM = get_rownum THEN
            DBMS_OUTPUT.PUT(RPAD(report_rec.name_id,6));
            DBMS_OUTPUT.PUT(RPAD(report_rec.name_last,16));
            DBMS_OUTPUT.PUT_LINE(LPAD(TO_CHAR(report_rec.ROWNUM,'999'),10));
            FETCH sample_cursor INTO get_rownum;
            EXIT WHEN sample_cursor%NOTFOUND;
        END IF;
    END LOOP;
    CLOSE sample_cursor;
END;
/

id     last                    rownum
----- --------------- ----------
@133  O'Leary                  2
@226  Sacco                    4
```

Figure 8-9: Randomly selecting a sample of report rows.

Constructed Functions

Oracle group functions provide several simple univariate measures such as the minimum, maximum, and average of a distribution. Often, however, other measures of a distribution would be useful. For example, in many cases the median is preferable to the mean as a measure of central tendency. While most statistical analyses should always be done with a statistical package instead of SQL, this section discusses two types of queries that extend the basic group functions provided by Oracle.

How do I find the median?

Oracle provides a function AVG that computes the average of data values for a group, but there is no function that computes the median. How can I find the median of a distribution of data values?

Approach

For many purposes the median is a better indicator of central tendency than the average. But it is more difficult to compute because the rows must be sorted first. With an odd number of data values, the median is that single value where the number of values less than it equals the number of values greater than it. For example, in a group of five data values, the median is the third value in rank order (i.e., two values are greater than it and two values are less than it). With an even number of data values, the median is determined by averaging the two middle values. For example, in a group of six data values, the median is the average of the third and fourth items in rank order.

Figure 8-10 shows training fees in descending order. There are 10 values; the median is the average of items 5 and 6 (i.e., 500 and 600).

```
id          fee
-----   -----------
a133        100
a226        200
a133        325
a226        400
a505        500    ◄
a925        610
a330        740
a925        740
a226       1200
a505       1500
```

Figure 8-10: Median of 10 student training fees.

Comments

▶ This group of training fees consists of 10 values. With an even number of values, the median is computed by rank ordering the data values and averaging the two middle values. In this case the two middle values are 500 and 610, making the median 555.

A pure SQL solution for the median has been proposed by several people. Celko (1995) provides a good discussion of these solutions. Many approaches rely on features available in SQL-92 and not yet available in commercial implementations of SQL. The solution shown in Figure 8-11 uses only standard features in Oracle7 Release 7.2. It does rely on a trick, however, using the implicit sorting that occurs with UNION compound queries to first sort the data values prior to computing the median.

```
BREAK ON REPORT
COMPUTE AVG LABEL 'Median' OF fee ON REPORT
COLUMN fee HEADING 'values|averaged|in median'
SELECT
      ROWNUM "rownum",
      student_total_fee "fee"
FROM
      (SELECT student_total_fee FROM student
      WHERE student_total_fee IS NOT NULL
      UNION
      SELECT 1 FROM DUAL WHERE 1=2)
GROUP BY
      student_total_fee,
      ROWNUM
HAVING
      ROWNUM >=
      (SELECT DECODE(MOD(total_freq,2),
            1,TRUNC(total_freq/2 + 1),
            0,TRUNC(total_freq/2))
      FROM
            (SELECT COUNT(*) AS total_freq FROM student
            WHERE student_total_fee IS NOT NULL))
      AND ROWNUM <=
      (SELECT DECODE(MOD(total_freq,2),
            1,TRUNC(total_freq/2 + 1),
            0,TRUNC(total_freq/2) + 1)
      FROM
            (SELECT COUNT(*) AS total_freq FROM student
            WHERE student_total_fee IS NOT NULL));

                  values
                  averaged
      rownum    in median
      ----------  ----------
            5          500
            6          610
                  ----------
Median                 555
```

Figure 8-11: SQL query that computes a median.

Comments

▶ The main query contains a subquery in the FROM clause. This subquery is actually a UNIONed compound query that implicitly sorts the data values for student_total_fee. Note that the second query in the UNION is a dummy that never equates to TRUE. It is included only to allow UNION to do an implicit sort.

▷ A HAVING clause selects the ROWNUMs from the sorted data values that will be used to compute the median. If there are an odd number of data values, then the median is one of the values in the group. However, if there are an even number of data values, the median must be computed by averaging the middle two values. The DECODE determines the correct ROWNUMs to use for the median based on whether there are an odd or even number of data values in the group.

▶ The total number of data values in the group is determined in this subquery. Note that it again illustrates the use of a subquery in the FROM clause.

You can simplify the solution in Figure 8-11 by creating a bind variable that counts the number of data values in the group. Figure 8-12 illustrates how this works.

Comments

▶ A PL/SQL cursor determines the total number of data values. This number then gets stored in a bind variable called total_freq.

▷ The HAVING clause is simplified compared with Figure 8-12 because it uses the bind variable total_freq and a simple query against DUAL to establish the ROWNUMs to include in the median calculation.

See Also

1. Sorting is a side-effect of the UNION set operation. Oracle does not recommend that you rely upon side-effects when writing ad hoc queries, in case they someday change the algorithm and the side-effect disappears. Until then, however, UNION does allow you to sort when you might otherwise be precluded from doing so. For examples, see Figure 8-4 in this chapter and Chapter 6 (Figure 6-24 on page 203).

2. With Oracle7 Release 7.2 and later releases, you can use

```
SET TRANSACTION READ ONLY;
VARIABLE total_freq NUMBER
DECLARE
    CURSOR c1 IS
    (SELECT COUNT(*) FROM student
    WHERE student_total_fee IS NOT NULL);   ◀1
BEGIN
    OPEN c1;
    FETCH c1 INTO :total_freq;   ◀1
    CLOSE c1;
END;
/
BREAK ON REPORT
COMPUTE AVG LABEL 'Median' OF fee ON REPORT
COLUMN fee HEADING 'values|averaged|in median'
SELECT
    ROWNUM "rownum",
    student_total_fee "fee"
FROM
    (SELECT student_total_fee FROM student
    WHERE student_total_fee IS NOT NULL
    UNION
    SELECT 1 FROM DUAL WHERE 1=2)
GROUP BY
    student_total_fee,
    ROWNUM
HAVING
    ROWNUM >=
    (SELECT DECODE(MOD(:total_freq,2),
        1,TRUNC(:total_freq/2 + 1),       ◀2
        0,TRUNC(:total_freq/2))
    FROM DUAL)
    AND ROWNUM <=
    (SELECT DECODE(MOD(:total_freq,2),
        1,TRUNC(:total_freq/2 + 1),       ◀2
        0,TRUNC(:total_freq/2) +1)
    FROM DUAL);

                        values
                        averaged
        rownum      in median
    ----------  ----------
             5             500
             6             610
                    ----------
Median                    555
```

Figure 8-12: Simplified median calculation using SQL and PL/SQL.

subqueries in the FROM clause. This makes a very nice addition to your query writing toolkit, because it allows you to create data views at runtime without using the CREATE VIEW command. For another example, see Chapter 10 (Figure 10-11 on page 301), or check the index under the heading FROM *clause*.

3. The DECODE function can be put to good use when you need

IF ... THEN ... ELSE logic and don't want to use a procedural language like PL/SQL. See the discussion beginning in Chapter 3 on page 92 for several uses of DECODE.

4. Computing a median with the SQL or PL/SQL in this section is pretty messy. Until Oracle gives us a median group function, save the logic in Figure 8-11 or Figure 8-12 as a SQL segment that you can reuse by cutting and pasting the next time you need it.

5. Performance comparisons between the two approaches used in this section to compute a median appear in Chapter 9 (Table 9-16 on page 287).

How do I find the mode?

I'd like to find the modal age (i.e., the most common age) for a group of undergraduate students. Is this possible with SQL?

Approach

Figure 8-13 shows a frequency distribution of the ages for 100 students.

```
          age          count
      ----------    ----------
          16            2
          17            7
          18           16
          19           17
          20           19      ◀
          21           15
          22           12
          23            9
          24            3
                    ----------
  sum                 100
```

Figure 8-13: Frequency distribution of ages for 100 students.

Comments

▶ The age with the largest frequency count is the modal age. In this case the mode occurs at age 20.

Determining the modal age with SQL is straightforward. The traditional method uses a subquery in the HAVING clause to select the age with the maximum frequency count. Figure 8-14 illustrates this approach.

```
COLUMN age HEADING 'modal|age'
SELECT
     undergrad_age "age",
     COUNT(*) "count"
FROM
     undergrad
GROUP BY
     undergrad_age
HAVING COUNT(*) =
     (SELECT MAX(COUNT(*))
     FROM undergrad                ◀
     GROUP BY undergrad_age);

     modal
      age          count
  ----------    ----------
        20           19
```

Figure 8-14: SQL query using a HAVING subquery to determine the mode.

Comments

▶ The main query groups rows by age. The HAVING clause in the main query retains for display only the single row with the maximum frequency count (i.e., the mode).

You also can find the mode of a distribution using a FROM clause subquery to create a runtime data view. When SQL-92 compliance is reached, a very simple query will produce the mode. For now, however, this approach still requires a subquery. Figure 8-15 illustrates how this works.

```
COLUMN age HEADING 'modal|age'
SELECT
     undergrad_age "age",
     freq "count"
FROM
     (SELECT undergrad_age, COUNT(*) AS freq
     FROM undergrad                                    ◀①
     GROUP BY undergrad_age)
WHERE
     freq =
     (SELECT MAX(freq1)
     FROM
          (SELECT COUNT(*) AS freq1      ◀②
          FROM undergrad
          GROUP BY undergrad_age));

     modal
       age          count
--------- ---------
        20               19
```

Figure 8-15: SQL query using a FROM clause subquery to determine mode.

Comments

▶ The FROM clause in the main query contains a subquery. In this case the subquery duplicates the effect of a view showing the frequency distribution by age. Note that one column in this on-the-fly view is given the alias "freq" and that this gets used in the WHERE clause of the main query.

▶ The subquery in the WHERE clause selects the row in the main query with the maximum frequency count (i.e., the mode). In the process, however, a second FROM clause subquery was used. This makes for a convoluted query. In SQL-92 the WHERE clause can be replaced with HAVING freq = MAX(freq).

See Also

1. A FROM clause subquery also was used in Figure 8-12 on page 247 to compute a median. For another example, also see Chapter 10 (Figure 10-11 on page 301).

Chapter 9
Performance

This chapter deviates from previous chapters in that it does not introduce any new frequently asked questions. Instead, it revisits questions from other chapters where two or more approaches solved the problem. Each alternative method of accomplishing the same action has performance implications. Basically, does one method run faster than the others? This chapter examines this issue.

All performance tests that appear in this chapter were based on simulated data values using the following procedures:

• Data values for all columns were simulated using Pump-It-Up Lite from The Client Server Factory.

• Primary keys were created for all tables, ensuring indexes were available for the data columns comprising the keys.

• Each alternative method was run in a new SQL*PLUS session in which the SQL_TRACE facility was enabled.

• Each alternative method was run 11 times and results from the first trial discarded. All trials used the rule-based optimizer.

• After each trial, TKPROF was run with the INSERT option enabled and trace file statistics were stored in a database table.

• Combined fetch and execute elapsed times were used to evaluate query performance.

• Results from the 10 trials of each method were averaged. The mean and standard deviations from the trials were used to compute *t*-test statistics to determine if the average performance times differed significantly among the functionally equivalent queries.

Functionally Equivalent Alternatives

Interpretation of the performance tests depends in part on knowing what
primary keys exist in each table. Table 9-1 lists these keys for reference.

Table	Key	Position
NAME	NAME_ID	1
	NAME_SERIESNO	2
ADDRESS	ADDRESS_ID	1
	ADDRESS_TYPE	2
	ADDRESS_SERIESNO	3
PERSON	PERSON_ID	1
STUDENT	STUDENT_ID	1
	STUDENT_REGSEQ	2
UNDERGRAD	UNDERGRAD_ID	1

Table 9-1: Primary keys in simulated data tables.

Which method of computing due dates is faster?

Chapter 3 presented two methods for determining due dates a specified
number of business days after a closing date. One method, shown in Figure 3-6 on page 87, used a complex SQL DECODE; the second method,
shown in Figure 3-8 on page 89, employed a PL/SQL function to return
the due date. Both produce the same results. Which one is faster?

Approach

For ease of reference, Figure 9-1 shows the two functionally equivalent
methods of determining due dates..

Table 9-2 compares the average elapsed time for 10 queries using
each method of computing due dates. The SQL solution using the
DECODE (i.e., Figure 3-6) is significantly faster than the PL/SQL function,
by almost a 3:1 factor. Depending on your particular circumstances, you
may want to trade the ease of interpretation provided by the PL/SQL
function for the improved performance of the DECODE.

See Also

1. The discussion about due dates begins in Chapter 3 on page 86.

2. Chapter 3 (Figure 3-7 on page 88) shows the due_date function.

```
Figure 3-6
SELECT
      seminar_code "class",
      TO_CHAR(seminar_end_date, 'dd-MON-yyyy, Day') "enddate",
      TO_CHAR(
         seminar_end_date +
         TRUNC(14/5)*7 +
         DECODE(
            mod(14,5),
            4, DECODE(TO_CHAR(seminar_end_date, 'D'),1,4,2,4,7,5,6),
            3, DECODE(TO_CHAR(seminar_end_date, 'D'),1,3,2,3,3,3,7,4,5),
            2, DECODE(TO_CHAR(seminar_end_date, 'D'),5,4,6,4,7,3,2),
            1, DECODE(TO_CHAR(seminar_end_date, 'D'),6,3,7,2,1),
            0, DECODE(TO_CHAR(seminar_end_date, 'D'),1,-2,7,-1,0)
            ),
      'dd-MON-yyyy, Day') "duedate"
FROM
      seminars
ORDER BY
      TO_CHAR(seminar_end_date, 'D');

Figure 3-8
SELECT
      seminar_code "class",
      TO_CHAR(seminar_end_date, 'dd-MON-yyyy, Day') "enddate",
      TO_CHAR(due_date(seminar_end_date, 14), 'dd-MON-yyyy, Day') "duedate"
FROM seminars
ORDER BY
      TO_CHAR(seminar_end_date, 'D');
```

Figure 9-1: Two methods of computing due dates.

| Query | --Elapsed Time (sec)-- | | | Mean | Statistical |
	Mean	StdDev	Trials	Ratio	Difference?
Figure 3-6	6.03	0.94	10	1.0	
Figure 3-8	15.53	1.46	10	2.6	Yes

```
Notes:
  1. Optimizer: Rule
  2. Hints: None
  3. Indexes: None
  4. Number of rows: 1000
  5. Statistical test: two-tailed t-test, 0.01 probability
  6. Elapsed time = elapsed execute + elapsed fetch
```

Table 9-2: Query performance for two methods of computing due dates.

Which method of recoding numeric data is faster?

Chapter 3 presented two methods for recoding numeric sales data into a discount rate based on the level of total sales. One method, shown in Figure 3-10 on page 92, used the DECODE and SIGN functions in a fairly formidable looking expression. The second method, shown in Figure 3-12 on page 94, used a PL/SQL function that removed the complexity from the query. Which method is faster?

Approach

For ease of reference, Figure 9-2 shows the queries for each of the two methods used in Chapter 3 to recode total sales into a discount rate.

```
Figure 3-10
SELECT
     sales_total "sales",
     DECODE(SIGN(sales_total - 100), -1, 0.03,
          DECODE(SIGN(sales_total - 200), -1, 0.04,
          DECODE(SIGN(sales_total - 350), -1, 0.05, 0, 0.05,
          0.06))) "discount1"
FROM
     xsales
ORDER BY 1;


Figure 3-12
SELECT
     sales_total "sales",
     discount(sales_total) "discount2"
FROM xsales
ORDER By 1;
```

Figure 9-2: Two methods of recoding numeric data.

Table 9-3 compares the elapsed time for 10 queries using each of the two methods of recoding numeric data. The table shows that the SQL approach using the DECODE and SIGN functions is significantly faster than the method employing a PL/SQL function, by an 8:1 ratio. Depending on the circumstances of your query, you may wish to trade the ease of interpretation provided by the PL/SQL function for the improved performance provided by the DECODE expression.

See Also

1. The discussion about recoding numeric data and discount rates begins in Chapter 3 on page 95.

2. Chapter 3 (Figure 3-11 on page 93) shows the discount function.

```
              --Elapsed Time  (sec)--    Mean     Statistical
Query            Mean    StdDev   Trials   Ratio    Difference?

Figure 3-10  7.09      0.51       10      1.0
Figure 3-12 58.58      1.84       10      8.3     Yes

Notes:
  1. Optimizer: Rule
  2. Hints: None
  3. Indexes: None
  4. Number of rows: 5000
  5. Statistical test: two-tailed t-test, 0.01 probability
  6. Elapsed time = elapsed execute + elapsed fetch
```

Table 9-3: Query performance for two methods of recoding numeric data.

Which method of returning an address hierarchy is faster?

Chapter 4 presented two methods for including an address hierarchy in queries, that is, for selecting one address if it exists but a second address if the first address does not exist. One method, shown in Figure 4-3 on page 111, used complex WHERE logic to retrieve the address hierarchy; the second method, shown in Figure 4-5 on page 113, used a PL/SQL function called address_hierarchy that makes the query much simpler and easier to understand. Which method performs better?

Approach

For ease of reference, Figure 9-3 shows the more complicated SQL method of producing an address hierarchy. Figure 9-4 shows the more elegant

```
Figure 4-3
SELECT
      count(distinct name_id) "count1",
      count(*) "count2"
FROM
      address a1,
      name
WHERE
      name_seriesno = name_now(name_id)
      AND a1.address_id = name_id
            AND
            (
            (a1.address_type = 'PR'
            AND a1.address_status = 'A'
            AND a1.address_seriesno =
                  max_address(name_id, a1.address_type))
            OR
            (a1.address_type = 'BU'
            AND a1.address_status = 'A'
            AND a1.address_seriesno =
                  max_address(name_id, a1.address_type)
                  AND NOT EXISTS
                  (SELECT 'x' FROM address a2
                  WHERE a2.address_id = name_id
                  AND a2.address_type = 'PR'
                  AND a2.address_status = 'A'))
            );
```

Figure 9-3: SQL method of returning an address hierarchy.

query that uses a PL/SQL function.

Table 9-4 compares the performance of both approaches to address hierarchies based on elapsed times for running each query 10 times. Note that the query with the complex WHERE condition is significantly faster than the query that uses the PL/SQL function. Again, the trade-off is performance for ease of query construction and interpretation.

```
Figure 4-5
SELECT
     count(distinct name_id) "count1",
     count(*) "count2"
FROM
     address a1,
     name
WHERE
     name_seriesno = name_now(name_id)
     AND a1.address_id = name_id
          AND a1.ROWID =
               address_hierarchy(name_id, 'PR', 'BU');
```

Figure 9-4: PL/SQL method of returning an address hierarchy.

Query	--Elapsed Time (sec)--			Mean Ratio	Statistical Difference?
	Mean	StdDev	Trials		
Figure 4-3	87.80	2.23	10	1.0	
Figure 4-5	121.92	5.68	10	1.4	Yes

Notes:
1. Optimizer: Rule
2. Hints: None
3. Indexes: Primary keys on *NAME* and *ADDRESS* tables
4. Number of rows: 1200
5. Statistical test: two-tailed t-test, 0.01 probability
6. Elapsed time = elapsed execute + elapsed fetch

Table 9-4: Query performance for two methods to do an address hierarchy.

See Also

1. The discussion about address hierarchies begins in Chapter 4 on page 109.

2. Several PL/SQL functions appear in the two methods used to construct address hierarchies. Chapter 1 (Figure 1-9 on page 13) shows the name_now function; Chapter 4 (Figure 4-4 on page 112) shows the max_address function; and Chapter 4 (Figure 4-6 on page 113) shows address_hierarchy.

Is a correlated subquery or a PL/SQL function faster?

Chapter 5 discussed one query that used a correlated subquery to return the most recent training data on students (see Figure 5-12 on page 149) and a second equivalent query that used a PL/SQL function instead of the subquery (see Figure 5-14 on page 152). Which method is faster?

Approach

For ease of reference, Figure 9-5 shows each of the two methods for returning the most recent student training data.

```
Figure 5-12
SELECT
      COUNT(*) "count1",
      COUNT(DISTINCT name_id) "count2"
FROM
      student s1,
      name
WHERE
      name_seriesno = name_now(name_id)
      AND s1.student_id = name_id
            AND s1.student_regseq =
            (SELECT MAX(s2.student_regseq)
            FROM student s2
            WHERE s2.student_id = name_id);


Figure 5-14
SELECT
      COUNT(*) "count1",
      COUNT(DISTINCT name_id) "count2"
FROM
      student,
      name
WHERE
      name_seriesno = name_now(name_id)
      AND student_id = name_id
            AND student_regseq = max_regseq(name_id);
```

Figure 9-5: Correlated subquery and equivalent PL/SQL function.

Table 9-5 compares the elapsed times for 10 trials with each query. Note that the correlated subquery is significantly faster than the PL/SQL function. The mean elapsed time for the query using the PL/SQL function is double that for the query using the correlated subquery. Again, depending on your circumstances, you may prefer to trade query clarity and ease of interpretation for the greater speed available with the more complex correlated subquery.

```
                --Elapsed Time  (sec)--    Mean     Statistical
    Query           Mean   StdDev   Trials   Ratio    Difference?

    Figure  5-12 44.47       1.66       10      1.0
    Figure  5-14 99.43       1.94       10      2.2      Yes

    Notes:
      1.  Optimizer:  Rule
      2.  Hints:  None
      3.  Indexes:  Primary  keys  on  NAME  and  STUDENT  tables
      4.  Number  of  rows:  1200
      5.  Statistical  test:  two-tailed  t-test,  0.01  probability
      6.  Elapsed  time  =  elapsed  execute  +  elapsed  fetch
```

Table 9-5: Query performance for correlated subquery and PL/SQL function.

See Also

1. The discussion about correlated subqueries and their alternatives begins in Chapter 5 on page 148.

2. The PL/SQL for the name_now function appears in Chapter 1 (Figure 1-9 on page 13). Chapter 5 (Figure 5-15 on page 153) shows the PL/SQL for the max_regseq function.

Which method of doing an outer join to a subquery is fastest?

Oracle's version of SQL does not permit an outer join to a subquery. Chapter 5 discussed three procedures that provide this functionality. One method, shown as Figure 5-20 on page 160, used a correlated subquery and an OR operator; a second method, shown as Figure 5-21 on page 161, achieved the same effect using a UNION compound query; and the third method, shown as Figure 5-22 on page 162, hid the complexity in each of the other methods by using a PL/SQL function. Which of the three methods is fastest?

Approach

For ease of reference, Figure 9-6 shows two approaches that are equivalent to doing an outer join to a subquery — one using a correlated subquery and the second a PL/SQL function. The method that uses the compound query appears in Figure 9-7.

```
Figure 5-20
SELECT
      count(*) "count1",
      count(distinct name_id) "count2"
FROM
      student s1,
      name
WHERE name_seriesno = name_now(name_id)
      AND  s1.student_id(+) = name_id
            and
            (
            s1.rowid IS NULL
            OR
            s1.student_regseq =
                  (SELECT MAX(s2.student_regseq)
                  FROM student s2
                  WHERE s2.student_id = name_id)
            );


Figure 5-22
SELECT
      count(*) "count1",
      count(distinct name_id) "count2"
FROM
      student s1,
      name
WHERE name_seriesno = name_now(name_id)
      AND  s1.student_id(+) = name_id
            AND s1.student_regseq(+) = max_regseq(name_id);
```

Figure 9-6: Two methods equivalent to an outer join to a subquery.

```
Figure 5-21
SELECT
    count(*) "count1",
    count(distinct name_id) "count2"
FROM
    name
WHERE name_seriesno = name_now(name_id)
    AND NOT EXISTS
    (SELECT 'x'
    FROM student
    WHERE student_id = name_id)
UNION
SELECT
    count(*) "count1",
    count(distinct name_id) "count2"
FROM
    student s1,
    name
WHERE name_seriesno = name_now(name_id)
    AND s1.student_id = name_id
        AND s1.student_regseq =
        (SELECT MAX(s2.student_regseq)
        FROM student s2
        WHERE s2.student_id = name_id);
```

Figure 9-7: A third method equivalent to an outer join to a subquery.

Table 9-6 compares the average elapsed times for 10 trials with each of the three queries. Note that the complex SQL method (Figure 5-20) proved fastest by a significant margin. This query completed in approximately one-half the time of the others. The UNION compound query also was significantly faster than the PL/SQL function by about 13%.

Query	--Elapsed Time (sec)-- Mean	StdDev	Trials	Mean Ratio	Statistical Difference?
Figure 5-20	46.60	4.49	10	1.0	
Figure 5-21	88.44	2.27	10	1.9	Yes
Figure 5-22	99.56	4.09	10	2.1	Yes

```
Notes:
  1. Optimizer: Rule
  2. Hints: None
  3. Indexes: Primary keys on NAME and STUDENT tables
  4. Number of rows: 1200
  5. Statistical test: two-tailed t-test, 0.01 probability
  6. Elapsed time = elapsed execute + elapsed fetch
```

Table 9-6: Performance for methods equivalent to a subquery outer join.

See Also

1. See Chapter 5 on page 159 for the discussion of outer joins and

subqueries, and how you can provide equivalent functionality.

2. Subqueries often pose their own unique problems for query writers. For a discussion of these problems, see the section beginning in Chapter 5 on page 148

3. See Chapter 1 (Figure 1-9 on page 13) for the name_now function and Chapter 5 (Figure 5-15 on page 153) for max_regseq.

Which method equivalent to an outer join with OR or IN is fastest?

Outer joins with OR or IN produce errors in Oracle SQL. Chapter 5 discussed three methods that provide this functionality. One approach, shown in Figure 5-24 on page 164, used a single SQL query with a complex WHERE clause requiring several OR conditions. A second method, shown in Figure 5-25 on page 165, used a compound UNION query to achieve the same effect. The third method, shown in Figure 5-26 on page 166, produced the same results using a PL/SQL function. Which of the three approaches is fastest?

Approach

For convenient reference, Figure 9-8 through Figure 9-10 show the three methods discussed in Chapter 5 that are equivalent to performing an outer join with the OR logical operator or with the IN comparison operator. Figure 9-8 shows the first solution based on a single SQL query and a complex WHERE clause.

```
Figure 5-24
SELECT
      COUNT(*) "count1",
      COUNT(DISTINCT name_id) "count2"
FROM
      student s1,
      name
WHERE name_seriesno = name_now(name_id)
      AND s1.student_id(+) = name_id
            AND
            (
            s1.ROWID IS NULL
            OR
            s1.student_sponsor IN ('Self','Employer')
                  AND s1.student_regseq =
                  (SELECT MAX(s2.student_regseq)
                  FROM student s2
                  WHERE s2.student_id = name_id
                  AND s2.student_sponsor IN ('Self','Employer'))
            OR
            s1.ROWID =
            (SELECT MAX(s2.ROWID)
            FROM student s2
            WHERE s2.student_id = name_id
                  AND NOT EXISTS
                  (SELECT 'x'
                  FROM student s3
                  WHERE s3.student_id = name_id
                  AND s3.student_sponsor IN
                        ('Self','Employer')))
            );
```

Figure 9-8: First method equivalent to an outer join with OR or IN.

Figure 9-9 shows the second solution, this one based on a compound UNION query.

```
Figure 5-25
SELECT
     COUNT(*) "count1",
     COUNT(DISTINCT name_id) "count2"
FROM
     student s1, name
WHERE
     name_seriesno = name_now(name_id)
     AND s1.student_id = name_id
          AND s1.student_sponsor IN ('Self','Employer')
          AND s1.student_regseq =
          (SELECT MAX(s2.student_regseq)
          FROM student s2
          where s2.student_id = name_id
          and s2.student_sponsor in ('Self','Employer'))
UNION
SELECT
     COUNT(*) "count1",
     COUNT(DISTINCT name_id) "count2"
FROM
     name
WHERE
     name_seriesno = name_now(name_id)
     AND NOT EXISTS
     (SELECT 'x'
     FROM student
     WHERE student_id = name_id
     AND student_sponsor IN ('Self','Employer'));
```

Figure 9-9: Second method equivalent to an outer join with OR or IN.

Figure 9-10 shows the third solution based on a PL/SQL function.

```
Figure 5-26
SELECT
     COUNT(*) "count1",
     COUNT(DISTINCT name_id) "count2"
FROM
     student s1,
     name
WHERE name_seriesno = name_now(name_id)
     AND s1.student_id(+) = name_id
          AND s1.ROWID(+) =
               sponsor_exist(name_id, 'Self', 'Employer');
```

Figure 9-10: Third method equivalent to an outer join with OR or IN.

Table 9-7 shows the results from 10 trials with each of the three queries. The single SQL query utilizing a complex WHERE clause is considerably faster than either of the other two approaches. Depending on your query circumstances, you may wish to avoid the conceptually cleaner PL/SQL function and choose the performance gains available in the more complex SQL query.

```
                --Elapsed Time  (sec)--      Mean      Statistical
    Query          Mean    StdDev   Trials   Ratio     Difference?

    Figure 5-24 46.37      1.66       10      1.0
    Figure 5-25 91.49      2.17       10      2.0       Yes
    Figure 5-26 83.19      4.35       10      1.8       Yes

    Notes:
      1. Optimizer: Rule
      2. Hints: None
      3. Indexes: Primary keys on NAME and STUDENT tables
      4. Number of rows: 1200
      5. Statistical test: two-tailed t-test, 0.01 probability
      6. Elapsed time = elapsed execute + elapsed fetch
```

Table 9-7: Performance for queries in Figure 9-8 through Figure 9-10.

See Also

1. The discussion about outer joins with IN and OR operators begins in Chapter 5 on page 163.

2. Chapter 1 (Figure 1-9 on page 13) shows the PL/SQL function name_now; Chapter 5 (Figure 5-27 on page 167) shows the sponsor_exist function.

Which method of constructing a traditional cross-tabulation is faster?

Chapter 6 discussed two methods for constructing a traditional cross-tabulation. This type of report appears as a table, with counts of the population items in the table cells and the rows and columns each containing categorical data columns. One method to do cross-tabulations relied on the DECODE function (see Figure 6-4 on page 180); a second method (see Figure 6-6 on page 182) used an identity matrix. Which of these methods is faster?

Approach

For convenient reference, the two methods that produce traditional cross-tabulations are shown in Figure 9-11.

```
Figure 6-4
BREAK ON REPORT
COMPUTE SUM OF col1 col2 count ON REPORT
SELECT
      NVL(student_sponsor, 'Unknown') "sponsor",
      SUM(DECODE(person_gender,'M',1,0)) "col1",
      SUM(DECODE(person_gender,'F',1,0)) "col2",
      COUNT(*) "count"
FROM
      person, student
WHERE
      student_regseq = max_regseq(student_id)
      AND person_id = student_id
GROUP BY
      NVL(student_sponsor, 'Unknown')
ORDER BY 1;


Figure 6-6
BREAK ON REPORT
COMPUTE SUM OF col1 col2 count ON REPORT
SELECT
      NVL(student_sponsor, 'Unknown') "sponsor",
      SUM(sexiden_male) "col1",
      SUM(sexiden_female) "col2",
      COUNT(*) "count"
FROM
      sexiden, person, student
WHERE
      student_regseq = max_regseq(student_id)
      AND person_id = student_id
      AND sexiden_code = person_gender
GROUP BY
      NVL(student_sponsor, 'Unknown')
ORDER BY 1;
```

Figure 9-11: Two methods for constructing traditional cross-tabulations.

Table 9-8 compares the average elapsed times in 10 trials with each of the two methods that produce cross-tabulations. Note that there is no significant difference in the average time. Choosing between these two methods should be a question of personal preference and not dictated by performance considerations.

```
             --Elapsed Time  (sec)--    Mean     Statistical
Query            Mean    StdDev    Trials     Ratio    Difference?

Figure 6-4   37.19      1.05        10       1.0
Figure 6-6   37.62      1.55        10       1.0      No

Notes:
  1. Optimizer: Rule
  2. Hints: None
  3. Indexes: Primary keys on STUDENT and PERSON tables
  4. Number of rows: 1400
  5. Statistical test: two-tailed t-test, 0.01 probability
  6. Elapsed time = elapsed execute + elapsed fetch
```

Table 9-8: Performance for two methods of constructing cross-tabulations.

See Also

1. The discussion on traditional cross-tabulation reports begins in Chapter 6 on page 180.

2. See Chapter 5 (Figure 5-15 on page 153) for the PL/SQL function max_regseq.

Which method of reporting running totals is faster?

Chapter 6 discussed two methods of preparing a report that showed running totals of a quantitative data column. One method, shown in Figure 6-15 on page 194, used a nonequi self-join. The second method, shown in Figure 6-16 on page 195, used a PL/SQL function to produce the running totals. Both methods refer to the simple situation where each population item has only one value in the data column used to compute the running total. Which of the two methods is faster?

Approach

Figure 9-12 shows the two methods that produce running total reports.

```
Figure 6-15
BREAK ON report
COMPUTE SUM OF fee1 ON REPORT
SELECT
      s1.student_id "id",
      s1.student_total_fee "fee1",
      SUM(s2.student_total_fee) "fee2"
FROM
      student s2,
      student s1
WHERE
      s2.student_id <= s1.student_id
GROUP BY
      s1.student_id,
      s1.student_total_fee
ORDER BY 1;


Figure 6-16
BREAK ON REPORT
COMPUTE SUM OF fee1 ON REPORT
SELECT
      student_id "id",
      student_total_fee "fee1",
      running_fee(student_id) "fee2"
FROM
      student
ORDER BY 1;
```

Figure 9-12: Two methods for constructing running totals.

Table 9-9 compares the average elapsed times for 10 trials with each query. The method that used the PL/SQL function (i.e., the method in Figure 6-16) ran about 6% faster than the method that used the nonequi self-join. This difference was statistically significant, but both methods exact a performance penalty. Depending on your circumstances, you may wish to produce running totals using a statistical package.

```
                --Elapsed Time  (sec)--     Mean   Statistical
    Query           Mean    StdDev   Trials   Ratio   Difference?

    Figure 6-15 58.76        1.67       10      1.0
    Figure 6-16 55.04        2.29       10      0.9    Yes

    Notes:
    1. Optimizer: Rule
    2. Hints: None
    3. Indexes: Primary keys on STUDENT and PERSON tables
    4. Number of rows: 325
    5. Statistical test: two-tailed t-test, 0.01 probability
    6. Elapsed time = elapsed execute + elapsed fetch
```

Table 9-9: Performance for two methods of constructing running totals.

See Also

1. The discussion about running total reports begins in Chapter 6 on page 194.

2. The PL/SQL for the running_fee function appears in Chapter 6 (Figure 6-17 on page 196).

Which method of preparing percentage distributions is faster?

Chapter 6 discussed two methods for constructing percentage distribution reports (i.e., reports that count population items by a categorical data column such as gender and show an associated percentage). Both methods require that the denominator in the percentage computations be determined separately from the main query. One method, shown in Figure 6-20 on page 199, used a view to determine the denominator; the second method, shown in Figure 6-22 on page 201, used PL/SQL to save the denominator value in a bind variable. Which method is faster?

Approach

For convenient reference, Figure 9-13 shows a view used to prepare percentage distribution reports. Figure 9-14 shows the PL/SQL approach.

```
Figure 6-20
BREAK ON REPORT
COMPUTE SUM OF count pct ON REPORT
SELECT
    person_gender "sex",
    COUNT(*) "count",
    ROUND(100*COUNT(*)/totname_total,0) "pct"
FROM
    person, name, totname
WHERE
    name_seriesno = name_now(name_id)
    AND person_id = name_id
GROUP BY
    person_gender,
    totname_total
ORDER BY 1;
```

Figure 9-13: View used to construct percentage distributions.

Table 9-10 shows the average elapsed times for 10 trials using each query method to produce percentage distributions. There is no statistically significant difference in the averages. Allow personal preference to guide your selection of a query method.

See Also

1. The discussion on percentage distribution reports begins in Chapter 6 on page 199.

2. See Chapter 6 (Figure 6-21 on page 200) for the *TOTNAME* view.

3. See Chapter 1 (Figure 1-9 on page 13) for the name_now function.

```
Figure 6-22
VARIABLE nametot NUMBER;
BEGIN
    SELECT COUNT(*) INTO :nametot
    FROM name
    WHERE name_seriesno = name_now(name_id);
END;
/
BREAK ON REPORT
COMPUTE SUM OF count pct ON REPORT
SELECT
    person_gender "sex",
    COUNT(*) "count",
    ROUND(100*COUNT(*)/:nametot,0) "pct"
FROM
    person, name
WHERE
    name_seriesno = name_now(name_id)
    AND person_id = name_id
GROUP BY
    person_gender
ORDER BY 1;
```

Figure 9-14: Bind variable used for percentage distributions.

Query	--Elapsed Time (sec)--			Mean	Statistical
	Mean	StdDev	Trials	Ratio	Difference?
Figure 6-20	85.61	2.29	10	1.0	
Figure 6-22	86.36	3.66	10	1.0	No

```
Notes:
 1. Optimizer: Rule
 2. Hints: None
 3. Indexes: Primary keys on NAME and PERSON tables
 4. Number of rows: 1200
 5. Statistical test: two-tailed t-test, 0.01 probability
 6. Elapsed time = elapsed execute + elapsed fetch
```

Table 9-10: Performance for two methods of doing percentage distributions.

Which method of preparing a top N report is faster?

Chapter 6 discussed two methods for reporting the top *N* values based on the rank order of a data column. One method, shown in Figure 6-25 on page 204, relied only on a nonequi self-join to select the correct rows. The second method, shown in Figure 6-26 on page 205, determined a cutoff value with a PL/SQL cursor, saved this value in a bind variable, and then used the bind variable in a query. Which method is faster?

Approach

Figure 9-15 shows the two methods discussed in Chapter 6 that produce a top *N* report.

```
Figure 6-25
SELECT
    s1.student_id "id",
    s1.student_total_fee "fee"
FROM
    student s1
WHERE
    3 >=
    (SELECT COUNT(DISTINCT s2.student_total_fee)
    FROM
    student s2
    WHERE s2.student_total_fee >= s1.student_total_fee)
ORDER BY 2 DESC;

Figure 6-26
SET TRANSACTION READ ONLY
VARIABLE cutoff NUMBER
DECLARE
    i NUMBER;
    CURSOR main_cursor IS
        SELECT student_total_fee
        FROM student
        ORDER BY 1 DESC;
BEGIN
    OPEN main_cursor;
    FOR i IN 1 .. 3
    LOOP
        FETCH main_cursor INTO :cutoff;
    END LOOP;
    CLOSE main_cursor;
END;
/
SELECT
    student_id "id",
    student_total_fee "fee"
FROM
    student
WHERE
    student_total_fee >= :cutoff
ORDER BY 2 DESC;
```

Figure 9-15: Two methods for constructing top *N* reports.

Table 9-11 compares the average elapsed times for 10 trials with each method for producing top *N* reports. Note that the PL/SQL approach is vastly superior to the SQL subquery. Stay away from nonequi self-joins!

Query	--Elapsed Time (sec)--			Mean Ratio	Statistical Difference?
	Mean	StdDev	Trials		
Figure 6-25	225.32	6.55	10	1.0	
Figure 6-26	0.52	0.03	10	0.0	Yes

```
Notes:
  1. Optimizer: Rule
  2. Hints: None
  3. Indexes: Primary keys on STUDENT table
  4. Number of rows: 1400
  5. Statistical test: two-tailed t-test, 0.01 probability
  6. Elapsed time = elapsed execute + elapsed fetch
```

Table 9-11: Performance for two methods of preparing top *N* reports.

See Also

1. The discussion about top *N* reports begins in Chapter 6 on page 202.

Which method of finding foreign key violations is fastest?

Chapter 7 discussed four approaches to the general problem of identifying rows in one table that do not have corresponding rows in a second table. This problem arises frequently when debugging SQL programs where population items fall through a join. The four methods appeared in Figure 7-9 on page 229. Which method is fastest?

Approach

One of the four approaches used an outer join and returned rows where ROWID is NULL; the second approach used a correlated subquery as predicate to NOT EXISTS; the third approach used a subquery and NOT IN; and the fourth approach used a compound query with the MINUS operation.

For purposes of tuning, specific queries are needed. Figure 9-16 through Figure 9-19 each illustrate one of the four methods. Figure 9-16 uses an outer join to find rows in the *NAME* table that do not have corresponding rows in the *STUDENT* table.

```
SELECT
     COUNT(*) "count1",
     COUNT(DISTINCT name_id) "count2"
FROM
     student,
     name
WHERE
     name_seriesno = name_now(name_id)
     AND student_id(+) = name_id
          AND student.ROWID IS NULL;
```

Figure 9-16: Outer join approach.

Figure 9-17 uses a correlated subquery to identify the same rows.

```
SELECT
     COUNT(*) "count1",
     COUNT(DISTINCT name_id) "count2"
FROM
     name
WHERE
     name_seriesno = name_now(name_id)
     AND NOT EXISTS
     (SELECT 'x'
     FROM student
     WHERE student_id = name_id);
```

Figure 9-17: Correlated subquery approach.

Figure 9-18 provides the same results using a subquery and NOT IN.

```
SELECT
    COUNT(*) "count1",
    COUNT(DISTINCT name_id) "count2"
FROM
    name
WHERE
    name_seriesno = name_now(name_id)
    AND name_id NOT IN
    (SELECT student_id FROM student);
```

Figure 9-18: Subquery and NOT IN approach.

Figure 9-19 uses a compound query with the MINUS operation to produce the same report.

```
SELECT
    COUNT(*) "count1",
    COUNT(DISTINCT name_id) "count2"
FROM
    name
WHERE
    name_id IN
    (SELECT name_id
    FROM name
    WHERE name_seriesno = name_now(name_id)
    MINUS
    SELECT student_id
    FROM student);
```

Figure 9-19: Compound query with MINUS approach.

Table 9-12 compares average elapsed times for 10 trials using each of the four queries. The NOT IN method required significantly longer processing time than any of the other approaches. None of the other three methods differed significantly among themselves. Choosing among the three can be based on personal preference or other features of a particular query that may tilt the decision in one direction.

See Also

1. See Chapter 7 on page 228 for the discussion of alternative methods to find rows in one table without corresponding rows in a second table.

2. The PL/SQL for the name_now function appears in Chapter 1 (Figure 1-9 on page 13).

| | --Elapsed Time (sec)-- | | | Mean | Statistical |
Query	Mean	StdDev	Trials	Ratio	Difference?
Figure 9-16	43.08	1.67	10	1.0	
Figure 9-17	42.59	1.22	10	1.0	No
Figure 9-18	104.13	2.01	10	2.4	Yes
Figure 9-19	42.73	1.69	10	1.0	No

Notes:
1. Optimizer: Rule
2. Hints: None
3. Indexes: Primary keys on *NAME* and *STUDENT* tables
4. Number of rows: 1200
5. Statistical test: two-tailed t-test, 0.01 probability
6. Elapsed time = elapsed execute + elapsed fetch

Table 9-12: Performance for queries in Figure 9-16 through Figure 9-19.

Which method of finding rows that multiply through a join is fastest?

Chapter 7 discussed three methods to find duplicate keys in a table. These methods also can be used to debug queries by finding rows that multiply through a join, that is, by finding rows in one table that have several corresponding rows in a second table. The three approaches appeared in Figure 7-11 on page 230. Which of the methods is fastest?

Approach

One of the three methods used a HAVING clause and COUNT(*) to identify rows in one table represented more than once in a second table. The second method used a correlated subquery; the third method used a self-join and WHERE criteria that included a ROWID mismatch.

To test the performance of the three methods, specific queries are required. Figure 9-20 through Figure 9-22 illustrate each approach to find rows in the *NAME* table that occur multiple times in the *STUDENT* table.

Figure 9-20 uses a HAVING clause as the key component.

```
SELECT
    name_id "id",
    COUNT(*) "count"
FROM
    student,
    name
WHERE
    name_seriesno = name_now(name_id)
    AND student_id = name_id
GROUP BY
    name_id
HAVING
    COUNT(*) > 1;
```

Figure 9-20: Approach that uses a HAVING clause.

Figure 9-21 relies on a correlated subquery to find the correct rows.

```
SELECT
    name_id
FROM
    name
WHERE
    name_seriesno = name_now(name_id)
    AND 1 <
    (SELECT COUNT(*)
    FROM student
    WHERE student_id = name_id);
```

Figure 9-21: Approach that uses a correlated subquery.

Figure 9-22 uses a third approach to the problem and employs a subquery in which a self-join of the *STUDENT* table occurs. The ROWIDs could only be different if more than *STUDENT* row existed for that person.

```
SELECT
      name_id
FROM
      name
WHERE
      name_seriesno = name_now(name_id)
      AND EXISTS
            (SELECT 'x'
            FROM
                  student s2,
                  student s1
            WHERE
                  s1.student_id = name_id
                  AND s2.student_id = name_id
                  AND s2.ROWID != s1.ROWID);
```

Figure 9-22: Approach that uses a self-join.

Table 9-13 compares the average elapsed times for 10 trials with each of the three queries. All three methods completed in about the same average time (i.e., there was no significant difference in the average times). The method you choose to identify rows in one table with multiple corresponding rows in a second table can be dictated by personal preference or by the circumstances of a specific query which favors one approach over the others..

Query	--Elapsed Time (sec)-- Mean	StdDev	Trials	Mean Ratio	Statistical Difference?
Figure 9-20	42.22	1.05	10	1.0	
Figure 9-21	41.76	1.20	10	1.0	No
Figure 9-22	43.46	1.92	10	1.1	No

```
Notes:
 1. Optimizer: Rule
 2. Hints: None
 3. Indexes: Primary keys on NAME and STUDENT tables
 4. Number of rows: 1200
 5. Statistical test: two-tailed t-test, 0.01 probability
 6. Elapsed time = elapsed execute + elapsed fetch
```

Table 9-13: Performance for queries in Figure 9-20 through Figure 9-22.

See Also

1. The discussion on finding rows that multiply through joins begins in Chapter 7 on page 230.

2. See Chapter 1 (Figure 1-9 on page 13) for the PL/SQL function called name_now.

Which method of sampling the Nth row from a query is faster?

Chapter 8 discussed two methods of sampling the *N*th row from a query. One method, shown in Figure 8-2 on page 234, used standard SQL with GROUP BY and HAVING clauses defining a ROWNUM to return. The second method, shown in Figure 8-3 on page 235, used a PL/SQL cursor to loop to the designated row, saved the ROWID as a bind variable, and then used this bind variable in a simple SQL query. Which method is faster?

Approach

For convenient reference, Figure 9-23 shows the two methods used in Chapter 8 to sample the *N*th row from a query.

```
Figure 8-2
SELECT
     name_id "id",
     ROWNUM "rownum"
FROM
     name
WHERE
     name_seriesno = name_now(name_id)
GROUP BY
     name_id,
     rownum
HAVING
     ROWNUM = 590;

Figure 8-3
SET TRANSACTION READ ONLY
VARIABLE rown VARCHAR2(20)
DECLARE
     i NUMBER;
     CURSOR main_cursor IS
         SELECT ROWIDTOCHAR(ROWID)
         FROM name
         WHERE name_seriesno = name_now(name_id);
BEGIN
     OPEN main_cursor;
     FOR i IN 1 .. 590
     LOOP
         FETCH main_cursor INTO :rown;
     END LOOP;
     CLOSE main_cursor;
END;
/
SELECT
     name_id "id"
FROM
     name
WHERE
     name.rowid = CHARTOROWID(:rown);
```

Figure 9-23: Two methods for sampling the *N*th row from a query.

Table 9-14 compares the average elapsed times for 10 trials with each of the two queries. The PL/SQL approach was about 20% faster in this performance test. If performance is a significant issue for your query, choose the PL/SQL method of sampling the Nth row from a query.

Query	--Elapsed Time (sec)-- Mean	StdDev	Trials	Mean Ratio	Statistical Difference?
Figure 8-2	42.68	2.17	10	1.0	
Figure 8-3	33.33	1.54	10	0.8	Yes

```
Notes:
 1. Optimizer: Rule
 2. Hints: None
 3. Indexes: Primary key on NAME table
 4. Number of rows: 1200
 5. Statistical test: two-tailed t-test, 0.01 probability
 6. Elapsed time = elapsed execute + elapsed fetch
```

Table 9-14: Performance for two methods of sampling the Nth row.

See Also

1. See Chapter 8 on page 234 for the discussion of sampling the Nth row of data in a query.

2. The PL/SQL for the name_now function appears in Chapter 1 (Figure 1-9 on page 13).

Which method of systematically sampling is faster?

Chapter 8 discussed two methods of systematically sampling rows from a query. One method, shown in Figure 8-5 on page 238, used standard SQL with a MOD function in a HAVING clause to perform the actual sampling. The second method, shown in Figure 8-6 on page 239, used a PL/SQL cursor and an FOR loop to accomplish the same task; it also used the DBMS_OUTPUT package to construct the report. Which method is faster?

Approach

For convenient reference, the two methods used in Chapter 8 to systematically sample are shown in Figure 9-24.

```
Figure 8-5
SELECT
     name_id "id",
     ROWNUM "rownum"
FROM
     name
WHERE
     name_seriesno = name_now(name_id)
GROUP BY
     name_id,
     ROWNUM
HAVING
     MOD(ROWNUM,15) = 0;

Figure 8-6
SET SERVEROUTPUT ON
DECLARE
     CURSOR main_cursor IS
        SELECT name_id, ROWNUM
        FROM name
        WHERE name_seriesno = name_now(name_id);
BEGIN
     DBMS_OUTPUT.PUT_LINE('id      last                    rownum');
     DBMS_OUTPUT.PUT_LINE('----- ---------------- ----------');
     FOR name_rec IN main_cursor
     LOOP
        IF MOD(name_rec.ROWNUM, 15) = 0 THEN
            DBMS_OUTPUT.PUT(RPAD(name_rec.name_id,6));
            DBMS_OUTPUT.PUT_LINE(LPAD(TO_CHAR(name_rec.ROWNUM,
               '999'),10));
        END IF;
     END LOOP;
END;
/
```

Figure 9-24: Two methods for systematically sampling every Nth row.

Table 9-15 compares the average elapsed times for 10 trials with each query. Note that the standard SQL approach is significantly faster than the PL/SQL approach.

```
              --Elapsed Time  (sec)--      Mean    Statistical
Query            Mean    StdDev   Trials   Ratio   Difference?

Figure 8-5   41.92      2.02        10     1.0
Figure 8-6   62.79      1.68        10     1.5     Yes

Notes:
  1. Optimizer: Rule
  2. Hints: None
  3. Indexes: Primary key on NAME table
  4. Number of rows: 1200
  5. Statistical test: two-tailed t-test, 0.01 probability
  6. Elapsed time = elapsed execute + elapsed fetch
```

Table 9-15: Performance for two methods of systematically sampling.

See Also

1. The discussion about systematic samples begins in Chapter 8 on page 238.

2. See Chapter 1 (Figure 1-9 on page 13) for the PL/SQL function name_now.

Which method of determining the median is faster?

Chapter 8 discussed two methods for finding the median value in a distribution. One approach, shown in Figure 8-11 on page 245, used a SQL query with a complex HAVING clause. The second approach, shown in Figure 8-12 on page 247, used a PL/SQL cursor to determine the total number of values in the distribution, saved this value in a bind variable, and finally used the bind variable in a SQL query. Which method is faster?

Approach

For convenient reference, Figure 9-25 shows the straight SQL method to find a median. Figure 9-26 shows the PL/SQL approach.

```
Figure 8-11
BREAK ON REPORT
COMPUTE AVG LABEL 'Median' OF fee ON REPORT
SELECT
    ROWNUM "rownum",
    student_total_fee "fee"
FROM
    (SELECT student_total_fee FROM student
    WHERE student_total_fee IS NOT NULL
    UNION
    SELECT 1 FROM DUAL WHERE 1=2)
GROUP BY
    student_total_fee,
    ROWNUM
HAVING
    ROWNUM >=
    (SELECT DECODE(MOD(total_freq,2),
        1,TRUNC(total_freq/2 + 1),
        0,TRUNC(total_freq/2))
    FROM
        (SELECT COUNT(*) AS total_freq FROM student
        WHERE student_total_fee IS NOT NULL))
    AND ROWNUM <=
    (SELECT DECODE(MOD(total_freq,2),
        1,TRUNC(total_freq/2 + 1),
        0,TRUNC(total_freq/2) + 1)
    FROM
        (SELECT COUNT(*) AS total_freq FROM student
        WHERE student_total_fee IS NOT NULL));
```

Figure 9-25: One method that determines the median of a distribution.

Table 9-16 shows no statistically significant performance differences between the two approaches..

See Also

1. The discussion on medians begins in Chapter 8 on page 244.

```
Figure 8-12
SET TRANSACTION READ ONLY
VARIABLE total_freq NUMBER
DECLARE
     CURSOR c1 IS
     (SELECT COUNT(*) FROM student
     WHERE student_total_fee IS NOT NULL);
BEGIN
     OPEN c1;
     FETCH c1 INTO :total_freq;
     CLOSE c1;
END;
/
BREAK ON REPORT
COMPUTE AVG LABEL 'Median' OF fee ON REPORT
SELECT
     ROWNUM "rownum",
     student_total_fee "fee"
FROM
     (SELECT student_total_fee FROM student
     WHERE student_total_fee IS NOT NULL
     UNION
     SELECT 1 FROM DUAL WHERE 1=2)
GROUP BY
     student_total_fee,
     ROWNUM
HAVING
     ROWNUM >=
     (SELECT DECODE(MOD(:total_freq,2),
            1,TRUNC(:total_freq/2 + 1),
            0,TRUNC(:total_freq/2))
      FROM DUAL)
      AND ROWNUM <=
      (SELECT DECODE(MOD(:total_freq,2),
            1,TRUNC(:total_freq/2 + 1),
            0,TRUNC(:total_freq/2) +1)
      FROM DUAL);
```

Figure 9-26: One method that determines the median of a distribution.

Query	--Elapsed Time (sec)-- Mean	StdDev	Trials	Mean Ratio	Statistical Difference?
Figure 8-11	1.30	0.32	10	1.0	
Figure 8-12	1.08	0.28	10	0.8	No

```
Notes:
 1. Optimizer: Rule
 2. Hints: None
 3. Indexes: Primary key on STUDENT table
 4. Number of rows: 1000
 5. Statistical test: two-tailed t-test, 0.01 probability
 6. Elapsed time = elapsed execute + elapsed fetch
```

Table 9-16: Performance for two methods of finding the median.

Which method of determining the mode is faster?

Chapter 8 discussed two methods for determining the modal value in a distribution. One approach, shown in Figure 8-14 on page 249, used GROUP BY and HAVING clauses in the main query. The second approach, shown in Figure 8-15 on page 250, used a subquery in the FROM clause and a second subquery in the WHERE clause to achieve the same effect. Which of the two methods is faster?

Approach

For convenient reference, Figure 9-27 shows the two methods to find the modal value of a distribution.

```
Figure 8-14
SELECT
     undergrad_age "age",
     COUNT(*) "count"
FROM
     undergrad
GROUP BY
     undergrad_age
HAVING COUNT(*) =
     (SELECT MAX(COUNT(*))
     FROM undergrad
     GROUP BY undergrad_age);

Figure 8-15
SELECT
     undergrad_age "age",
     freq "count"
FROM
     (SELECT undergrad_age, COUNT(*) AS freq
     FROM undergrad
     GROUP BY undergrad_age)
WHERE
     freq =
     (SELECT MAX(freq1)
     FROM
          (SELECT COUNT(*) AS freq1
          FROM undergrad
          GROUP BY undergrad_age));
```

Figure 9-27: Two methods that determine the mode of a distribution.

Table 9-17 shows that there were no performance differences between the two approaches used to determine the mode.

See Also

1. The discussion about finding the mode of a distribution begins in Chapter 8 on page 249.

```
               --Elapsed Time  (sec)--      Mean     Statistical
  Query            Mean    StdDev   Trials    Ratio    Difference?

  Figure 8-14   0.39      0.03       10       1.0
  Figure 8-15   0.39      0.04       10       1.0      No

  Notes:
   1. Optimizer: Rule
   2. Hints: None
   3. Indexes: Primary key on UNDERGRAD table
   4. Number of rows: 1000
   5. Statistical test: two-tailed t-test, 0.01 probability
   6. Elapsed time = elapsed execute + elapsed fetch
```

Table 9-17: Performance for two methods of finding the mode.

Chapter 10
Interesting Queries

This chapter departs from the format used in earlier chapters. Rather than dealing with frequently asked questions and grouping those questions into common categories, this chapter examines several queries that pose interesting problems.

Some of the problems discussed in this chapter require only simple solutions (e.g., using UNION ALL instead of UNION), but these problems can still be subtle to identify and correct. In hindsight, many query problems appear simple, but when you're stuck, it's baffling.

Other problems discussed in this chapter require more complicated solutions. For example, one query is a brief journey into statistics. The query writer wishes to select two objects from a population of N objects when the order of the objects does not matter. In this case she wanted to list unique combinations of cities (e.g., Boston-Chicago) and report the distance between those two cities. The solution discussed in this chapter uses a cartesian product of data views defined by FROM clause subqueries. There are indeed times when a cartesian product proves useful.

You'll also again find an emphasis on performance in this chapter. SQL, SQL*PLUS, and PL/SQL are very flexible tools. While this flexibility provides definite advantages, it frequently produces several possible solutions to problems. Yet not all solutions, even if they're functionally equivalent, are equal. Queries that run faster and are more elegant are preferable to queries that run slower and are more cumbersome to decipher. This chapter discusses one situation in which the query writer got the correct results but used four correlated subqueries in the process. Performance suffered as the query ground through these subqueries. This chapter discusses two alternative approaches, one of which ran 15 times faster than the original query.

How can I write a query functionally equivalent to a NOT DISTINCT?

I'd like to get a list of column A and column B where the two columns are not unique, that is, where the same combination of column A and column B occurs more than once in a table. Functionally, this seems the opposite of the DISTINCT keyword, yet when I use NOT DISTINCT, I get an error message. How can I construct a query that will identify all non-unique combinations of two data columns?

Approach

Figure 10-1 shows three approaches to this problem.

```
Method 1
SELECT
      colA,
      colB,
      COUNT(*)
FROM
      tab1
GROUP BY
      colA,
      colB
HAVING
      COUNT(*) > 1;

Method 2
SELECT DISTINCT
      t1.colA,
      t1.colB
FROM
      tab1 t1
WHERE
      2 <=
      (SELECT COUNT(*)
      FROM tab1 t2
      WHERE t2.colA = t1.colA
      AND t2.colB = t1.colB);

Method 3
SELECT DISTINCT
      t1.colA,
      t1.colB
FROM
      tab1 t1
WHERE
      EXISTS
      (SELECT 'x'
      FROM tab1 t2
      WHERE t2.colA = t1.colA
      AND t2.colB = t1.colB
      AND t2.ROWID != t1.ROWID);
```

Figure 10-1: Three queries equivalent to NOT DISTINCT.

Comments

▶ Method 1 uses a single query with GROUP BY and HAVING clauses to identify the nonunique combinations of two columns.
▶ Method 2 uses a correlated subquery that identifies when the combination of the two columns occurs more than once.
▶ Method 3 also uses a correlated subquery but with an EXISTS that stops the subquery whenever the combination of the two columns in the main query occurs in the subquery and the ROWIDs differ. Methods 2 and 3 would only be appropriate when indexes existed on the two columns in question

Table 10-1 shows the results of performance tests with the three methods. The single query using GROUP BY and HAVING ran considerably faster than either of the two methods using subqueries. As expected, the subquery method that required only partial execution (Method 3) ran faster than the method that required complete execution.

```
              --Elapsed Time  (sec)--    Mean    Statistical
  Query         Mean    StdDev   Trials  Ratio   Difference?

  Method 1      0.36    0.03       10     1.0
  Method 2      1.35    0.03       10     3.8     Yes
  Method 3      1.19    0.05       10     3.3     Yes

  Notes:
   1. Optimizer: Rule
   2. Hints: None
   3. Indexes: Nonunique index on colA and colB
   4. Number of rows: 1000
   5. Statistical test: two-tailed t-test, 0.01 probability
```

Table 10-1: Performance for queries in Figure 10-1.

See Also

1. Method 1 is nearly identical to one of the techniques used to find rows that multiply through joins when you're debugging join problems. For examples that use this procedure, see Chapter 7 on page 226 and Chapter 7 on page 230. For another test of performance using this method, see Chapter 9 (Table 9-13 on page 280).

2. The DISTINCT keyword can sometimes pose special problems for query writers. For a discussion of these problems, see Chapter 5 on page 170.

How can I get a frequency distribution by a time interval?

A table that I use contains date and time information showing when users log on and log off our administrative database. I'd like to prepare a report that counts the number of logons by duration of connect time. The duration should be displayed in categories (e.g., ≤ 5 minutes, 5–10 minutes, etc.). How can I do this?

Approach

Figure 10-2 describes a table containing logon start and end times. The connect duration must be computed by subtracting the start time from the end time. This computation can then be recoded into categories such as 5 minutes or less, and the categories used in a standard frequency distribution query.

```
SQL> DESC logtime
 Name                                        Null?    Type
 --------------------------------------  --------  ----
 LOGTIME_ID                                  NOT NULL NUMBER(4)
 LOGTIME_SEQNO                               NOT NULL NUMBER(4)
 LOGTIME_LOGON                                        DATE
 LOGTIME_LOGOFF                                       DATE

 Primary key: LOGTIME_ID, LOGTIME_SEQNO
 Index: on primary key

SQL> SELECT COUNT(*) "count" FROM logtime;

     count
 ----------
       995
```

Figure 10-2: *LOGTIME* table described.

This report can be handled easily with straight SQL, but not without creating a messy query that's difficult to understand, test, and debug. Figure 10-3 shows one approach that produces the desired report.

Comments

▶ Connect time is computed by first converting logtime_logoff and logtime_logon date and time into a numeric value. The 'sssss' that appears in the format converts the time into the number of seconds past midnight. Subtracting the converted logtime_logon value from the converted logtime_logoff value produces the connect time in seconds.

```
BREAK ON REPORT
COMPUTE SUM OF count ON REPORT
COLUMN online FORMAT A20
SELECT
     DECODE(
     DECODE(SIGN((TO_NUMBER(TO_CHAR(logtime_logoff,'YYMMDDSSSSS'))
            -
            TO_NUMBER(TO_CHAR(logtime_logon,'YYMMDDSSSSS'))) - 300),  ◀❶
            -1, 0, 0, 0,
            DECODE(SIGN((TO_NUMBER(TO_CHAR(logtime_logoff,'YYMMDDSSSSS'))
            -
            TO_NUMBER(TO_CHAR(logtime_logon,'YYMMDDSSSSS'))) - 600),  ◀❷
            -1, 1, 0, 1,
            2)),
       0, '0: <=5 min',
       1, '1: >5 and <=10 min',                ◀❸
       2, '2: >10 min') "online",
     COUNT(*) "count"
FROM logtime
GROUP BY
     DECODE(
     DECODE(SIGN((TO_NUMBER(TO_CHAR(logtime_logoff,'YYMMDDSSSSS'))
            -
            TO_NUMBER(TO_CHAR(logtime_logon,'YYMMDDSSSSS'))) - 300),
            -1, 0, 0, 0,
            DECODE(SIGN((TO_NUMBER(TO_CHAR(logtime_logoff,'YYMMDDSSSSS'))
            -
            TO_NUMBER(TO_CHAR(logtime_logon,'YYMMDDSSSSS'))) - 600),
            -1, 1, 0, 1,
            2)),
       0, '0: <=5 min',
       1, '1: >5 and <=10 min',
       2, '2: >10 min')
ORDER BY 1;


online                         count
--------------------  ----------
0: <=5 min                       196
1: >5 and <=10 min               188
2: >10 min                       611
                      ----------
sum                              995
```

Figure 10-3: SQL query that produces a frequency distribution by a time interval.

❷ The DECODE and SIGN functions get used to create categories based on the connect time. In this case the connect time (in seconds) is compared with 600 (i.e., 10 minutes). If connect time minus 600 is negative or zero, the DECODE assigns the category 1 to the value.

❸ The outermost DECODE attaches descriptions to the time intervals. For example, the category 0 is given the label '0: <=5 min'. The leading zero in the label ensures that the categories sort in the proper order in the report. You could handle the category codes and the descriptions separately if this seemed preferable, but it would require an even messier query.

The query in Figure 10-3 can be greatly simplified using PL/SQL functions. Figure 10-4 shows a query that uses two PL/SQL functions to produce the identical frequency distribution shown earlier. Note how easy it is to interpret the query, in part because the query itself is smaller, but also because the PL/SQL function names convey their purpose.

```
BREAK ON REPORT
COMPUTE SUM OF count ON REPORT
COLUMN online FORMAT A20
SELECT
    time_cat(online_duration(logtime_logon, logtime_logoff)) "online",
    COUNT(*) "count"
FROM
    logtime
GROUP BY
    time_cat(online_duration(logtime_logon, logtime_logoff))
ORDER BY 1;
```

Figure 10-4: Frequency distribution by time interval using two PL/SQL functions.

Comment

▶ This query uses two PL/SQL functions. One, named online_duration, uses the logtime_logon and logtime_logoff times to compute connect time. The second, named time_cat, uses the connect time to determine which time interval the value belongs in.

For completeness, Figure 10-5 shows the online_duration function and Figure 10-6 shows the time_cat function.

```
CREATE OR REPLACE FUNCTION online_duration
    (start_time IN DATE,
    end_time IN DATE)
RETURN NUMBER
AS
    duration_in_seconds NUMBER(8);

BEGIN
    duration_in_seconds :=
        TO_NUMBER(TO_CHAR(end_time,'YYMMDDSSSSS'))
        -
        TO_NUMBER(TO_CHAR(start_time,'YYMMDDSSSSS'));
    RETURN duration_in_seconds;
END;
/
```

Figure 10-5: PL/SQL function named online_duration.

If ease of interpretation, testing, and debugging are your primary concerns, then the query in Figure 10-4 that uses the two PL/SQL

```
CREATE OR REPLACE FUNCTION time_cat
    (duration_in_seconds IN NUMBER)
RETURN VARCHAR2
AS
    time_category VARCHAR2(20);
    minute_duration NUMBER(8,2);

BEGIN
    minute_duration := duration_in_seconds/60;

    IF minute_duration <= 5.0 THEN
            time_category := '0: <=5 min';
    ELSIF minute_duration > 5.0
      AND minute_duration <= 10.0 THEN
            time_category := '1: <5 AND <= 10 min';
    ELSIF minute_duration > 10.0 THEN
            time_category := '2: >10 min';
    END IF;

    RETURN time_category;
END;
/
```

Figure 10-6: PL/SQL function named time_cat.

functions is definitely the better choice. However, as the following table makes clear, the query with the PL/SQL functions is also considerably slower than the messier but faster SQL query in Figure 10-3. Again, there's a trade-off to make between performance and elegance.

Query	--Elapsed Time (sec)-- Mean	StdDev	Trials	Mean Ratio	Statistical Difference?
Figure 10-3	1.93	0.13	10	1.0	
Figure 10-4	23.99	0.27	10	12.4	Yes

Notes:
1. Optimizer: Rule
2. Hints: None
3. Indexes: on primary key in *LOGTIME* table
4. Number of rows: 995
5. Statistical test: two-tailed t-test, 0.01 probability

Table 10-2: Performance for queries in Figure 10-3 and Figure 10-4.

See Also

1. For another example that uses DECODE and SIGN to recode numeric data, see Chapter 3 (Figure 3-10 on page 92).

How can I cross-tabulate dates by week and day of the week?

One of the tables that I use tracks overtime hours by date and department. I'd like to prepare a cross-tabulated report with days of the week as report columns and weeks as the rows. Totals by week and by day of the week and a grand total also should appear in the report. And finally, if one week has no overtime hours, that week should still appear in the report even though the cell values will all be zero. How can I prepare a report like this?

Approach

Let's discuss a partial solution first, for the well-behaved situation where at least one day in each week of the report contains overtime hours. Figure 10-7 describes a simple *OVERTIME* table, where the primary key is the department code and the date the overtime hours occurred.

```
SQL> DESC overtime
     Name                                    Null?      Type
     ----------------------------------      --------   ----
     OVERTIME_UNIT_CODE                      NOT NULL   NUMBER(4)
     OVERTIME_DATE                           NOT NULL   DATE
     OVERTIME_HOURS                                     NUMBER(2)

     Primary key: overtime_unit_code, overtime_date
     Index: none

SQL> SELECT count(*) "count" FROM overtime;

        count
     ----------
           24
```

Figure 10-7: Description of an *OVERTIME* table.

Several methods exist to categorize dates by week. One convenient approach uses the TRUNC function with a DAY format that truncates dates to the starting date of a week. Starting days differ by NLS_TERRITORY; in the AMERICA territory, the start day for a week is Sunday. The query in Figure 10-8 uses this technique. It also relies on the DECODE function to create the report columns. As an alternative to the DECODE approach, you could use an identity table as discussed in Chapter 6.

The query in Figure 10-8 works fine for every week in which overtime hours exist. Suppose, however, that overtime hours are only inserted into the table when they occur so that no entry is made on days when overtime does not occur. In this case, if an entire week has no overtime

```
BREAK ON REPORT
COMPUTE SUM OF sun mon tue wed thu fri sat total ON REPORT
SELECT
        TRUNC(overtime_date, 'DAY') "week",
        SUM(DECODE(TO_CHAR(overtime_date, 'DY'), 'SUN', overtime_hours, 0)) "sun",
        SUM(DECODE(TO_CHAR(overtime_date, 'DY'), 'MON', overtime_hours, 0)) "mon",
        SUM(DECODE(TO_CHAR(overtime_date, 'DY'), 'TUE', overtime_hours, 0)) "tue",
        SUM(DECODE(TO_CHAR(overtime_date, 'DY'), 'WED', overtime_hours, 0)) "wed",
        SUM(DECODE(TO_CHAR(overtime_date, 'DY'), 'THU', overtime_hours, 0)) "thu",
        SUM(DECODE(TO_CHAR(overtime_date, 'DY'), 'FRI', overtime_hours, 0)) "fri",
        SUM(DECODE(TO_CHAR(overtime_date, 'DY'), 'SAT', overtime_hours, 0)) "sat",
        SUM(overtime_hours) "total"
FROM
        overtime
WHERE
        overtime_date BETWEEN '29-SEP-96' AND '02-NOV-96'
GROUP BY
        TRUNC(overtime_date, 'DAY')
ORDER BY 1;


week         sun  mon  tue  wed  thu  fri  sat  total
---------  ---- ---- ---- ---- ---- ---- ---- ------
29-SEP-96   11    3    0    0    4   51    4     73
06-OCT-96   32   15    4    0    0    0    4     55
13-OCT-96    0    0   22    0    0   27   11     60
20-OCT-96    0   14   17    5    0    0    0     36
27-OCT-96   14   15    0    0   21    0    0     50
           ---- ---- ---- ---- ---- ---- ---- ------
sum         57   47   43    5   25   78   19    274
```

Figure 10-8: Overtime hours by week and day of the week.

hours, then that week will not appear in the report. To ensure that each week appears in the report, even if the overtime hours for that week are zero, you'll need to revise the query in Figure 10-8.

One revision employs a second table populated with each date covered by the report (i.e., for each date defined by the WHERE clause). Suppose you created and populated a table called *TABL1996* that contained each day in the year 1996. An outer join between this table and the *OVERTIME* table would ensure that each week appeared in the report even if no overtime hours existed for that week.

See Also

1. See Chapter 3 (Figure 3-5 on page 84) for another example that uses the TRUNC function to collapse days into weeks. This section also discusses how the starting day of weeks vary depending upon NLS_TERRITORY.

2. Chapter 6 (Figure 6-6 on page 182) shows an identity matrix table used to produce a cross-tabulated report.

How can I count items across two tables?

At present, I track sales at two stores in two separate tables. Frequently, I want to know the total number of sales and the total quantity sold. This means combining the data from the two tables. I tried creating a view using UNION, but this doesn't always seem to give the correct result. Figure 10-9 shows the SQL that I used to create the view.

```
CREATE OR REPLACE VIEW flower_sales
(flower_name,
flower_quantity)
AS
(SELECT f1_name, f1_quantity FROM f1
UNION
SELECT f2_name, f2_quantity FROM f2);
```

Figure 10-9: View for *FLOWER_SALES*.

Figure 10-10 shows sample data that illustrate the problem. The counts and sums of Cacti are clearly wrong using the view.

```
Data
name                    seqno      quantity
---------------      ----------   ----------
Dracaena                 1            50
Cacti                    1            20
Cacti                    2            40
Cacti                    3            25
Cacti                    1            25
Cacti                    2            75
Dracaena                 1            35
Philodendron             1            10

Query
BREAK ON REPORT
COMPUTE SUM OF quantity count ON REPORT
COLUMN flower HEADING 'flower|group'
SELECT
     flower_name "flower",
     SUM(flower_quantity) "quantity",
     COUNT(*) "count"
FROM flower_sales
GROUP BY flower_name
ORDER BY 1;

Report
group                   quantity        count
---------------      ----------      ----------
Cacti                    160             4
Dracaena                 85              2
Philodendron             10              1
                     ----------      ----------
sum                      255             7
```

Figure 10-10: Query that gives the wrong result from *FLOWER_SALES*.

Approach

The problem is actually fairly simple. The view was created as a compound query that UNIONed two data columns from each of the tables. In the UNION process an implicit DISTINCT eliminates duplicate rows. Note in Figure 10-10 that two rows have identical names and quantities (i.e., Cacti and 25, respectively). Only one of these rows gets retained with UNION. Thus the solution to the problem merely requires that the view be recreated with UNION ALL instead of UNION.

However, you also may want to consider replacing the view entirely. Oracle7 Release 7.2 allows the use of subqueries in the FROM clause, meaning you can achieve the same effect of the view by using a subquery. Figure 10-11 illustrates how this works.

```
Query
BREAK ON REPORT
COMPUTE SUM OF quantity count ON REPORT
COLUMN flower heading 'flower|group'
SELECT
     flower_name "flower",
     sum(qty) "quantity",
     count(*) "count"                        ▼①
FROM
     (SELECT f1_name AS flower_name,f1_quantity AS qty FROM f1
     UNION ALL
     SELECT f2_name, f2_quantity FROM f2)
GROUP BY
     flower_name
ORDER BY 1;

Report
flower
group                    quantity          count
----------------      ----------      ----------
Cacti                         185               5
Dracaena                       85               2
Philodendron                   10               1
                      ----------      ----------
sum                           280               8
```

Figure 10-11: Correct results using UNION ALL and a FROM subquery.

Comments

▶ The *FLOWER_SALES* view gets replaced in this query by a FROM clause subquery that uses UNION ALL.

See Also

1. See Chapter 8 (Figure 8-15 on page 250) for another example using a FROM clause subquery.

How do I select distinct combinations of two objects from N objects?

One of my tables contains information on cities and their locations. I want to use the location data to compute distance between any two cities. However, I only want each combination of cities to appear once in the report. For example, the report should include the distance between Boston and Chicago, but the distance between Chicago and Boston is redundant and should not appear. Is this possible?

Approach

There are $N!/[r!(N-r)!]$ distinct combinations of r objects selected from a population of N objects when the order of the items selected does not matter. In this case we wish to select two cities (i.e., $r = 2$) from N cities. When $r = 2$ the formula simplifies to $N(N-1)/2$ distinct combinations. If, for example, there are three cities (i.e., $N = 3$), then there will be $3 \cdot 2/2 = 3$ distinct combinations of cities. Assume that the cities are Boston, Chicago, and Atlanta. The distinct combinations are Boston-Chicago, Boston-Atlanta, and Chicago-Atlanta.

With this bit of statistical review, it's possible to consider the query that will display only distinct combinations of cities. Figure 10-12 describes a simple table containing data on city locations; it also shows the data in the table. Note that there are four cities in the table. We expect $4 \cdot 3/2 = 6$ distinct combinations of cities in the report.

```
SQL> desc cityloc
 Name                                    Null?    Type
 -------------------------------------- -------- ----
 CITY                                   NOT NULL VARCHAR2(3)
 XPOS                                   NOT NULL NUMBER(2)
 YPOS                                   NOT NULL NUMBER(2)

SQL> select * from cityloc;
 city         xpos          ypos
 ----    ----------    ----------
 LA            0             0
 CHI           3             0
 ATL           3             4
 BOS           1             6
```

Figure 10-12: Description of *CITYLOC* table.

Figure 10-13 shows a query that returns only distinct combinations of cities. It is interesting in two respects. First, it uses a cartesian product of the *CITYLOC* table. But second, the cartesian product actually occurs between two versions of *CITYLOC* created by FROM clause subqueries.

This allows the addition of ROWNUM to each of the *CITYLOC* tables, which in turn makes it possible to construct a WHERE clause that ensures only distinct combinations get returned.

```
SELECT
      city1,
      city2
from
      (SELECT city AS city1, ROWNUM AS row1 FROM cityloc),  ◀1
      (SELECT city AS city2, ROWNUM AS row2 FROM cityloc)
WHERE
      row2 < row1;  ◀2


city1 city2
----- -----
CHI    LA
ATL    LA
BOS    LA
ATL    CHI
BOS    CHI
BOS    ATL
```

Figure 10-13: Query that displays only distinct combinations of two cities.

Comments

▶ Two versions of the *CITYLOC* table get used in the query, each created by a FROM clause subquery. This allows the addition of ROWNUM to each view of the *CITYLOC* data.

▶ Note that no join criterion exists; there is a cartesian product between the two *CITYLOC* views. Requiring that ROWNUM from the first view is less than ROWNUM from the second view ensures that only distinct combinations of cities will appear in the report. Note that the report does, as expected, include six distinct combinations of cities.

See Also

1. Cartestian products generally mean trouble, because in most cases they occur when a query writer forgets to join two tables. This can seriously degrade system performance if the tables in question are large. But there are other times, like the query in Figure 10-13, when you can use a cartesian product with good effect. For another example, see Chapter 3 (Figure 3-20 on page 104).

How do I find the maximum number of contacts any one customer has?

I'd like to write a query that returns the maximum number of contacts made with any of our customers. I can, of course, count contacts by customer and order the report in descending order to get the information. But all I really need is just the first line from this report. Is there some way I can prepare a report that shows only this one number?

Approach

Figure 10-14 describes a simple *CONTACT* table. It includes data columns that capture the customer identification number, the sequence number of the contact, the type of contact, and the date of the contact. The identification and sequence number columns comprise the primary key. The table contains approximately 4400 contacts with 990 customers.

```
SQL> DESC contact
  Name                                     Null?      Type
  -------------------------------------    --------   ----
  CONTACT_ID                               NOT NULL   NUMBER(4)
  CONTACT_SEQNO                            NOT NULL   NUMBER(3)
  CONTACT_TYPE                             NOT NULL   VARCHAR2(4)
  CONTACT_DATE                             NOT NULL   DATE

  Primary key: CONTACT_ID, CONTACT_SEQNO
  Index: on primary key

SQL> SELECT COUNT(*) "contacts",
  2    COUNT(DISTINCT contact_id) "customers"
  3    FROM contact;

  contacts   customers
  ---------- ----------
      4398         990
```

Figure 10-14: Customer *CONTACT* table described.

Finding the number of contacts for each customer is simple enough; you merely GROUP BY contact_id and count the contacts. The trick becomes reporting only the maximum count. Several approaches exist:

• Create a view that counts contacts by each contact_id, and then write the query to return the maximum number from this view;

• Use a FROM clause subquery to duplicate the effect of a view without the need to first create the view.

• Use a PL/SQL cursor and a bind variable to return the maximum contact count.

The following three figures illustrate each approach. Figure 10-15 shows a view used to return the maximum contact count.

```
View
CREATE VIEW contacts_by_id
     (id, num_contacts)
AS
     (SELECT contact_id, COUNT(*)
     FROM contact
     GROUP BY contact_id);
Query
SELECT MAX(num_contacts) FROM contacts_by_id;
```

Figure 10-15: Maximum contact count with a view.

Figure 10-16 provides the same result but uses a single query with a FROM clause subquery to replace the view.

```
SELECT
     MAX(num_contacts)
FROM
     (SELECT contact_id AS id, COUNT(*) AS num_contacts
     FROM contact
     GROUP BY contact_id);
```

Figure 10-16: Maximum contact count with FROM clause subquery.

Finally, Figure 10-17 uses a PL/SQL cursor and a bind variable to produce the same effect as the other two approaches.

```
PL/SQL
SET TRANSACTION READ ONLY;
VARIABLE max_contacts NUMBER
DECLARE
     CURSOR main_cursor IS
        SELECT COUNT(*)
        FROM contact
        GROUP BY contact_id
        ORDER BY 1 DESC;
BEGIN
     OPEN main_cursor;
     FETCH main_cursor INTO :max_contacts;
     CLOSE main_cursor;
END;
/
Query
SELECT :max_contacts FROM DUAL;
```

Figure 10-17: Maximum contact count with a PL/SQL cursor and bind variable.

Table 10-3 presents performance results based on 10 trials with each query. Note that none of the three methods is significantly faster than the others. In this case, personal preference can best guide your selection of a query strategy.

```
                  --Elapsed Time  (sec)--    Mean    Statistical
   Query            Mean    StdDev   Trials   Ratio   Difference?

   Figure 10-15 1.39      0.19       10       1.0
   Figure 10-16 1.42      0.27       10       1.0     No
   Figure 10-17 1.62      0.27       10       1.1     No

   Notes:
    1. Optimizer: Rule
    2. Hints: None
    3. Indexes: on primary key in CONTACT table
    4. Number of rows: 4400
    5. Statistical test: two-tailed t-test, 0.01 probability
```

Table 10-3: Performance for queries in Figure 10-15 through Figure 10-17.

See Also

1. FROM clause subqueries give query writers added flexibility when approaching some query problems. For other examples of this type of subquery, see Figure 10-11 on page 301 in this chapter and also Chapter 8 (Figure 8-15 on page 250).

How do I improve the performance of a query?

I've got a simple problem, but the query I wrote takes forever to complete. Since the query will be run frequently, I'd like to make it faster.

I'm using a table called **LOC** (for location) that contains data on the branch location of employees, several characteristics of their employment, and the date when any change became effective. Employees can only be assigned to one location at a time. However, they may work in several locations during their employment with the company, including the same location more than once. Whenever any of the characteristics of employment change, a new row is added to the table. Figure 10-18 describes the table columns and provides basic information about the table.

```
SQL> DESC loc
 Name                                    Null?    Type
 -------------------------------------   -------- ----
 LOC_STAFF_ID                            NOT NULL NUMBER(4)
 LOC_LOCATION                            NOT NULL VARCHAR2(15)
 LOC_EFF_DATE                            NOT NULL DATE
 other employment columns

 Primary key: LOC_STAFF_ID, LOC_EFF_DATE
 Index: on primary key

SQL> SELECT COUNT(*) "rows",
  2     COUNT(DISTINCT loc_staff_id) "employees"
  3     FROM loc;

     rows    employees
 ----------  ----------
     9944         1000
```

Figure 10-18: Employee location table (*LOC*) described.

I need to determine the date when the current location became effective for each employee. Here's the approach I took. The current location is loc_location at MAX(loc_eff_date); that is, it's the most recent location. I then found the MIN(loc_eff_date) for the current location. But in case the person had worked at the current location more than once, I also had to add logic that no other location could have a loc_eff_date > MIN(loc_eff_date) for the current location. Figure 10-19 shows data for one employee and identifies the correct row that the query should return.

Comments

▶ The current location for this employee is Newark. She worked previously at Newark, but this was followed by a transfer to Nashville. Her present assignment began on 16-May-1997.

```
          id location        eff_date
--------- --------------- ---------
         8 Newark          25-JUL-95
         8 Nashville       16-JUN-96
         8 Newark          16-MAY-97  ◀1
         8 Newark          04-SEP-97
```

Figure 10-19: Sample data from the employee location table.

Figure 10-20 shows the SQL query that I wrote based on this approach. The query gives the correct results but it takes a very long time to complete. I'd like to revise the query so it runs faster. How can I do that?

```
SELECT
    l1.loc_staff_id,
    l1.loc_location,
    l1.loc_eff_date
FROM loc l1
WHERE l1.loc_eff_date =
    (SELECT MIN(l2.loc_eff_date)
     FROM loc l2                                              ◀1
     WHERE l2.loc_staff_id = l1.loc_staff_id
     AND l2.loc_location =
            (SELECT l3.loc_location
             FROM loc l3
             WHERE l3.loc_staff_id = l1.loc_staff_id          ◀2
             AND l3.loc_eff_date =
                    (SELECT MAX(l4.loc_eff_date)
                     FROM loc l4                              ◀3
                     WHERE l4.loc_staff_id = l1.loc_staff_id))
    AND NOT EXISTS
    (SELECT 'x'
     FROM loc l5
     WHERE l5.loc_staff_id = l1.loc_staff_id                 ◀4
     AND l5.loc_eff_date > l2.loc_eff_date
     AND l5.loc_location != l2.loc_location));
```

Figure 10-20: Query approach 1.

Comments

▶1 For each employee, choose the minimum effective date . . .

▶2 For the location . . .

▶3 That is the most recent . . .

▶4 And where no other location has a later effective date. This ensures that you're not picking up an earlier employment at the current location that was followed by employment in other branch locations.

Approach

Tuning a query is still more artform than standard practice, despite the common advice about optimizer goals, access paths, hints, driving tables, inadvertent disabling of indexes, and other dangers to avoid or improvements to seek. Often the most dramatic performance gains occur when you rephrase your definitions and recast your query logic. The query in Figure 10-20 uses four correlated subqueries. Let's see if we can't make it less complicated.

The query in Figure 10-20 defines the current location as the location with the most recent effective date (i.e., it is loc_location at MAX(loc_eff_date)). This is certainly accurate. But the current location is also the location at the MIN(loc_eff_date) where no other location has a later effective date. Using this definition simplifies the query, as shown in Figure 10-21. The revised query reduces the number of correlated subqueries from four to two. Performance should improve (and does, as we'll see shortly).

```
SELECT
      l1.loc_staff_id,
      l1.loc_location,
      l1.loc_eff_date
FROM  loc l1
WHERE l1.loc_eff_date =
      (SELECT MIN(l2.loc_eff_date)
      FROM  loc l2                                       ◀1
      WHERE l2.loc_staff_id = l1.loc_staff_id
         AND NOT EXISTS
         (SELECT 'x'
         FROM  loc l3
         WHERE l3.loc_staff_id = l1.loc_staff_id         ◀2
         AND l3.loc_eff_date > l2.loc_eff_date
         AND l3.loc_location != l2.loc_location));
```

Figure 10-21: Query approach 2.

Comments

▶1 For each employee, choose the minimum effective date . . .
▶2 Where no other location has a later effective date.

The query in Figure 10-21 still uses two correlated subqueries, one of which merely returns a minimum effective date. You could accomplish the same thing with a MIN group function. Figure 10-22 shows how the MIN group function simplifies the query even more.

```
SELECT
     loc_staff_id,
     loc_location,
     MIN(loc_eff_date)  ◀①
FROM
     loc l1
WHERE
     NOT EXISTS
     (SELECT 'x'
     FROM loc l2
     WHERE l2.loc_staff_id = l1.loc_staff_id     ◀②
     AND l2.loc_eff_date > l1.loc_eff_date
     AND l2.loc_location != l1.loc_location)
GROUP BY
     loc_staff_id,
     loc_location;
```

Figure 10-22: Query approach 3.

Comments

▶① For each employee, choose the minimum effective date . . .

▶② Where no other location has a later effective date.

The performance tests in Table 10-4 show that reducing the number of correlated subqueries from four to two improved performance significantly. But the dramatic improvement occurred when using a group function to reduce the number of correlated subqueries to one. Compared with the original query, the final query ran nearly 15 times faster. If the query will be run against an enormous database or if it will be run repeatedly, even a 1500 percent improvement may not be sufficient. But it does demonstrate the potential for improved performance when you rethink your definitions and query strategy.

Query	---Elapsed Time (sec)--			Mean Ratio	Statistical Difference?
	Mean	StdDev	Trials		
Figure 10-20	648.66	42.20	10	1.00	
Figure 10-21	400.05	15.52	10	0.62	Yes
Figure 10-22	43.70	1.30	10	0.07	Yes

```
Notes:
  1. Optimizer: Rule
  2. Hints: None
  3. Indexes: Primary key on LOC table
  4. Number of rows: 9944
  5. Statistical test: two-tailed t-test, 0.01 probability
```

Table 10-4: Performance for the queries in Figure 10-20 to Figure 10-22.

See Also

1. Correlated subqueries are marvelous query tools, but don't go overboard using them. To replace correlated subqueries with PL/SQL functions, see the discussion in Chapter 5 on page 152 — but also see the performance comparisons in Chapter 9 (Table 9-5 on page 261).

Appendix A
SQL Scripts

Many of the SQL and SQL*PLUS programs appearing in this book are general enough that they could prove useful in a variety of ad hoc query situations. This appendix collects these programs in one place.

Utilities

Several programs get used repeatedly by other ad hoc query programs, much like subroutines or procedural calls in structured programming languages. These utilities get executed with the START or @ commands.

Utility programs include those which perform housekeeping functions, date and time stamp reports, create SQL*PLUS environments suitable for reports intended for the monitor or the printer, define default column headers for reports, and capture standard user prompts for reuse.

clears.sql

This program (see Figure A-1) clears any preexisting BREAK, COMPUTE, or COLUMN settings. It's a good idea to run clears.sql prior to and after each query. In this way you ensure a tabula rasa for each query and you also tidy up after the query to prevent conflicts with subsequent queries.

```
CLEAR BREAKS
CLEAR COMPUTES
CLEAR COLUMNS
```

Figure A-1: Clears.sql

date.sql

This date utility (see Figure A-2) retrieves the current system date, formats it as dd-MON-yyyy, and captures the formatted value in a user variable to use when datestamping reports with the TTITLE command.

```
COLUMN today NEW_VALUE xDate
SELECT TO_CHAR(SYSDATE, 'dd-MON-yyyy') "today" FROM DUAL;
```

Figure A-2: Date.sql

time.sql

This program (see Figure A-3) retrieves SYSDATE, formats the time as hh24:mi, and captures the value in a user variable called xTime that can be used to timestamp a report with the TTITLE command.

```
COLUMN now NEW_VALUE xTime
SELECT TO_CHAR(SYSDATE, 'hh24:mi') "now" FROM DUAL;
```

Figure A-3: Time.sql

screen.sql

Query writers work in the SQL environment via their monitor screens. While working at the screen or spooling quick reports to the screen, you'll want to customize the SQL environment one way. When spooling reports to an output file, however, you'll usually change several environment settings. This screen utility customizes the SQL environment for work at the monitor. Run it at login and again after the completion of any ad hoc reports spooled to output files that require special formatting.

Screen settings depend largely on individual preferences. The program screen.sql (see Figure A-4) shows one way to customize the screen. It sets the screen size as 24 lines by 80 characters, pauses after each screen in long reports, eliminates top titles, echoes the SQL to the screen, deactivates any forced formfeeds appropriate for printed reports (with NEWPAGE 1), undefines the escape character (\) to use in strings such as path names, and ensures that output spools to the screen.

```
SET PAUSE "ENTER to continue..."
SET PAUSE ON
SET LINESIZE 80
SET PAGESIZE 24
SET NEWPAGE 1
TTITLE OFF
SET ESCAPE OFF
SET ECHO ON
SET TERMOUT ON
```

Figure A-4: Screen.sql

printer.sql

There are different ways to control the printing of reports. The SPOOL OUT command will print a report at your default printer. Using this technique, any special printing instructions must be embedded in the output report, or the printer must first be configured to accommodate the spooled report. More options exist, however, if you first spool to an output file instead of directly to the printer. You can then pass the report file through any number of intermediate programs that allow you to change fonts, point sizes, styles, margins, page layouts, and many other features. You could, for example, open the report file with a word processing program and then execute a macro to set standard report characteristics.

The utility printer.sql (see Figure A-5) illustrates this latter technique. It assumes that the report will be printed in landscape mode with an 8-point monospaced font. In Microsoft Word using the MS Line Draw font, this nicely duplicates the standard green-bar printout of 132 characters. Depending on your software, some experimentation with PAGESIZE and LINESIZE settings may be necessary. PAGESIZE 65 and LINESIZE 80 is suitable for portrait reports using 9-point MS Line Draw.

```
SET  PAUSE  OFF
SET  PAGESIZE  52
SET  LINESIZE  85
SET  ECHO  OFF
SET  TIMING  OFF
SET  FEEDBACK  ON
SET  TTITLE  ON
SET  DOC  OFF
```

Figure A-5: Printer.sql

This program turns off pausing so that the report spools continuously to the report file, sets echoing off so that the SQL does not appear with the report, turns FEEDBACK on so that a summary line appears at the end of the report, and ensures that no timing statistics appear in the report.

Many of the programs appearing later in this appendix are formatted for landscape mode with a LINESIZE width of 85. This formatting made it easy to import the report files directly into the software that produced this book. For spooling to printers that can accommodate larger line sizes, change some of the COLUMN formats in the programs.

owncol.sql

Query writers tend to concentrate on portions of a database. They work with one or two modules (e.g., a finance or a human resource module), and within these modules they typically work with only selected tables. Consequently, certain data columns get used repeatedly.

It is helpful to use column headings that are consistent from report to report. You'll also save considerable time because you no longer need to create headings in each query. You simply start a command file to use your default column headings. Then only the adjustments to these defaults must be made. Over time this program will grow in size to include hundreds of data columns you use most frequently. The version shown in Figure A-6 provides only an example of what's possible.

```
/* name */
COLUMN name_id HEADING 'id'
COLUMN name_last HEADING 'last|name'
COLUMN name_first HEADING 'first|name'
COLUMN name_middle HEADING 'middle|name' FORMAT A6
COLUMN name_seriesno HEADING 'name|seqnum' FORMAT 999999

/* address */
COLUMN address_id HEADING 'id'
COLUMN address_type HEADING 'address|type' FORMAT A7
COLUMN address_street HEADING 'street|address'
COLUMN address_city HEADING 'city|address'
COLUMN address_loc HEADING 'state|prov|etc' FORMAT A5
COLUMN address_pcode HEADING 'postal|code'
COLUMN address_country HEADING 'nation|addr|code' FORMAT A7
COLUMN address_seriesno HEADING 'addr|seqnum' FORMAT 9999999
```

Figure A-6: Owncol.sql

getowner.sql

As you write queries that prompt users for runtime information, you'll find that some prompts get used repeatedly. These can be conveniently captured in SQL programs and then used by issuing a START command in your query shell. The program getowner.sql (see Figure A-7) prompts a the user for a table owner and then stores the response in the variable called xOwner. The VERIFY setting is disabled to suppress a listing of the SQL whenever the xOwner variable gets used in your program. The same technique can be used for capturing other user responses.

```
SET VERIFY OFF
SET TERMOUT ON
ACCEPT Owner PROMPT 'Enter table owner: '
SET TERMOUT OFF

COLUMN owner NEW_VALUE xOwner NOPRINT
SELECT UPPER('&&Owner') "owner" FROM DUAL;
```

Figure A-7: Getowner.sql

gettable.sql

The program gettable.sql (see Figure A-8), which is exactly analogous to getowner.sql, prompts the user for a table name and then captures the response by defining a user variable called xTable.

```
SET VERIFY OFF
SET TERMOUT ON
ACCEPT Table PROMPT 'Enter table name: '
SET TERMOUT OFF

COLUMN tablename NEW_VALUE xTable NOPRINT
SELECT UPPER('&&Table') "tablename" FROM DUAL;
```

Figure A-8: Gettable.sql

Login Settings

SQL*PLUS supports something called a *site profile*, which is an SQL*PLUS command file generally named glogin.sql that allows the database administrator to create a default SQL environment for all users. The default name and location are system dependent.

SQL*PLUS also supports a *user profile*, which is a command file named login.sql that's run after glogin.sql. Each time you enter the SQL*PLUS environment, login.sql gets executed from your current directory if it exists or from a system-dependent path if it is not in your current directory. This allows you to customize the SQL environment to your choosing.

The login.sql command file shown in Figure A-9 defines a number of path names, establishes a default editor, and executes the screen utility listed above. It is, of course, operating system specific. You'll want to modify the login.sql program to reflect your own circumstances.

Defining path names in login.sql provides two advantages: (1) you can change the location of utilities without making changes to individual SQL queries that call these programs (by making a single change in the path definition in login.sql), and (2) if the defined names are short, they're much more convenient to use at the SQL prompt than longer path names. Modify the login.sql shown below to reflect your own preferences. You might, for example, wish to capture the user name and the Oracle instance and then reset the SQL prompt with these values.

```
SET TERMOUT OFF
DEFINE object = d:\orawin95\komenda\objects
DEFINE tool = d:\orawin95\komenda\tools
DEFINE query = d:\orawin95\komenda\query
DEFINE _EDITOR = c:\windows\notepad.exe
START &&object.\screen
SET TERMOUT ON
```

Figure A-9: Login.sql

Owners

Examining a frequency distribution of data tables listed by their owners provides one overview of an Oracle database. In databases with multiple modules, for example, the modules often will have different table owners that are revealed in the frequency report.

Shell: owners.sql

Running the program owner.sql (see Figure A-10) produces a frequency report of database tables by their owner. Information for the report is retrieved through a second program (xowners.sql) started by the shell.

```
SET TERMOUT OFF
START &&object.\clears
START &&object.\printer
START &&object.\date
START &&object.\time

TTITLE 'Database tables and views by owner' SKIP 1 -
    LEFT 'Date: ' xDate '        Time: ' xTime -
    RIGHT 'Page: ' FORMAT 999 SQL.PNO SKIP 1 -
    LEFT 'Report name: owners.lis' -
    RIGHT 'SQL name: owners.sql' SKIP 2;

SPOOL &&query.\owners.lis
    start &&tool.\xowners
SPOOL OFF

START &&object.\clears
START &&object.\screen
```

Figure A-10: Owners.sql

Data program: xowners.sql

The program xowners.sql (see Figure A-11) retrieves data needed for the report. The BREAK and COMPUTE commands produce the grand total that appears in the report.

```
BREAK ON REPORT
COMPUTE SUM OF count ON REPORT
SELECT
    owner "owner",
    count(*) "count"
FROM
    ALL_CATALOG
WHERE
    table_type in ('TABLE','VIEW')
GROUP BY
    owner
ORDER BY 1;
```

Figure A-11: Xowners.sql

Tables

Lists of data tables that include a brief description of each table's purpose prove very useful for ad hoc query writers.

Shell: tables.sql

Running table.sql (see Figure A-12) produces a report of all tables for a specified owner. The table owner gets specified by the user at runtime.

```
SET TERMOUT OFF
START &&object.\clears
START &&object.\printer
START &&object.\date
START &&object.\time
START &&object.\getowner
START &&tool.\deftabl

TTITLE 'Tables for owner: ' xOwner SKIP 1 -
    LEFT 'Date: ' xDate '      Time: ' xTime -
    RIGHT 'Page: ' FORMAT 999 SQL.PNO SKIP 1 -
    LEFT 'Report name: ' xReport -
    RIGHT 'SQL name: tables.sql' SKIP 2;

SPOOL &&query.\&&xReport
    START &&tool.\xtables
SPOOL OFF

START &&object.\clears
START &&object.\screen
```

Figure A-12: Tables.sql

Data program: xtables.sql

The program xtables.sql (see Figure A-13) retrieves data needed for the report. If the comments in the report are blank, it means that the database designer or table owner neglected to include documentation.

```
COLUMN comments FORMAT A40 WORD_WRAP
BREAK ON type SKIP 1
SELECT
    t.table_name "name",
    t.table_type "type",
    c.comments "comments"
FROM
    ALL_TAB_COMMENTS C,
    ALL_CATALOG T
WHERE
    t.owner = '&&xOwner'
    AND c.owner = t.owner
        AND c.table_name = t.table_name
        AND c.table_type = t.table_type
ORDER BY 2, 1;
```

Figure A-13: Xtables.sql

Defined variables: deftabl.sql

The shell program runs deftabl.sql (see Figure A-14) to create a user variable called xReport that defines the output report name.

```
COLUMN reportname NEW_VALUE xReport NOPRINT
SELECT '&&xOwner'||'.tab' "reportname" FROM DUAL;
```

Figure A-14: Deftabl.sql

Dictionaries

Data dictionaries list each data column in a table, describe its datatype and characteristics such as length or precision, and describe its meaning.

Shell: tabldict.sql

Running the program tabldict.sql (see Figure A-15) produces a data dictionary. The table name and owner get specified by the user at runtime.

```
SET TERMOUT OFF
START &&object.\clears
START &&object.\printer
START &&object.\date
START &&object.\time
START &&object.\gettable
START &&object.\getowner
START &&tool.\defdict

TTITLE LEFT xDate '   ' xTime CENTER xType ': ' xTable -
    RIGHT 'Page: ' FORMAT 999 SQL.PNO SKIP 1 -
    LEFT 'Report: ' xReport CENTER 'Owner: ' xOwner -
    RIGHT 'SQL: tabldict.sql' SKIP 1 -
    CENTER xTable_desc SKIP 2 -
    LEFT 'Column Name' COL 22 'Type' COL 32 'Width' -
    COL 39 'Scale Nulls' COL 55 'Column comments' SKIP 1 -
    LEFT xLine SKIP 1;

SPOOL &&query.\&&xReport
    START &&tool.\xtabldic
SPOOL OFF

START &&object.\clears
START &&object.\screen
```

Figure A-15: Tabldict.sql

Normally, HEADING is enabled; here it is disabled and the TTITLE command provides the report headings. This technique proves useful whenever you want specially formatted report headers.

Data program: xtabldic.sql

The program xtabldic.sql (see Figure A-16) retrieves data used in the dictionary report. Note that if the datatype is NUMBER, the dictionary contains the precision of the column. However, if the datatype is CHAR or VARCHAR2, the length of the data column appears in the report.

Defined variables: defdict.sql

At runtime the user is prompted for a table name and owner. An output report name is then concatenated from the table name and a file

```
SET HEADING OFF
SET RECSEP OFF
COLUMN name FORMAT A20
COLUMN type FORMAT A8
COLUMN width FORMAT 99999
COLUMN scale FORMAT 99999
COLUMN nulls FORMAT A9
COLUMN comments FORMAT A30 WORD_WRAP
SELECT
    t.column_name "name",
    t.data_type "type",
    DECODE(t.data_type, 'NUMBER', t.data_precision,
        t.data_length) "width",
    t.data_scale "scale",
    DECODE(t.nullable, 'N', 'NOT NULL', 'Y', 'NULL') "nulls",
    c.comments "comments"
FROM ALL_COL_COMMENTS C, ALL_TAB_COLUMNS T
WHERE t.owner = '&&xOwner'
        AND t.table_name = '&&xTable'
    AND c.owner = t.owner
        AND c.table_name = t.table_name
        AND c.column_name = t.column_name
ORDER BY column_id;
```

Figure A-16: Xtabldic.sql

extension (.dic). The table and owner responses are also used to access ALL_TAB_COMMENTS to retrieve the table type (view or table) and any table comments to use as documentation in the report title.

The program defdict.sql (see Figure A-17) illustrates a useful technique in which several user variables get defined in a single query. This requires only a small trick in which each DEFINE after the first one is forced to start on a new line (see the NextLine alias). The variable xLine is used in the TTITLE command to separate headers from the report body.

```
/* construct a report name */
COLUMN reportname NEW_VALUE xReport NOPRINT
SELECT '&&xTable'||'.dic' "reportname" FROM DUAL;

/* get several column values from all_tab_comments */
COLUMN tabletype NEW_VALUE xType NOPRINT
COLUMN table_comments NEW_VALUE xTable_desc NOPRINT
SELECT
    table_type "tabletype",
    DECODE(comments, NULL, 'No description available',
        ''''||comments||'''') "table_comments"
FROM ALL_TAB_COMMENTS
WHERE owner = UPPER('&&xOwner')
    AND table_name = UPPER('&&xTable');

DEFINE xLine =
'================================================================
===================================='
```

Figure A-17: Defdict.sql

Indexes

Indexes are essential for tuning queries that affect system performance. But they're also helpful if you must ensure that only one row gets returned for each item in the report population. Examining unique indexes can help you craft a query to have the intended effect.

Shell: indexes.sql

The shell program indexes.sql (see Figure A-18) prompts the user for a table owner, uses this response to create an output report name, and then calls the data retrieval program. The report shows all indexes for tables with the specified owner.

```
SET TERMOUT OFF
START &&object.\clears
START &&object.\printer
START &&object.\date
START &&object.\time
START &&object.\getowner
START &&tool.\defindx

TTITLE LEFT 'Indexes on tables owned by: ' xOwner SKIP 1 -
     LEFT 'Date: ' xDate '       Time: ' xTime -
     RIGHT 'Page: ' FORMAT 999 SQL.PNO SKIP 1 -
     LEFT 'Report name: ' xReport -
     RIGHT 'SQL name: indexes.sql' SKIP 2;

SPOOL &&query.\&&xReport
     START &&tool.\xindexes
SPOOL OFF

START &&object.\clears
START &&object.\screen
```

Figure A-18: Indexes.sql

Data program: xindexes.sql

The program xindexes.sql (see Figure A-19 on page 325) retrieves data used in the index report. Note that the report identifies the position of each data column included in an index. This item is important. You can inadvertently but dramatically affect query performance by constructing a query so that the leading edge of an index is unknown and unavailable.

Defined variables: defindx.sql

The shell program runs defindx.sql (see Figure A-20 on page 325) to create a user variable called xReport that defines the output report name. The NEW_VALUE option in the COLUMN command coordinates with a SELECT against the DUAL table to implicitly define xReport.

```
COLUMN table FORMAT A15
COLUMN index FORMAT A25
COLUMN uniqueness FORMAT A10
COLUMN column FORMAT A25
COLUMN position HEADING 'pos' FORMAT 999
BREAK ON table ON index ON uniqueness SKIP 1
SELECT
    a.table_name "table",
    a.index_name "index",
    b.uniqueness "uniqueness",
    a.column_name "column",
    a.column_position "position"
FROM
    ALL_IND_COLUMNS A,
    ALL_INDEXES B
WHERE
    b.owner = '&&xOwner'
    AND a.index_owner = b.owner
            AND a.index_name = b.index_name
            AND a.table_owner = b.table_owner
            AND a.table_name = b.table_name
ORDER BY 1, 2, 5
;
```

Figure A-19: Xindexes.sql

```
COLUMN reportname NEW_VALUE xReport NOPRINT
SELECT '&&xOwner'||'.idx' "reportname" FROM DUAL;
```

Figure A-20: Defindx.sql

Constraints

Constraint reports help query writers identify the primary and unique keys in a table, determine if any foreign keys reference primary or unique keys in other tables, and find the conditions enforced on data columns.

Shell: constrnt.sql

Running constrnt.sql (see Figure A-21) produces a constraint report. At runtime the user is prompted for a table name and owner. The report includes the constraint name and type, any conditions enforced by the constraint, the names of other constraints referenced by the constraint, whether the constraint is enabled, and the data columns included in the constraint.

```
SET TERMOUT OFF
START &&object.\clears
START &&object.\printer
START &&object.\date
START &&object.\time
START &&object.\gettable
START &&object.\getowner
START &&tool.\defcnsrt

TTITLE LEFT 'Constraints on ' xOwnerTable SKIP 1 -
    LEFT 'Date: ' xDate '      Time: ' xTime -
    RIGHT 'Page: ' FORMAT 999 SQL.PNO SKIP 1 -
    LEFT 'Report name: ' xReport -
    RIGHT 'SQL name: constrnt.sql' SKIP 2;

SPOOL &&query.\&&xReport
    START &&tool.\xconstrn
SPOOL OFF

START &&object.\clears
START &&object.\screen
```

Figure A-21: Constrnt.sql

Data program: xconstrn.sql

The program xconstrn.sql (see Figure A-22 on page 327) retrieves data needed for the constraint report.

Defined variables: defcnsrt.sql

Two user variables get defined in defcnsrt.sql (see Figure A-23 on page 327). The first names the output report by concatenating a file extension (.cst) to the table name. The second concatenates the owner and table names to use in the report title.

```
COLUMN cname HEADING 'constraint' FORMAT A26
COLUMN type HEADING 't|y|p|e' FORMAT A1
COLUMN search HEADING 'search' FORMAT A18 WORD_WRAP
COLUMN rconstraint HEADING 'referential|constraint' FORMAT A11
COLUMN stat HEADING 'status' FORMAT A7
COLUMN col HEADING 'column' FORMAT A16
COLUMN pos HEADING 'pos' FORMAT 99
BREAK ON cname ON type ON search ON rconstraint ON stat SKIP 1
SELECT
    a.constraint_name cname,
    a.constraint_type type,
    a.search_condition search,
    a.r_constraint_name rconstraint,
    a.status stat,
    b.column_name col,
    b.position pos
FROM
    ALL_CONS_COLUMNS B,
    ALL_CONSTRAINTS A
WHERE
    a.owner = '&&xOwner'
        AND a.table_name = '&&xTable'
    AND b.owner = a.owner
        AND b.table_name = a.table_name
        AND b.constraint_name = a.constraint_name
ORDER BY 2, 1, 7;
```

Figure A-22: Xconstrn.sql

```
COLUMN reportname NEW_VALUE xReport NOPRINT
SELECT '&&xTable'||'.cst' "reportname" FROM DUAL;

COLUMN ownertable NEW_VALUE xOwnerTable NOPRINT
SELECT '&&xOwner'||'.'||'&&xTable' "ownertable" FROM DUAL;
```

Figure A-23: Defcnsrt.sql

Linesize

When space is at a premium in a report, it's important to know precisely what LINESIZE is required to accommodate the requested columns. If the columns require more characters than you have available on a page, then you'll need to compress them. The program linesize.sql prompts for data columns you intend to use and then computes the LINESIZE needed.

Shell: linesize.sql

The shell program linesize.sql (see Figure A-24) prompts for data column names, sets a LONG display width, retrieves the DATE format in effect, and then computes the LINESIZE required for the report.

```
SET TERMOUT OFF
START &&object.\clears
START &&object.\screen2
START &&object.\date
START &&object.\time
START &&object.\getcolmn
START &&tool.\defline

SET TERMOUT ON
TTITLE 'Minimum report linesize needed' SKIP 1 -
     LEFT 'Date: ' xDate '      Time: ' xTime SKIP 2;

START &&tool.\xlinesiz
SET TERMOUT OFF

START &&object.\clears
START &&object.\screen
```

Figure A-24: Linesize.sql

Data program: xlinesiz.sql

This program (see Figure A-25) computes the LINESIZE needed to include all requested data columns in the report.

```
SELECT
    (SUM(DECODE(data_type,
            'NUMBER', DECODE(data_scale,
                        0, data_precision + 2,
                        data_precision + 3),
            'CHAR', data_length + 1,
            'VARCHAR2', data_length + 1,
            'DATE', TO_NUMBER(&&xDate_length) + 1,
            'LONG', 81,
            data_length + 1
            )) - 1) "length"
FROM ALL_TAB_COLUMNS
WHERE owner||'.'||table_name||'.'||column_name IN &&ColumnName;
```

Figure A-25: Xlinesiz.sql

Utility program: screen2.sql

Output from the linesize report is one number showing how many characters you need across a page. The program screen2.sql (see Figure A-26) sets the SQL*PLUS environment for displaying this number at the screen.

```
SET PAUSE OFF
SET LINESIZE 80
SET PAGESIZE 24
SET NEWPAGE 1
SET ECHO OFF
```

Figure A-26: Screen2.sql

Defined variables: getcolmn.sql

To compute report line size, you must specify the data columns by table owner, table name, and data column name. The program getcolmn.sql (see Figure A-27) prompts for these columns and accepts the response.

```
SET VERIFY OFF
SET TERMOUT ON
PROMPT Enter data columns: owner.table_name.column_name
PROMPT Use single quotes around entries and enclose within ().
PROMPT Use uppercase only.
PROMPT
ACCEPT ColumnName PROMPT 'Enter column names: '
SET TERMOUT OFF
```

Figure A-27: Getcolmn.sql

Defined variables: defline.sql

Data columns with a LONG datatype display by default at the smaller of the LONG or LONGCHUNKSIZE system variables. The program defline.sql sets each of these system variables to 80 characters. It also retrieves the NLS parameters in effect for the session and determines the display width needed for DATE data columns.

```
    -- set LONG and LONGCHUNKSIZE so know display width
    -- for LONG datatype
SET LONG 80
SET LONGCHUNKSIZE 80
    -- determine length of date format being used
COLUMN datelength NEW_VALUE xDate_length NOPRINT
SELECT
    LTRIM(length(value),' ') "datelength"
FROM NLS_SESSION_PARAMETERS
WHERE parameter = 'NLS_DATE_FORMAT';
```

Figure A-28: Defline.sql

References

Celko, Joe. *Joe Celko's SQL for Smarties: Advanced SQL Programming*. San Francisco: Morgan Kaufmann Publishers, 1995.

Feuerstein, Steven. *Oracle PL/SQL Programming*. Sebastopol, CA: O'Reilly & Associates, 1995.

Lewis, Gary. *Oracle Reporting: Queries with SQL Objects*. Cambridge, MA: Komenda Publishing, 1995.

Oracle Corporation. *Oracle7 Server Concepts, Release 7.2*. Redwood City, CA: Oracle Corporation, 1995.

Oracle Corporation. *Oracle7 Server Reference, Release 7.2*. Redwood City, CA: Oracle Corporation, 1995.

Oracle Corporation. *Oracle7 Server SQL Reference, Release 7.2*. Redwood City, CA: Oracle Corporation, 1995.

Oracle Corporation. *Oracle7 Server Tuning, Release 7.2*. Redwood City, CA: Oracle Corporation, 1995.

Oracle Corporation. *PL/SQL User's Guide and Reference, Release 2.2*. Redwood City, CA, 1995.

Oracle Corporation. *SQL*Plus User's Guide and Reference, Release 3.2*. Redwood City, CA: Oracle Corporation, 1995.

Press, William H.; Teukolsky, Saul A.; Vetterling, William T.; and Flannery, Brian P. *Numerical Recipes in C: The Art of Scientific Computing*. Cambridge: Cambridge University Press, 1992.

Index

Colophon

Design and illustration

Composition software:	Adobe FrameMaker 5.1
Text typeface:	Janson Text
Display typeface:	Avenir 55
Typeface in figures:	OCRB Alternate

Credits

Cover designers:	Lightbourne Images
	Gaelyn Larrick
	Shannon Bodie
Copy editor:	James Madru
Interior designer:	Gary Lewis
Indexer:	Gary Lewis
Printer:	Thomson-Shore, Inc.